Acknowledgments

JuEunhae: I would like to acknowledge Chris Gair and Helen Stoddart for their support in all my endeavors, and to the University of Glasgow for helping to make our original Reading #Instapoetry conference possible, even in the midst of a pandemic. Most of all, I am thankful to my family for always being there for me, especially my amazing husband, Alan, who has encouraged me every step of the way, and my precious son Ransom, the sunshine of my life.

James: I am lucky enough to work with a genuinely lovely group of colleagues, and would like to thank Stavros, Charis, Petra, and Dimitra for their patience in putting up with me over the years. I'd also like to acknowledge the undergraduate students from my Contemporary Poetry class in 2016 and 2017, whose reactions to Rupi Kaur convinced me to take Instapoetry seriously. Finally, I'd like to send love to my parents, Robin and Marianna, who raised me to be curious about this world, and also to my kids, Sophia and Ethan, who help keep that curiosity alive.

Introduction

JuEunhae Knox and James Mackay

Instapoetry, a portmanteau of "Instagram" and poetry—and thus a portmanteau of a portmanteau—has in a short time changed the publishing industry's perception of poetry and reached a far bigger audience than any previous mass literary movement. Its roots admittedly lie further afield than just the one social media platform, containing within its imprecise and shifting boundaries not only poets who emerged on Instagram, but also ones who have mainly published on Tumblr, Twitter, even Facebook. Not every poet on Instagram is an Instapoet, nor is every poem by those writers gathered under this label an Instapoem, but there are now enough commonalities between these works for a sense of a genre to have emerged.

The work of the masked and anonymous poet, Atticus, who cannily utilizes the neophilia of social media to build and maintain an audience, exemplifies the challenge and potential of Instapoems. Take, from his debut collection, the couplets "I can't think of a more beautiful reason / for it all to exist" or, from a different poem, "as if all the universe / came more alive" (Atticus, locs 87 & 198).[1] Depending on the reader's tastes and their angle of analysis, these sentiments could be seen as deeply meaningful or utterly vacuous, their intention either the Romantic sublime or the student poster cliché, the form of the poems from which they come either classically simple or an example of digital dumbing-down. And this is not even to mention the question of how to "read" a poem, the impact of which depends just as much on the poet's use of typewriter fonts, monochrome photographs, and delicately off-white backgrounds. This is just one example from a highly successful practitioner: with over 11.4 combined million hashtags dedicated to #instapoet, #instapoetry, and #instapoem, Instapoetry has proliferated far beyond any one person's ability to encompass, while attracting almost no critical attention. Indeed, more than almost any other genre of poetry for the past century or more, Instapoetry is wildly popular. Cleo

Wade, Tyler Knott Gregson, Bridgett Devoue, Samantha King Holmes, r.h. Sin, Nayyirah Waheed, Lang Leav, Nikita Gill, Courtney Peppernell, Najwa Zebian, Upile Chisala, and many others, with the help of the publisher Andrews McMeel, have all achieved sales that would make most established writers experience at least a twinge of envy.

Despite its prevalence both online and in print, the "Instapoem" is still remarkably difficult to define. Certainly, at the surface, the movement appears to be visually composed of glib aphorisms, primarily focused on topics of love and loss, universal empowerment, and vague spirituality. The galleries are extremely attractive to look at, coordinating font, background, and images crafted to draw users' eyes as they scroll through the rest of Instagram's endless, gorgeous feed. Although the posts are free to view, the platform still promotes a continual flow of exchange in the form of likes and follows, which can eventually become monetary profit. Those who gain a large following are able to become "influencers," receiving lucrative sponsorship from top brands, and even those who do not attain such celebrity status can still benefit commercially by merchandizing their poems. Atticus's best known six-word poem appears on sun-kissed, female bathing-suit models displayed in tattoo adverts, as well as printed on kitschy tea towels on Etsy. R. M. Drake sells poems as 75-cm motivational posters. Amanda Lovelace offers a 45-card "oracle deck." The sheer marketability of this poetry seems to present a new height of commodified literature, all the more consumable on account of its rapid-fire platform.

Instagram itself had one of the fastest-growing markets at its generation, collecting 25,000 users in a single day. Adapting its name from the combination of the terms "instant" and "telegram," the app owed its immediate popularity to its wide range of photo-sharing capabilities, with filters and editing features that were unique amongst other networks at the time (Frier 2020: 26–7). The platform has only continued to grow in traction with over billion users, 88 percent of whom are now based outside of the United States, and is prevalently used by those under the age of thirty-five, who compose 90 percent of the platform's demographics (Dixon 2023). Such demographics certainly influence the makeup of both writers and readers of Instapoetry, with many praising Instapoets for paving the way for more marginalized voices to be heard, from international women of color to those openly discussing mental health struggles.

One of the most famous of these voices is undoubtedly that of the influencer Rupi Kaur, whose name has become so synonymous with Instapoetry that budding, amateur poets now even use her name as a generic hashtag to draw in those browsing for more Instapoems. While there are many other poets who have capitalized on the genre's widespread acclaim, none can top that of Kaur, who first became renowned for her infamous menstrual picture that was banned on Instagram. It was not until the rallying cries of offended users made the young Canadian suburbanite a social media darling that Kaur was handed the platform to evolve into the sophisticated icon that she is today. Kaur's typewritten poems, accompanied by ink sketchings, really started drawing attention in 2016, when her collection *Milk and Honey* was featured in the *New York Times* bestseller list. Since then, she has inspired countless numbers of young poets to borrow her style, tone, and boldness, even if critics note that she too readily exploits vulnerability for commercial means, or too broadly obscures the voices of individual trauma under a blanket "minority experience" (which in turn has caused other poets like Nayyira Waheed to censure Kaur for her own version of plagiarism).

Yet even though Kaur has had an undoubtable influence upon Instapoetry, this does not bring us closer to an actual definition of the genre itself. If the platform with its unique haptics and tokens is what delineates the poems, are they still Instapoetry if they leave Instagram, whether reposted on another site, such as Tumblr, Instagram's precursor, or printed in a self-published book? Even more tenuously, do they still count as Instapoems if they never actually made it onto the platform, but were directly published in the typical Instapoetry "style"? Moreover, if this style primarily consists of short and aphorismic phrases, who is to discount older poets who also used such "techniques" in their work, from Maya Angelou to William Carlos Williams.? Some of Emily Dickinson's and William Blake's poems sound like they came straight out of an Instagram gallery—in fact, some poetry fans are apt to place short quotes from "classical" poems in stereotypical typewriter font and aesthetic backgrounds, posting them on the platform as if they *were* Instapoems. Even some ancient biblical proverbs like "The banner over me is love" and "There is a time for mourning and a time for dancing" from the Song of Songs or Ecclesiastes would fit right into a quintessential grayscale Instapoetry collage. Interpreted too broadly or too narrowly, either nothing is Instapoetry or everything is Instapoetry.

Despite these clear challenges of making precise delineations—and how could one hope for a perfect definition, when prescribing "poetry" itself is wrought with controversy—in these past few years a general formulation of common Instapoetry trends has emerged. Poems tend to consist of a minimalist prosaic phrase or set of phrases, usually 1–4 lines long (depending on spacing). The use of traditional rhetorical devices, from meter to rhyme to even imagery, is often nonexistent, in order to keep the message unmitigatedly clear to the reader. In terms of format, since appearance is extremely important, Instapoets can choose whatever fonts and spacing they desire, but backgrounds are especially significant, since these catch the users' eye first. Thus, the feed for Instapoetry can be filled with soft pastels or bright neons, or images ranging from sunset montages to flowery meadows. Many also feature female subjects, either clothed in ethereal gowns or partially nude, demurely looking away into the distance. However, the most popular styling format is still a white or cream backdrop with black serif fonts like Courier, Olivetti, or even Weary Thesis Typewriter—or the exact opposite, with a pitch-black setting and white sans-serif Helvetica font.

One could spend much time surveying these distinct contrasts alone. Is there a growing dichotomy between those clinging to an antiquarian look and "feeling" of a book, and those purposefully reflecting our modern black mirrors, radiating a pale glow back onto our faces as we scroll throughout the night? Yet more pressing than a study of such formalist differences is a study of the goals and behaviors of Instapoets, struggling to remain relevant on Instagram's public "affect world" by balancing the oxymoronic extremes of sincere intimacy and clockwork consistency. Uniformity is the principal method of drawing and keeping readers' attention; galleries must not only be homogeneous and orderly, so that anyone visiting the page will be treated to a gorgeous, matching array in a single holistic style, but they must also be consistent with the norms that have come to frame Instapoetry. Instagram's feed is constantly refreshed by such masses of new content that simply being followed once by a user is no guarantee that your posts will ever be seen again. Thus, algorithms award visibility to those who both produce regular, large streams of content as well as actually receive more impressions (likes, or better yet, comments) from their readers. The practices of the platform become as important as the practices of the individual author, more than was ever the case in traditional publishing and bookselling.

To even find these followers in the first place, and then maintain their engagement, Instapoets must make sure that they regularly post poems that are recognizable as Instapoems. This way, anyone rapidly swiping through the feed might see that tell-tale, center-spaced typewritten axiom—and without even being able to yet read the tiny words, simply click on the post because it fits with their already established conception of an Instapoem. The platform's consumerist purposes are thus ingrained in the very acts of making, formatting, and publishing Instapoetry. Even those who want to use alternate forms and devices to craft their poem into something that requires more time, effort, or multiple readings to grapple with images and language and emotion are stymied from the outset. Since longer or denser writing does not immediately resemble an Instapoem, it is less likely to be discovered. This dilemma, combined with the fact that such users are rarely able to afford the fancy photographers or stylists of Rupi Kaur, nor the daily £1,000 demanded by Instagram to supposedly increase one's platform ranking, means that those seeking to escape Instapoetry tropes have little chance of gaining an equal stage. In a hypercapitalist society, even would-be "rebel" Instapoets must ultimately succumb to satisfying the algorithm by using certain promotional tactics, from follow4follow messages to tactical hashtagging—or else be content with having a mere 1k followers.

To readers with a more traditional view of literature, many of these calculations of influence as a constitutive element of poem writing may seem in some way shocking. This rejection is inherent in the neologism "Instapoetry" itself. Few genres of writing have been associated so directly and so insistently with their platform: imagine, for instance, calling Ezra Pound a "little magazine poet." More, the association of writers with specific technologies often means that they would be considered as experimental writers—for instance, Mark Danielewski, who would never have been able to produce *House of Leaves* without the QuarkXpress program. In the case of less formally experimental writers, however, the effect is often intended as insulting—Jack Kerouac's spontaneous prose was not described as "typing" by Truman Capote as a compliment, and it is equally noticeable how many of Stephen King's detractors like to refer to him as a "paperback writer." In the case of Instapoetry, there is often a conscious association by the genre's detractors with phrases such as "instantly disposable," a fact that may explain why so many Instapoets are reluctant to allow themselves to be described as such. The fact that some readers have chosen to tattoo Atticus's six-word poem on their bodies, perhaps the most permanent way to hold a poem close, represents a significant contradiction of this view, but it cannot be denied that most Instapoems were designed for a scrolling readership and a digital screen in a way that lends them a weightless affect.

Instapoetry has been defined by its enemies in other ways as well, none more so than in Rebecca Watts' broadside "The Cult of the Noble Amateur," published in *PN Review* in 2018. Watts, herself an accomplished poet, lays out a charge sheet against the genre, arguing that it is artless, that it disrespects language, that it prioritizes a shallow emotional authenticity over craft, that many Instapoets have read little to no poetry from previous generations and, as such, what they produce can never be more than teenage diary scribblings. Other articles in newspapers and high-profile literary magazines have continued the assault. Claire Bucknell, in an article for the *London Review of Books*, tries to give a sympathetic ear to the claim that Instapoetry may represent a new literary movement, misunderstood and undervalued in the manner of the Bloomsbury group or the Beat Generation, but she cannot resist finally concluding that Instapoetry "is a badly wrought urn, self-contained, free-floating, divorced from history. It would be a New Critic's dream if it weren't so barren of interest." Such sentiments are not restricted to establishment literary gatekeepers, either: a YouTube search for "Instapoetry" brings up several Gen-Z rants about these poems having in some indefinable way ruined twenty-first-century poetry.

For some, the question of whether poems are "good" or "bad" is the ultimate purpose of literary criticism. In the end, for those taking such a stance, the purpose is to recognize poems that have inherent literary merit (however that is defined), promote them, and explicate their workings. As editors of this volume, we recognize the validity of such feelings, and the idea that Instapoetry en masse lacks any form of literary skill that would have been recognized by I. A. Richards is not inaccurate. However, another and equally valid question then arises, of who gets to decide on the ideal standards of poetry, and who therefore gets to be the ideal(ized) Dear Reader. From this standpoint, the fact that Instapoetry speaks—and not only that, it speaks deeply and meaningfully—to a large audience, makes it worthy of discussion. In the absence of survey data, one can make some inferences from the published Instapoets and from a wider look at those publishing poems on the Instagram platform that this audience is young, predominantly but by no means exclusively female, and highly ethnically diverse. First- and second-generation immigrants make up a significant number of the most successful writers.

With the virtual Instagram platform effecting the same function that Grasmere and Keswick did for the Lake Poets, or that Sylvia Beach's Shakespeare & Co. bookshop performed for the Lost Generation, Instapoetry has also become highly geographically diverse—indeed, we would make the bold claim that no other genre of writing has spread anything like as rapidly past multiple language barriers. Instapoems are being written in English, Urdu, Mandarin, Spanish, Arabic, Norwegian, and many other languages besides, and there are prominent Instapoets from countries as diverse as Iran, India, or Malawi. We argue, with this in mind, that serious examination of Instapoetry as a literary phenomenon is long overdue.

This collection began with a conference, also called *Reading #Instapoetry*, which we organized at the University of Glasgow in 2020. (Actually, it began a year earlier over bad coffee on the streets of Angers in France, the first time either of the editors had met anyone else remotely interested in the study of this genre.) Only when we received such a flood of submissions for our conference that we were forced to change what had been planned to be just one day to a three-day event did we realize just how many other people, spread across the world, were also working on these poems. We were also lucky enough to have several submissions from poets who had made Instagram part of their poetic practice, which had a great effect on the conversation and significantly deepened our understanding of the labor that goes into constructing seemingly simple poems. What was also quickly notable was just how diverse were the approaches they were taking: affect theory, posthumanism, ecocriticism, hashtag studies, digital humanities, feminist and transnational theories, readings based on Instapoetry's relationship to classical myth, and readings of Instapoetry's relationship to e-literature. Indeed, one peer reviewer of this volume suggested that this collection could easily serve as a primer to the major currents of literary criticism, especially given the easy to grasp nature of Instapoems.

We begin with platform studies, situating Instapoetry as the third generation of electronic literatures. Leonardo Flores was one of the first critics to articulate this generational shift, in his appropriately titled essay "Third Generation Electronic Literature," arguing that while most literary critics "grew up at a time where we could see the digital materiality sharply most 3rd generation e-lit writers are a younger generation who have naturalized what was experimental to us," and as a result the production of e-literature had shifted from an aesthetic of experimentation with form to one of simply working with preexisting tools. Kathi Inman Berens builds on this insight, asking whether an art form that lacks the aesthetic of difficulty that characterized previous waves can really be considered e-lit. Her essay, reprinted here with a new introduction, argues for new reading strategies that consider printed collections of Instapoetry in their proper context, as the result of algorithmic manipulations and invisible interactions in metadata. As such, Instapoetry gives us a way to read the platforms, and by extension the entire apparatus of digital surveillance capitalism, from whence it springs.

Such an approach, via consideration of hashtags and user interactions, is typified by JuEunhae Knox's essay, "#Tagged." By concentrating on the ways that users tag, share, and reshare excerpts from both Instapoets and highly canonical, traditional poets, a practice she christens "poe(t/m)-tagging," Knox

a self-described "Fat, Fly, Brown, Poet." In her classroom, Sánchez's students embrace the anti-elitism of Salgado's poems, seeing something that most poetry lacks for them—a direct connection to their lived experience. Salgado also participates in community-making activities including workshops and collaborations, making poetry that is intensely democratic, potentially providing a way into literature for students who feel excluded by more traditional offerings.

Yet despite these opportunities for democratization, it is dangerous to uncritically embrace a movement that contains diverse poets as necessarily promoting diverse perspectives. Millicent Lovelock's chapter, for example, uses affect theory as a way of understanding much of Instapoetry's tendency to promulgate heartfelt yet somehow superficial feminism. Drawing on Lauren Berlant's concept of the intimate public, and Eva Illouz's discussions of emotional capitalism, Lovelock reads the overt feminism of Rupi Kaur as primarily something that establishes a sense of personal connection between the poet and her audience. Recognizing the unequal nature of gender relations in a heteronormative and patriarchal society, however, is not in itself a sufficient gesture to effect political change. Lovelock shows that the economic paradigm of the pop-psychology that pervades Kaur's work and public statements, in which each individual is responsible for working to overcome her individual trauma, results in a commercialized form of feminism in which healing can be bought at a price, and in which the idea of social change is subsumed into self-work.

Lovelock's chapter broaches conversations around Instapoetry as an intensely capitalist art, the theme of the final section of essays. We open with a provocation from Ryan Prewitt and Max Accardi, who test a common criticism of Instapoetry—that the poems are so formulaic that they might as well be written by computer. Using a corpus of existing Instapoems, they create an algorithm based on the concept of Markov chains to automatically write new works in the genre. This experimental literary study calls into question the entire idea of Instapoetry as a purposive genre, and leads us back to the circulation of Instapoems as that which gives the genre value: at the same time, they trace the hollowing out of meaning and human intentionality this implies as a product of late-stage capitalism.

In making this argument, Prewitt and Accardi draw on the ideas of Jean Baudrillard, particularly orders of simulacra, arguing that their artificial Instapoems represent a fourth order of simulation. In the following chapter, Melissa Sarakaya picks up this theme to look at the British Instapoet Hollie McNish via Baudrillard's concept of the hyperreal, which she argues predicts the environment of Instagram. For Sarakaya, an important element to consider becomes McNish's marketing and branding strategy. The poet employs confessional snippets of personal information and discussion of feelings to invite readers to form a community in which the poet, rather than controlling the discourse, becomes just another active participant: importantly, however, via captions rather than comments. While such a strategy would seem to accord with the platform's insatiable appetite for the commodification of personal lives, Sarakaya argues that McNish subverts the algorithm by highlighting the artificiality of the digital environment and by moving readers into real-world interactions with her work and with each other.

Zak Bronson and Warren Steele also look at Instapoetry as a business which requires personal branding, though with much less optimism. They argue that while it is true that self-publishing on Instagram has proven to be an excellent route to market for marginalized voices, their achievements have come at the expense of any ability to develop an authentic or individual voice. Public statements by Instapoets demonstrate an obsessive interest in both the visible and invisible architectures of social media, something that the authors argue also inflects the poetry they produce. Moreover, the constant shifts in metrics of discoverability on multiple platforms create conditions of precarity among a group of poets entirely reliant on likes and shares for their readership: poetry becomes just another gig economy job that makes enormous demands on the time of producers for little or no reward unless they follow the imperatives of the algorithm.

Gig economy jobs take place in the context of a rapidly degrading environment and global warming, conditions that form the context for James Mackay and Polina Mackay's final chapter. Discussing the physical conditions of the Instapoetry reader, scrolling and receiving haptic feedback from their mobile phones, the authors ask whether the alien, artificial feel of the screen serves as an insistent reminder of the reader's position on the edge of civilizational and ecological collapse. Close reading of a single two-line Instapoem on various scales, from the immediate to that of the geological epoch in which it was produced, demonstrates the constant avoidance of eco-anxiety that characterizes life in the twenty-first century.

From these diverse but connected examinations of Instapoetry, we hope it will be clear how fascinating this genre is, and how worthy of additional study. Like the platform to which it is inextricably linked, Instapoetry can be used in multidimensional ways, whether as acts of performance to spark ethical and political interventions, or as linguistic tokens to sell kitschy cottage-core accessories. At their best, the Instapoets who juggle multiple roles of writer, publisher, marketer, therapist, and more may smash crystal ceilings of gender and class, or at their worst, they may reinforce hegemonic stances beneath a new aesthetic patina of "selfie-empowerment." Yet regardless of its use, there is no denying that this massively growing body of literature should be of great interest to scholars and leaders of industry alike. What other movement (besides interim flurries of war-time newspaper rhymes) has so extensively and immediately reflected the rapidly changing aspirations and anxieties of its society, particularly a movement that is largely written for the public and by the public? Each paneled window in the interminable feed, organized in tidy 3-by-3 grids, displays in real time the events and values that consume us in a post-digital gig economy world, and that do so on a global scale. Moreover, no other movement thus far has had the same intermediacy of Instapoetry, which simply cannot be fully transferred or detached from its virtual contexts. We would do well to not only pay attention to who is reading, who is writing, and what is being written, but how the haptics, hypertext, and marginalia of a social media platform can transfigure the concept of "engagement" itself. With this critical collection, therefore, we seek to spur future explorations of a movement that is constantly shifting and evolving, transforming our ideas not only of what it means to read poetry, but what reading digitally means in the first place.

Note

1 Copyright is a significant barrier to the discussion of Instapoetry. In the first draft of this Introduction, we had focused on a single well-known six-word poem by Atticus, which we felt exemplified the tension in the genre between feminist affirmation and vacuous statements. However, due to the laws on copyright that pertain, we cannot use this six-word poem (itself freely published and viewed in its digital format) without paying a significant sum of money. Ironically, the ambiguity of an Instapoem's blended identity as both a social media post and a poem, along with its brevity, means that it is actually more vulnerable to being enclosed by stringent copyright rules in print, which traditional literary forms usually circumnavigate with fair use practices. These issues with uncertainties of copyright law as it pertains to reproducing social media posts have also meant that some contributors have needed to modify their chapters when permission was not forthcoming. One chapter, which focused on close readings of a specific Instapoet,

had to be withdrawn late in the process when that poet would not give permission for reproduction of their work. In a genre made up of poems that are usually extremely short and have often first been posted online, these copyright restrictions in both the United States and United Kingdom can have a genuinely chilling effect on the discussion of literary works, as well as further scholarship in burgeoning digital-born and hybrid forms.

References

Dixon, Stacy Jo. 2023. "Distribution of Instagram Users Worldwide as of January 2023, by Age and Gender." *Statista*, February 14. Available online: https://www.statista.com/statistics/248769/age-distribution-of-worldwide-instagram-users/. Accessed June 1, 2023.

Frier, Sarah. 2020. *No Filter: The Inside Story of Instagram*. New York: Simon & Schuster.

1

E-Lit's #1 Hit: Is Instagram Poetry E-literature?

Kathi Inman Berens
Portland State University

Preface to the Republished Essay

A lot has happened in the world, and in e-literature, since my essay débuted as a conference presentation then a publication in *electronic book review* in 2018. Global protests against the murders of George Floyd and Breonna Taylor during the pandemic summer of 2020 sparked reckoning with how banal, mainstream, and lethal is white supremacy. Six months later, in response to specific critiques about access and equity inside the Electronic Literature Organization, its Board of Directors published a statement about Equity, Diversity and Inclusion (EDI) as a core value. As an editor of the *Electronic Literature Collective Volume 4*, I can attest that we centered EDI in our search for and evaluation of works to include in the fourth installment of the field's canonical anthology. In "Excavating Logics of White Supremacy in Electronic Literature: Antiracism as Infrastructural Critique," Ryan Ikeda shares his experience of searching the ELMCIP database for "'critical race theory,' 'Black feminism' and 'Asian American studies'—all of which yielded zero results." As a cultural act, "these serialized zeroes affirmed an all-too-familiar affective state …. Care and community building begin by organizing the symbolic structures of an institution to reflect its constituents" (2021).

The history of exclusion is Instapoetry's foundational moment. Instapoetry began with two immigrant, millennial women of color, Rupi Kaur and Lang Leav, selling directly to social media publics circa 2014 after having been repeatedly rejected by publishing house acquisitions editors. Today, Instapoetry's community of makers is too broad and diffuse to generalize about whether its practitioners "critically engage" readers, or otherwise meet the aesthetic standards articulated by editors in four volumes of the *Electronic Literature Collection*. But that shouldn't stop us from taking a keen interest in Instapoetry's field development. It has morphed from the feminism of Kaur and Leav to that of Noor Unnahar (@noor_unnahar) and the humorous Arti Gollapudi (@artifartypoems) and Aly Dixon (@aly__dixon). Sylvia Castelán (@ 💐💐💐) and Liliana Vasques (@robot_sorridente [smiling_robot]) use the Instagram platform for wry self-expression rather than as springboards to book sales. The field is now distributed rather than centralized in a few hit makers, though Andrews McMeel Publishing remains the preeminent publisher of printed Instapoetry. Robert M. Drake (@rmdrk) and Reuben Holmes (@r.h.sin), both men of color, female-affirming, and self-published, have attained *New York Times* bestseller status.

Instapoetry gives agency to poets typically shut out of prestige economies such as book publishing and academia. Without gigantic social media response in 2014, and thousands of self-published book sales, publishers wouldn't have taken a chance on Instapoetry. Rupi Kaur doesn't code her Instapoems—that option exists for no one. But in 2014 Kaur wrote, edited, and hand-built the design of her first book, *milk and honey*, as an end-run around gatekeeping poetry publishers. This exactly the kind of digital self-agency the ELO EDI statement is meant to acknowledge and invite. Those of us who read the code of an e-lit work alongside its user interface find the experience of reading e-lit published in social media flat. Shorn of its code, a work can feel like just a fragment.

Although most readers may not think of it this way, to buy a printed volume of Instapoetry is to buy the entire meaning-making apparatus. It is a contestatory act, owning a book and doing with it what you will. Read and share the book without being tracked. Browsing and preferences are the mother lode of an individual's value to media platforms, which harvest one's data in exchange for serving algorithmically customized content for "free." Harvard Business School Professor Emerita Shoshana Zuboff calls this "surveillance capitalism": the commodification of personal data for the sole purpose of profit-making (2020: v). Users of social media have no idea whether giving away their browsing data in exchange for more relevant search returns is a fair exchange because no regulatory body has compelled media companies to disclose the value of the information, or give people the ability to opt out. Want to pay a subscription fee to stop the collection of your data? That option doesn't exist. The richest and most powerful global companies trade human-derived commodities mostly free from regulatory constraint. It's immoral.

In the context of limitless data surveillance, one printed copy of Rupi Kaur's third volume of poetry, *Home Body*, is a bargain. For just $7.48 you can have a private Instapoetry reading experience because Kaur's publisher, Andrews

McMeel, overestimated demand; the book is remaindered. Imagine! Private reading discounted 50 percent.

Eugenio Tisselli and Rui Torres believe that "being peripheral may actually be the role of e-literature. To critically engage from the inside of a system is to guarantee that readers are not passive or merely entertained watchers." Critical awareness and resistance are excellent cultural contributions. So are access, inclusion, and community. This chapter is one exploration of the tensions between those things in Instapoetry.

***

Toward E-Lit's #1 Hit[1]

If ever there were e-literature that could fill a stadium, it's Instagram poetry.

This chapter, which I presented on the panel "Toward E-Lit's #1 Hit" at the Electronic Literature Organization 2018 conference in Montréal, responds to Matthew Kirschenbaum's keynote at the prior year's conference. Kirschenbaum traced the coincident development of stadium ("prog") rock—specifically Electric Light Orchestra—and electronic literature, a twinning that led some of us to speculate about what might constitute massively popular e-literature, its "#1 hit."

Formally more akin to a greeting card than traditional poetry because of its sentimentality and combination of text and image, Instagram poetry is a book publishing phenomenon, accounting for a stunning 47 percent of all the poetry books sold in the United States in 2017. In Canada, Instapoets' domination of the genre peaked in 2017 with their books making up 80 percent of all poetry books sold that year, according to BookNet Canada (2021). Since the peak year 2017, printed volumes of Instapoetry remained a market force: 52 percent of all poetry books sold in Canada were penned by poets with 50,000+ followers on Instagram in 2019; in 2020 "Instapoets held on to a respectable 49%."

Whether it is the top seller, Rupi Kaur, with her pen-and-ink feminist drawings and confessional verse, or R. M. Drake, whose Insta profile announces "$12 FOUR BOOK BUNDLE BACK IN STOCK: link below," or the handwritten-on-parchment and IBM Selectric typewriter aesthetic of Tyler Knott Gregson, Instapoetry is simplistic, little more taxing than reading a meme. It is almost always inspirational or emotional. Printed books of Instapoetry collect exactly the same content accessible for free in the Instagram app. Printed volumes eliminate the social features of the app such as reader comments, nested conversations, and quantification of reposts and likes. In this sense, printed Instapoetry is more like traditionally printed poetry because it is deliberately sequenced in book form and stripped of the social features that make it "viral," or "spreadable." In *Spreadable Media*, Henry Jenkins, Sam Ford, and Joshua Green critique the metaphor of virality as too passive, undercutting fan agency in spreading content they like. Jenkins, Ford, and Green suggest instead that massively shared content is like peanut butter: "content that remains sticky even as it's spread" (2013: 9). Instagram poetry is peanut butter.

Year-over-year annual poetry sales indicate a walloping 21 percent annual compound growth rate 2013–17, a growth corresponding with when Lang Leav self-published the first volume of printed social media poetry *Love and Misadventures*, which originally appeared in Tumblr (NPD 2018). Rupi Kaur's début volume of printed Instapoetry, *milk and honey* sold three million copies worldwide and has been translated into twenty-five languages. NPD Group [now called Circana] reports 2,067,164 copies of *milk and honey* sold as of January 9, 2019. This figure does not include Amazon sales, which Amazon never shares. In 2017, Kaur's second volume *the sun and her flowers* outsold #3 on the poetry bestseller list, Homer, at a ratio of 10:1. But the hits are not just by Kaur: Instapoets comprised *twelve* of 2017's top twenty bestselling poets. That's *60% of bestsellers* in a publishing field that had been considered moribund.

Instapoetry is definitely a #1 hit. But is it e-literature?

More precisely, can a literary work be e-lit if it's not self-consciously engaged in the aesthetic of difficulty that characterizes e-literature's first and second generations?

While I am persuaded by Leonardo Flores's argument that there's a wealth of digital writing among people who have never heard of ELO nor studied e-lit in college, I wonder if the radical expansion of e-lit's aesthetic from difficulty to ease violates one of e-literature's founding principles: that to read e-lit requires "non-trivial" effort, whether that effort is physical interaction and/or cognitive complexity? This 1997 definition from Espen Aarseth's *Cybertexts*, and N. Katherine Hayles's definition of *technotexts* (2002) describe the mechanics by which e-lit artists align its practices with modernist poetry, not populist bestsellers. The e-literature field remains committed to self-conscious reading practices, where the interaction between a work's physical properties and its semantic strategies engages in "reflexive loops" (Hayles 2008). Stephanie Strickland suggests that "reading e-lit requires taking an aesthetic attitude toward the textscape as an object that stimulates the sense. To read e-works is to operate or play them (more like an instrument than a game, though some e-works have gamelike elements)" (2009). An experimental, hand-built interface is very different from a pre-packaged, self-evident social media interface. In this chapter, I explore whether or not Instapoetry participates in the defined aesthetics of electronic literature, and I argue that Instagram poetry's aesthetic is indivisible from the surveillance capitalism infrastructure of social media metadata that makes algorithms agentic in "reading" the reader.

I conceptualize Instapoetry as a watershed moment in bibliography, where scholars writing about digital literary interactivity must reckon not only with the gestures we can see—the "likes," comments, reposts, or "@s"—but the platform code and data harvesting we cannot see. Perhaps we could agree that a "like" is "trivial" engagement. But what about the terabytes of data shed by and then harvested from Instapoetry fans? It cannot be "trivial" when 160,000 people "touching" just one Instapoem leave behind so much information that is quite literally out of their hands—is, in fact, a loss they can neither feel nor tally?

Instapoetry is especially interesting generically because "poetry" connotes the pinnacle of the literary highbrow. Poetic language is the most condensed and figurative of literary modes and there's a special wing of the Interwebs devoted to explaining why poetry is so hard to understand, items like "how to read poetry like a professor" (hint: reread) and David Biespeil's list of "Ten Things Successful Poets Do." Number one: "embrace toxicity;" number two: "assume the worst;" number three: "Let negative thoughts hijack [your] brain," and so forth (2013). Poetry, since the early-twentieth-century moderns, has been a difficult business, both in the reading and making: think Pound's debt to Chinese ideograms, and Eliot's endnotes to *The Waste Land*, which reviewers at the time found both necessary and risible. It's no wonder there are guides today on Goodreads for how to make poetry less intimidating.

It is into this highbrow literary context that printed Instagram "poetry" became a phenomenon in 2013 when Lang Leav, a woman born in a Thai refugee camp, sold the rights to her self-published book *Love and Misadventures* to Andrews McMeel Publishing, who sold cookbooks, gift books, and comic strip collections until Instapoetry made its fortune. AMP understood the value proposition of moving *Love and Misadventures* onto their roster, and Leav, whose 5,000-unit print-run sold out in a week, understood she needed help to meet demand.

It's worth lingering over how self-publishing a poetry book is different from self-publishing poetry via a social media website like Tumblr or Instagram.

The most salient difference is in the type of capital that circulates in these transactions. Reposts, likes, and comments are the currency of social media, where the financial value of those transactions is harvested by media platforms, not the authors. Every form of interaction, from simply seeing the post in one's feed ("lurking") to reposting it with a comment sheds reader data that becomes volumetric with each increased level of engagement.

Think of the information on the user interface—that is, what the reader engages with on the screen—as the informational tip of the iceberg: the vast majority of data in any social media post is, like an iceberg, hidden from view.

A famous visualization of a Tweet's metadata made by Raffi Kirkorian (2010; viewable as a public resource) indicates the types of information Twitter collects on a single Tweet during this paleolithic era of Twitter. At the top of the image is the actual tweet that users would have seen in their feeds. The rest of the metadata is the invisible bulk of the iceberg. This is sheerly descriptive metadata. It is not the code that moves packets of information from author to device to server and out through a vast, dispersed distribution system.

It's interesting that this annotated metadata of a 2010 tweet is a rare disclosure of metadata that the company collects. Obviously, a lot changed for Twitter during the ten years since Kirkorian's annotation—not to mention the disruptions that have happened since Elon Musk bought Twitter. Some changes that happened between 2010 and 2020:

The text count doubled to 280 characters;

Tweets embed images and short videos;

Tweets harvest much more precise GPS data, down to what aisle one is standing in at a store.

Bots, hate speech, and "dog whistles" are effects of the platform.

A more recent analysis of Twitter metadata (Barrero 2017) includes new classes such as Klout scores, sentiment and "sentiment category probability," emotion and "emotion category probability." This is also a very basic view of contemporary social media metadata. The focus on emotion and sentiment is raw data for behavioral marketing. What Flores has dubbed "Third Generation E-literature" is inextricably co-constituted with such metadata, which is to say, engaging its literary and artistic meaning comes at the cost of shedding behavioral data that is collected, collated, and auctioned. Reading e-literature in this context inscribes the reading with acts of commercial marking that are locked away from the reader and visible to the human and nonhuman agents gathering and auctioning such information. In *The Metainterface—The Art of*

Platforms, Cities and Clouds (2018), Christian Ulrik Andersen and Søren Bro Pold track what it means that "today's cultural interfaces disappear by blending immaculately into the environment" (10) and propose net art and e-literature as materially self-conscious practices that reveal "fissures" in "habitual" (159) ubiquitous computing. What is the "metainterface"? It's the movement of human/computer interaction from the desktop to the smartphone and cloud. Humans are both agents and quarry, where they use smartphones to electively inscribe themselves on the network, but also shed enormous quantities of data harvested by media companies such as Facebook and Google. Instapoetry is the alluring blossom that attracts users' attention and engagement. Such readers' social media wanderings pollinate sites with data both shed and accumulated. The datafication of reader response *is an essential part of the poem*, one whose effects are visible to readers only indirectly in ads prompted by the reader's engagement with the poem. This is a new kind of "reader response," where algorithms are agentic: the human reader is herself "read" by behavioral targeting algorithms, parsed for commercial susceptibility, and served new information or ads designed to entice transaction, even if that transaction is only a click.

Let's imagine Instapoetry in the wild. One poem by Rupi Kaur about the Trump administration's policy of separating refugee families at the US border published June 19, 2018, illustrates what made Kaur a destination site for so many people, and revitalized sales of poetry books.

Kaur, speaking as an immigrant, excites a lively discourse in multiple spoken languages and emoji, a visual communication format underwritten by Unicode and meant to provide "all the characters needed for writing the majority of living languages in use on computers" (W3C, quoted in Reed 2016). The blend of spoken word and emoji is characteristic of the types of populist formats of third-generation electronic literature. Instagram organizes conversation into a time-stamped database too large for humans to read closely. Sample selection delivers a snippet of a political debate about whether incarcerating children is a just implementation of US immigration law. The problem for literary critics or book publishing scholars who are taking the measure of this kind of discourse is how to cull evidence and make the case for exemplarity when the dataset is so large? Some of the tools of distant reading [most frequent word counts or co-locations] are only so good as the query. How to measure significance in an environment of rapidly proliferating superabundance, where hundreds of thousands of pieces of data are created each day—and that's just what's visible on the user interface, let alone the volume of invisible but material metadata sparked by each digital touch.

In the case of Instagram comments, to stabilize the data is to denature it.

To take the measure of Instagram as a platform for electronic literature, consider Shelley Jackson's *SNOW* (2014), a sequential text/image poem where each of the 428 lexia is hand-drawn with sticks and brushes to look like type pressed into snow in various stages of melt and drift. *SNOW* is a time-based work. Its first lexia was published January 22, 2014, and the most recent was published, at time of writing this chapter, March 3, 2023. The still-in-progress poem cuts off mid-sentence.

There are several aspects of *SNOW* that mark its second-gen e-lit aesthetic. First, it has reading instructions: "A story in progress, weather permitting. (Read in reverse order.)" Five of twenty-four comments on the first lexia also instruct others how to read it. Second, *SNOW* repays close reading. Anna Nacher, Søren Pold, and Christian Ulrik Anderson, and Scott Rettberg have all prepared conference papers or published work about *SNOW*. Third, Jackson's status as a vaunted first-gen e-literature artist imbues *SNOW* with literary prestige. *Patchwork Girl* is the second most frequently cited work of electronic literature, according to Jill Walker Rettberg's distant reading of dissertations about electronic literature. Jackson's reputation casts a highbrow aura of modernist difficulty despite this poem being set in a populist platform. Fourth, Jackson disengages from the circulation of social capital on Instagram. She treats the Instagram platform as a printing press that distributes a hand-drawn emulation of machine writing. Jackson does not respond to comments posted to lexia, nor does she "like" or repost them. The profile picture of Jackson in winter coat bending over a snow bank like a scribe leaning over vellum reinforces the materiality and ancient human labor of her endeavor. The profile picture frames Jackson in the act of writing. She is resolutely removed from the scene of reading, making *SNOW* categorically different from Instapoetry where authors interact with fans.

Aesthetically, *SNOW* has more in common with Jim Andrews' "Seattle Drift" (1997) than Instapoetry. As is the case of the one-word lexia in *SNOW*, each of the div tags in "Seattle Drift" holds one word of the poem. In the code comments of this visual, kinetic poem, Andrews says of "Seattle Drift":

> Stylistically … the text talks about itself. I like this approach because it focusses [*sic*] attention on the questions and also allows me to develop character. *The character is the text itself.* [My emphasis]

Both Jackson and Andrews are interested in the autonomous behavior of text, whether machine-mediated or snow-mediated. For them, text is a nonhuman "character," and "drift" is a pivot point of interactivity. Andrews's poem begs the reader to make it drift, to "do me." For Jackson, drift is non-interactive. Snow and climate, not humans, are the agents influencing drift and display. Visually the poem reinforces snow's way of looking like a blank page awaiting inscription; but unlike the nineteenth-century British male romantic poets, for whom nature was a handmaiden to their own poetic expression, *SNOW* is a page that resists human inscription by melting.

On the surface, assessing digital-born Instapoetry through close reading as I've just done with *SNOW* and "Seattle Drift," Instapoetry seems not to be a technotext. But ludostylistic scholarship gives us tools for reading Instapoetry's bibliographic code. Calling upon us to "keep in view the need to let go of the object-centered approach that is at the heart of book history," Johanna Drucker articulates a vision of book history that decenters the book as object and considers instead the logics by which a book is an "event space" (2014).

Book publishers have found a way to extract extraordinary financial value from printed Instapoetry as a dynamic playable event space. While social media capital is a routine part of any book marketing campaign, and influences which authors are or are not offered publishing contracts, converting social media capital into sales remains hard to correlate. In Instapoetry, book publishers have a direct conversion of social media capital to financial capital. Unlike other social media celebrities such as YouTube personalities, Instapoets don't face the awkward task of converting a fanbase from one medium (vlogging) to another (printed books). Printed Instapoetry shifts the "content" seamlessly from digital to print. But stripped of liveness, printed Instapoetry ends up looking banal. Its treacly insights, absent the warm glow emanating from fans inside the app, harden into branding. A Goodreads review, visible on the first page of returns about *milk and honey* circa 2018, sums up the skepticism Instapoetry can evoke outside the app:

> So if I
> write my review
> like this
> will it
> automatically
> become poetry?

I've argued in various contexts that even in physically interactive collaborative poetry such as *The Poetry Machine* and virtually interactive literary games like netprov (see my "Live/Archive" essay), printed or archival repositories of live experience always distort the live experience. Nothing, neither digital traces nor printed artifacts, replicates liveness. But that doesn't stop us from wanting mementos of pleasurable live experience: think about the enormous market for live music "merch" such as concert t-shirts, hats, programs, shot glasses. A printed book of Instagram poetry is also a souvenir, though one stripped of playfulness in a dynamic event space like the Instagram app. Nevertheless, printed poetry books participate in the ongoing flow of play and comment by stopping the flow, performing that it's possible to stop paddling in digital currents.

The bibliographic intervention I propose layers a new valence onto "play" where gestural interactivity is foundational, but not the primary object of study. This would be a new turn in ludosemiotic scholarship. Commenting on the book as a physical medium, Serge Bouchardon notes that "[w]ith the Digital, it is not only the medium, but the content itself which becomes manipulable. Manipulability is the very principle of the Digital" (2018: 25). Katarzyna Bazarnik defines *Liberature* as specifically "a Book-bound Genre … _better understood as 'expanded' literature, aware of its spatial, embodied nature" (2018: 43). Agnieska Przybyszewska suggests that liberature is not a genre, but can be classed according to gradations of physical play that transpire both within and outside the printed book format, such as in mobile electronic literature (her monograph *Liberackość dzieła literackiego* is cited and discussed in Bazarnik, particularly 103–4). Astrid Ensslin, in *Literary Games* (2014), situates works on quadrants where physical play is relative to literary ambiguity. Alexandra Saemmer has speculated that the intensity of physical touch in a digital-born literary work affects the reader's process of identification with the protagonist (2013). These and other scholars of ludosemiotics, including Amaranth Borsuk's recent *The Book* in the M.I.T. Press "Essential Knowledge" series, use close reading techniques to consider how play and physical manipulation influence how we read literature.

What I'm proposing is slightly different.

A book of printed Instapoetry is not like a gem in a setting that is somehow lifted up and out of the data-harvesting context. Instead, such a book is brought into being by the social media transactions that make Instapoetry phenomenal—even as the printed volume seems to offer respite from tracking and behavioral marketing. In fact, the site of tracking and reader datafication shifts from the social media platform to the book distributor, whether it's Amazon or a brick-and-mortar bookseller. Even books purchased anonymously with cash are still tracked as sales. *The reader being converted into a datastream is not a byproduct of reading poetry. It is part of the poem itself.* As we think about the memetics of Third Generation electronic literature, an aesthetic inextricable from tactical media and surveillance capitalism, we ask: What does it mean that the first highly profitable digital-born literature, Instagram poetry, makes its money in the walled gardens of the "post-Web" in ways we can only imagine because the code on which those proprietary social media platforms are built is not inspectable, even to government regulators?

Nick Montfort asks:

> [W]hat has happened to Hypertext in the post-Web world? Just to stick to Twitter, for a moment: You can still put links into tweets, but corporate enclosure of communications means that the wild wild wild linking of the Web tends to be more constrained. Links in tweets look like often-cryptic partial URLs instead of looking like text, as they do in pre-Web and Web hypertexts. You essentially get to make a Web citation or reference, not build a hypertext, by tweeting. And hypertext links have gotten *more* abstruse in this third, post-Web generation! When you're on Twitter, you're supposed to be consuming that linear feed—automatically produced for you in the same way that birds feed their young—not clicking away of your own volition to see what the Web has to offer and exploring a network of media. (2018)

I began this research project wondering why people would pay $13 for a book that reprints exactly the same content that can be had for free, on-demand, in the Instagram app. Why buy the book? Now I understand that printed Instagram poetry wouldn't be a phenomenon without its origin in post-Web, walled-garden engagement. Is Instapoetry e-literature? Yes. The performative materiality of social media platforms reshapes the contemporary literary field. The e-lit aesthetic of difficulty moves from close reading the medium-specificity of first- and second-generation works, to skimming the content and close reading the promiscuous read/write capacities of social media metadata, and guessing at the black-boxed code that undergirds third-generation e-lit.

Note

1 This version of the chapter strips all figures from the chapter and replaces them with textual description to comply with permissions restrictions.

References

Anderson, Christian Ulrik and Søren Bro Pold. 2018. *The Metainterface: The Art of Platforms, Cities and Clouds*. Cambridge, MA: The M.I.T. Press.

Andrews, Jim. 1997. "Seattle Drift." *Vizpo*. http://www.vispo.com/animisms/SeattleDrift.html

Barrero, Carlos. 2017. "The Metadata from a Single Social Media Post." October 2. https://www.crimsonhexagon.com/blog/metadata-from-a-social-media-post

Bazarnik, Katarzyna. 2018. *Liberature: A Book-bound Genre*. New York: Columbia University Press [U.S. distribution of original publication by Jagiellonian University Press, 2016].

Berens, Kathi Inman. 2015. "Live/Archive: *Occupy MLA*." *Hyperrhiz: New Media Cultures*, 11 (Spring). http://hyperrhiz.io/hyperrhiz11/essays/live-archive-occupy-mla.html

Biespiel, David. 2013. "Ten Things Successful Poets Do." *The Rumpus*. https://therumpus.net/2013/12/david-biespiels-poetry-wire-10-things-successful-poets-do/

Borsuk, Amaranth. 2018. *The Book*. Cambridge, MA: The M.I.T. Press.

Bouchardon, Serge. 2018. "Mind the Gap! 10 Gaps for Digital Literature?" Keynote presentation at the 2018 Electronic Literature Organization Conference. Montréal. http://www.utc.fr/~bouchard/Bouchardon-ELO18-English.pdf

Castelán, Sylvia. 🥀🥀🥀, https://brokenenglish.lol/🥀🥀🥀/

Dixon, Aly. https://www.instagram.com/aly__dixon/

Drucker, Johanna. 2014. "Distributed and Conditional Documents: Conceptualizing Bibliographical Alterities." *MATLIT: Materialities of Literature*, 2 (1): 11–29. https://doi.org/10.14195/2182-8830_2-1_1

Electronic Literature Organization. 2021. "Addressing EDI in ELO." March 8. https://eliterature.org/2021/03/addressing-edi-in-elo/

Ensslin, Astrid. 2014. *Literary Gaming*. Cambridge, MA: The M.I.T. Press.

Gollapudi, Arti. https://www.instagram.com/artifartypoems/?hl=en

Hayles, N. Katherine. 2008. "Distributed Cognition at/in Work: Strickland, Lawson Jaramillo, and Ryan's *seippingglimpse*." *Frame*, 21 (1): 15–29.

Ikeda, Ryan. 2021. "Excavating Logics of White Supremacy in Electronic Literature: Antiracism as Infrastructural Critique." *Electronic Book Review*, January 3. https://electronicbookreview.com/essay/excavating-logics-of-white-supremacy-in-electronic-literature-antiracism-as-infrastructural-critique/ DOI: 10.7273/cctw-4415.

Jackson, Shelley. 2014-present. SNOW. https://www.instagram.com/snowshelleyjackson/

Jenkins, Henry, Sam Ford, and Joshua Green. 2013. *Spreadable Media: Creating Value and Meaning in a Networked Culture*. New York: NYU Press.

Kaur, Rupi. 2016. *Milk and Honey*. Kansas City: Andrews McMeel Publishing.

Kaur, Rupi. 2018. "You Split the World into Pieces." *Instagram*, June 19. https://www.instagram.com/p/BkOyGTxlAWf/

Kirkorian, Raffi. 2010. "Map of a Twitter Status Object." *The Wall Street Journal*, April 18. http://online.wsj.com/public/resources/documents/TweetMetadata.pdf

Kirschenbaum, Matthew. 2017. "ELO and the Electric Light Orchestra: Lessons for Electronic Literature from Prog Rock." Keynote at the 2017 Electronic Literature Organization conference. Porto, Portugal.

Mongeon, Monique. 2021. "Stars and Stanzas: Social Media, Stardom, and Poetry in 2020." *BookNet Canada*, January 7. https://www.booknetcanada.ca/blog/2021/1/7/stars-and-stanzas-social-media-stardom-and-poetry-in-2020

Montfort, Nick. 2018. "A Web Reply to the Post-Web Generation." August 26. https://nickm.com/post/2018/08/a-web-reply-to-the-post-web-generation/

Nacher, Anna. 2017. "The Creative Process as a Dance of Agency: Shelley Jackson's Snow: Performing Literary Texts with Elements." In *Digital Media and Textuality: From Creation to Archiving*, edited by Daniela Côrtes Maduro, 169–86. Bremen: Transcript verlag.

NPD Group. 2018. "Instapoets Rekindling U.S. Poetry Book Sales." https://www.npd.com/wps/portal/npd/us/news/press-releases/2018/instapoets-rekindling-u-s–poetry-book-sales–the-npd-group-says/.

Reed, Rob. 2016. "Everything You Need to Know about Emoji." *Smashing Magazine*, November 14. https://www.smashingmagazine.com/2016/11/character-sets-encoding-emoji/

Rettberg, Jill Walker. 2013. "A Network Analysis of Dissertations about Electronic Literature." Paper presented at the 2013 Electronic Literature Conference. Paris. http://conference.eliterature.org/sites/default/files/papers/Jill-Walker-Rettberg-A%20Network%20Analysis%20of%20Dissertations%20About%20Electronic%20Literature.pdf

Rettberg, Scott. 2019. "Room for So Much World: A Conversation with Shelley Jackson." *EBR*, January 6. https://electronicbookreview.com/essay/room-for-so-much-world-a-conversation-with-shelley-jackson/

Saemmer, Alexandra. 2013. "Hyperfiction as a Medium for Drifting Times: A Close Reading of the German Hyperfiction *Zeit für die Bombe*." In *Analyzing Digital Fictions*, edited by Alice Bell, Astrid Ensslin, and Hans Rustad, 176–96. London: Routledge.

Strickland, Stephanie. 2009. "Born Digital." *The Poetry Foundation*. https://www.poetryfoundation.org/articles/69224/born-digital

Tisselli, Eugenio and Rui Torres. 2020. "In Defense of the Difficult." *electronic book review*, May 20. https://electronicbookreview.com/essay/in-defense-of-the-difficult/ DOI: 10.7273/y2vs-1949.

Vasques, Liliana. "The Name Is Woman" [Instagram account]. https://www.instagram.com/robot.sorridente/

Zuboff, Shoshana. 2020. *The Age of Surveillance Capitalism: The Fight for a Human Future at the New Frontier of Power*. New York: PublicAffairs.

2

#Tagged: Hashing Meaning through Poe(t/m)-tagging

JuEunhae Knox
University of Sheffield

The term "gig," abbreviated from the word "engagement," was originally conceived by 1920s jazz players, performing at sporadic events while they sought steady patrons. No longer confined to musicians, the word now represents a vast, intricate economy, where any job, from food delivery to freelance transcription, is crowdsourced to the masses of self-managing and self-marketing entrepreneurs endeavoring to fulfill "on-demand" work. Many pro-capitalist psychologists and economy gurus heartily approve of this efficacy of freelance commerce, claiming that those who de-compartmentalize the boundaries of labor and life—while fervently believing in their autonomous, creative labor—will achieve true self-actualization (Maslow 1965; Reeves 2001; Sinicki 2019). Others have observed, however, that the gig economy severely exploits the quality of work and on workers' lives. In this model, many people subsist on incessant, menial tasks for pittance wages, vainly hoping to eventually earn enough to pursue their real passions (Petriglieri, Ashford, and Wrzesniewski 2018). The digital nature of the modern gig economy enforces even subtler restraints upon those relying on crowdsourcing for their livelihood, as apps designed to curate consumers' personalized experiences tightly control workers through algorithms optimizing location, availability, qualifications, and accumulated ratings (Morgan and Nelligan 2018; Prassl 2018).

Artists, the original gig-seekers and most endangered species of precariats, are certainly also bound to these constraints. They must constantly juggle desires for both elite approval consecration and financial stability, while still struggling with the old illusion privileging art as somehow pure and as something that transcends commercial agendas (Bourdieu 1996; Bernes 2017). Yet of all the movements increasingly subsumed by the creative economy, few have been as impacted by hegemonic cultural commodification as much as Instapoetry, a form permanently being re-engineered to sustain multitudes of para-social kinships on its platform. Instagram itself is currently the leading social media network for 67 percent of the world's Top 50 influencers, from Cristiano Ronaldo to Kylie Jenner (Wallach 2021). Their Insta-followers not only outrank those combined on Facebook, Twitter, YouTube, and TikTok by several hundred million but greatly affect these influencers' brand-generated wealth; a single post by Ronaldo is worth $889,000 (Chakraborty 2020). Because the platform overtly encourages users to gain external rewards of microcelebrity and money by boosting their visibility, it is no wonder that the genre of Instapoetry, uniquely shaped by its technological tokens of likes, follows, and view-counts, is also entrenched in digital optimization.

Despite its clear hypercapitalist interconnections, there is an understandable, though still reprehensible, scholarly lacuna regarding Instapoetry's place in today's digital market. At first glance, Instapoetry still appears to be technically "free," unlike other traditional gig employment services, like ridesharing. And as poems—particularly ones that broadcast highly emotional themes like love, rejection, and self-empowerment—they still draw upon the inherited belief that poetry is a mutually beneficial "gift," forging shared intimacies between the reader and writer community (Craig 2007). Yet the existence of, for example, popup on-demand Instapoetry sessions where customized "typewriter poems" are sold for $50–$96 each, demonstrate that Instapoets, at least those hoping to increase their brand, are fully invested in the rewards of manufacturing and rationalizing intimacy.

The question becomes how to examine such behaviors since the value of poetry as cultural capital is extremely difficult to quantify. This is where it became crucial to examine one of Instagram's most significant digital tokens: the hashtag. Because of its combined technicity and grammatization, this protean and ambivalent symbol enables us to examine the nuanced methods utilized by Instapoets and Insta-venders alike. Through poe(t/m)-tagging, which I define below, users often reterritorialize disparate poets and poems as productive assemblages, both to promote their services and goods and to exploit the in-egalitarian popularity enjoyed by highly visible influencers. Despite the seeming possibility for online activism, however, Instagram's omnipotent algorithms, which restrain, exclude, and scatter posts in the name of user relevance, mean that a massive structural change would be needed before fractured Instapoems could ever produce true amelioration of digital hegemony.

A History of Poe(t/m)-tagging

The hashtag is not unique to Instagram, as it was first used to systemize channels in Internet Relay Chat before it was adapted by social media networks to organize content and profiles. However, these handy meta-discursive hyperlinks have become especially prevalent on Instagram's platform, which directly rewards users who are both prolific and strategic in tagging with greater visibility.[1] Clicking a tag now directs one to a never-ending communal feed amassing loosely related posts, from viral memes to celebrity co-opted brands. Because they are neither purely material nor wholly conceptual, hashtags embody both extrinsic and intrinsic contexts like discursive "statements" (Foucault 1972: 86). This transformation from merely syntactical symbols to semantic ones enables intricate reflexive meta-commentary, for example using #excited to sarcastically signify the opposite emotion. Marginalized activist groups can even repurpose tags to resist elitist misrepresentation (Bernard 2019), an attribute that I will examine later in the chapter.

Although tagging people, places, things, and ideas is nothing new, there is currently an unexplored trend that has increasingly gained traction on Instagram, a practice that I have labeled "poe(t/m)-tagging." Pronounced po-tum-tagging, this neologism does not merely abbreviate "the act of tagging poets (and/or) poems," but incorporates those who purposefully tag poets and poems to promote any product for external, commercial rewards. Rupi Kaur's *milk and honey* greatly helped to popularize Instapoetry from 2016 onwards, but the seeds of poe(t/m)-tagging were laid as early as 2011, when the platform first introduced the hashtag function. While people have of course quoted poets and poems for numerous reasons across the centuries, there has never been a distinct method for calculating the values of such references. With hashtags, however, one can quantifiably track a poet's platform popularity, a critical step before qualitatively analyzing the distinctions of tag patterns, motivations, deviations, and ambiguities. Under Instagram's current API, hashtags not only operate with navigational technicity, but exhibit standardization through reproduced fluxes (Omena, Rabello, and Mintz 2020). Analyzing the grammatization of poe(t/m)-tagging could thus produce large sampling parameters as well as indicating how these tags directly affect users' collective action.

To build my qualitative–quantitative database, I googled "Famous Poets," and compared the top 26 poets by number of Google searches with their number of Instagram tags. Many categories paralleled in popularity across the two search bars. This is a predictable fact considering that users' exposure to poetry is often limited to classics learned in high school, which is why Frost, Poe, Whitman, and Blake are all ranked so high. Nevertheless, there were some interesting surprises, indicating that the folksonomy of Instagram could influence even the marbled halls of a predominantly white, Western, male canon. Maya Angelou has the highest number of tags after Shakespeare, while Plath and Dickinson outrank most of their male peers, and Neruda gains a huge audience, predominantly through his Spanish Insta-readers. And of course, the newly famous Instapoets, with the advantage of being alive to self-tag and promote, have high tag counts on the platform instead of on Google—although there are significant distinctions in how these tags are reappropriated, which will be examined further in the chapter.

Table 2.1 Tables of Classical and Instapoet Poet Popularity. Results were compiled by the author on June 2, 2020

Poet's Name/Username	Number of Searches on Google	Instagram Tags
William Shakespeare/ #shakespeare	145,000,000 results (0.87 seconds)	2,605,796
William Blake #williamblake	135,000,000 results (0.83 seconds)	127,374
Dylan Thomas/ #dylanthomas	113,000,000 results (0.72 seconds)	64,522
Robert Frost/ #robertfrost	85,500,000 results (0.68 seconds)	189,433
Walt Whitman #waltwhitman	23,100,000 results (0.64 seconds)	177,953
Edgar Allan Poe #edgarallanpoe	42,000,000 results (0.67 seconds)	636,354
Lord Byron #lordbyron	52,900,000 results (0.72 seconds)	92,737
#Emily Dickinson/ #emilydickinson	51,000,000 results (0.63 seconds)	197,058
Pablo Neruda #pabloneruda	15,000,000 results (0.59 seconds)	477,993
John Keats #johnkeats	12,800,000 results (0.56 seconds)	53,374

Poet's Name/Username	Number of Searches on Google	Instagram Tags
William Wordsworth #williamwordsworth	11,900,000 results (0.56 seconds)	32,244
Maya Angelou #mayaangelou	11,300,000 results (0.65 seconds)	882,787
Langston Hughes #langstonhughes	9,160,000 results (0.71 seconds)	78,138
William Butler Yeats #williambutleryeats	8,980,000 results (0.74 seconds)	14,210
Sylvia Plath/ #sylviaplath	8,610,000 results (0.49 seconds)	224,438

Instapoet's Name/ Username	Number of Searches on Google	Instagram Tags
R. M. Drake #rmddrake	42,200,000 results (0.48 seconds)	506,524
Cleo Wade #cleowade	16,000,000 results (0.63 seconds)	25,294
Rupi Kaur #rupikaur	3,990,000 results (0.51 seconds)	698,013
Atticus (Poet) #langleav	2,860,000 results (0.47 seconds)	423,395
Lang Leav #langleav	1,390,000 results (0.49 seconds)	208,716
Tyler Knott Gregson #tylerknottgregson	433,000 results (0.49 seconds)	76,039

From November 2017, I kept a daily running tally of the top 9 posts and most recent 200 posts dedicated to each poet for four weeks, reassessing multiple intervals every four months throughout the last three years. This evolving collection generated such extensive data that I could easily develop unique studies for each poet. For instance, #emilydickinson initially had mostly complete poems, as Dickinson's aesthetic, dash-filled verse was fittingly concise and attractive to adapt into typewriter posts. Yet since AppleTV's 2019 release of *Dickinson*, the feed is now mainly filled with photos of Hailee Steinfeld, who plays the titular role. The images do not necessarily relate to Dickinson's own life, but primarily feature Steinfeld posing as a model and fashion icon, or passionately kissing her female co-star in various stages of déshabillé, exemplifying that images of young, nude, female bodies still receive the most attention. In contrast, #dylanthomas used to be filled with many random photos featuring coffee, dogs, yoga, babies. It also included shots of the actor Dylan O'Brien, who plays teenage heartthrob Thomas in the YA *Mazerunner*: the fan-made profile, which daily crowded the feed with adoring montages of their idol, seemed happy to capitalize on the poet's tag to garner more traffic. Now, however, the feed is almost entirely composed of images of Thomas: at his writing desk, with different translations of his poetry and plays, and in his scenic home in Laugharne.

Equally as fascinating as the evolving tags of poets, however, is the practice of poem-tagging. Poems have a more niche following but reveal key insights about language on the platform. Take, for example, the surprising popularity of Thomas's famous "Do Not Go Gentle into That Good Night." Of all the pieces explicitly recognized as poetry on Instagram, Thomas's poem has one of the largest numbers of tags. The tags #donotgogentleintothatgoodnight and #rageagainstthedyingofthelight, or any combination of the two, have collectively accumulated 31,209 posts on Instagram, a surprising statistic considering the sheer number of characters. Lengthy tags jamming words together without spaces are not only more time-consuming to write and difficult to read, but simply look unaesthetic on a network obsessed with appearance. Yet Thomas's poem steadily continues to gain posts, with 2,030 even dedicated to #ragerageagainstthedyingofthelight—a rare exception, since users usually avoid the tacky redundancy of repeating words.

While there are many reasons why Thomas's poem might continue to resonate with readers, not least the fact that it is included within many American high school syllabuses, I would argue that the lines possess distinct aural and rhetorical qualities that make them memorable (and therefore commonly taught by teachers). The poem is driven by a rigidly steady and diagrammable villanelle beat, yet forceful monosyllables like "rage rage," made wilder by repetition, continually foil any potential lulls. Multiple, hard plosives starting with "g" and "d" and "b" reverberate against soft or silent consonants like those found in "gentle" and "sight," while tidy, exact rhymes contrast starkly against opposite images and themes, such as "night" and "light." The contradictory combinations of clashing sound and unusual meter fully drive the poem's forlornness, arresting even the most novice reader.

I am not suggesting that most users could clearly explain these striking linguistic qualities in critical language, of course. More realistically, the poem's overall sentiment combined with its eye-catching rhetoric can be easily adapted into captions for pretentious sunset selfies or Botox ads. In contrast to a vague aphorism like Kaur's #ifthehurtcomessowillthehappiness, which has only twenty-eight re-tags, Thomas's vivid diction is just more attention-grabbing. For all the doomsday prophesies over recent decades of poetry's inevitable demise, and even Thomas's own mournful sigh about words' inability to permanently "fork lightning," the continual re-tagging of classical poems suggests that many Instagram users have taken his petition to heart: neither the human race, nor the art of poetry, must gently resign itself to death, but go out burning and blazing. However, there is a critical distinction between Thomas's poem that weeps for dying fathers and the futility of men's transient wisdom, and the faux carpe diem attitude touted by gurus, life-coaches, and digital merchants profiting from this reterritorialized tag—a difference more closely examined in the following section.

Poe(t/m)-tagging Delineations

To understand the grammatization of poe(t/m)-tagging, it is important to first discuss the kinds of users tagging on the platform. According to Omena, Rabello, and Mintz's 3L model, Instagram users are categorized either in the majority of "ordinary" users, or in the minority of high-visible actors, with vast, consistent levels of audience engagement reach (2020). This initial concept is helpful because it first helps to exclude many ordinary poetry fans who post photos of poets and poems out of pure "enjoyment," or apply poetry to personal or social circumstances. This group also included those who stumbled across poets or poems by accident, perhaps inspired by picturesque headstones or provoked by lines scrawled under a motorway. Posts from this category were far more likely to feature entire or partial poems or incorporate detailed commentary. This does not mean that such users are all altruistically un-narcissistic, since any social media post is an act of self-promotion, but they still greatly diverge from users I classify as actual poe(t/m)-taggers, purposefully manipulating poetic references to sell products, services, or even lifestyles.

This group incorporates both Instapoets and general "commercial" users, all the way from MLM hustlers selling essential oils, to multi-experienced spiritualists whose Renaissance-diverse services often include yoga, fashion, and mindset change. Of the two forms of agents in a gig-economy, both sets of users can act as "sharers" and "direct sellers." As direct sellers, both groups are capable of directly offering their customers tangible products, particularly those working for established companies such as Avon. However, these users also operate in lateral exchange markets, rendering services to unknown customers (Gleim, Johnson, and Lawson 2019). The fact that both groups utilize such practices interchangeably does not hinder my argument, since I am not attempting to categorize what counts as "true" Instapoetry. Rather, the fact that these poe(t/m)-taggers are virtually indistinguishable unless they use direct tags like #mypoetry or #iamapoet precisely demonstrates just how deeply hypercapitalism has embedded itself into tagging practices, whether users are selling Vans or verses.

I argue that almost all poe(t/m)-tagging is still practiced by "ordinary" users, in the sense that high-visible influencers, at least Instapoets such as Kaur, Drake, Leav, and others, do not need to tag others to increase impressions—and in fact would eschew this tactic to avoid losing their followers to other profiles.[2] However, unlike the first group of individuals who occasionally tag poets or poems to celebrate them, this second category resorts to tagging in hopes of gaining high visibility. As unsuspecting readers search a hyperlink, they are instantly redirected to an assemblage of vaguely related tags including the poe(t/m)-tagger's own clickbait post. For this reason, certain canny users devote themselves to consistently choking the feed with their own tags. The user omnipotentvision, who labels himself as a "POETRY GOD" and recommends using only one "nice" recognizable style, effectively out-floods competition by saturating the feed for #realpoet and #1bestseller with over 400 posts a day, featuring the same image of his self-authored book.

The issue then becomes which tags should be used, since they could become undiscoverable by being either too broad or too narrow. This is particularly challenging for novice Instapoets, who have difficulty exposing their work outside the platform anyway without the support of a brick-and-mortar brand, a situation even more onerous because their poetry usually does not feature literary "manifattura," Bourdieu's term for artists' unique craft distinctions that make them identifiable (1996). Currently, Instagram's overtly visual platform still only allows a hashtag "word" search rather than a picture search because managing and categorizing images would be too vast and difficult, especially when photos are constantly re-shared. Yet since their aphorisms are so vague, many Instapoets can only be distinguished from each other (if at all) by their gallery style, background color, or image pattern—such as the inclusion of dried wildflowers or typewriter keys.

This is detrimental to Instapoems' discoverability, even those of high-visible Instapoets. Rupi Kaur's post #fallinlovewithyoursolitude, currently liked by 346,449 followers, only has 238 tags. Another popular poem, "Our backs tell stories no books have the spine to carry" (rupikaur_ 2020), only has forty-two hyperlinks, even for the more condensed tag #ourbackstellstories. Other influential Instapoets do not fare well in terms of poem discoverability either. Despite the thousands of likes for Tyler Knott Gregson's popular axiom: "You are the poem I never knew how to write" (tylerknott 2020), the hashtag #youarethepoem has 100 posts, while the line in its entirety has been linked just once. By tagging classical poets, however, Instapoets and commercial users alike can profit from semi-broad, semi-narrow tags to maximize audience attraction, particularly through a few selective methodologies.

Poe(t/m)-tagging Practice 1: Connecting to the Canon

While poe(t/m)-taggers utilize hyperlinks in a myriad of ways, three primary methodologies have gained particular traction. The first of these—that of tagging well-known poets—is quite familiar, since many, from Milton to Eliot, have utilized name-dropping. Yet there are multiple variances of how poe(t/m)-taggers manipulate these captions. Some posts tag in a cursory fashion, barely connecting to the central image. These posts often take a poem completely out of context for commercial means, to the point of rendering oppositional meanings. Quoting "Fern Hill" to advertise anti-aging moisturizing cream is built on the principle that we are *not* futilely held "green and dying" by Time. A white user's appropriation of "Still I Rise" to promote his energy drink directly flies in the face of Angelou's fierce anthem, crescendo-ing from dusk to daybreak. Notably, such users do not often clearly state that they did not write the poem. Instead, they either bury the original poet's attribution within a long list of hashtags, or at least omit quotation marks, meaning that only attentive users might recognize the quote. For example, one photo by the user @lassenl displays an image of himself shirtless and flexing his abdominal muscles, with the first stanza of Robert Frost's "The Road Not Taken" in the margins, accompanied by motivational quotes like #bumpyroad and #roadtosuccess. Because the poem does not contain quotation marks, those who are unfamiliar with the poem may not be immediately aware that lassenl is reappropriating Frost—which another user points out on the post with the critique: "Usually people add the name of the author, otherwise people think you clain [*sic*] this work as your own" (@t.kjaergaard in response to @lassenl 2020). This example does not necessarily mean all users are purposefully plagiarizing texts, but certainly highlights the fact that literary accuracy is not of utmost importance, since the post's main feature is framing the user's attractive selfie or product.

Other poe(t/m)-taggers make more of an effort, using intimate captions to express how antiquarian poets have inspired them to choose their own destinies, love more authentically, and show their true colors. Such poe(t/m)-taggers commonly choose hues and fonts demonstrating their appreciation for everything vintage. Sepia filters and Courier fonts instill a nostalgic ambiance to compel users to purchase the poe(t/m)-tagger's distressed leather satchels or retro spectacles. There are also poe(t/m)-taggers whose connections to established poets are not as perfunctory, whose tags serve to demonstrate their legitimacy by exhibiting their own literary knowledge. The poet Mallory Rowe, whose profile @petitspoemes had over 10,000 followers at the time of writing, also has published five collections on Amazon featuring micro poems similar to "You can break my heart / In the best way possible / With just your glances" (petitspoemes 2018). Despite her commercial success as an Instapoet, however, Rowe also demonstrates her literary authenticity in connection to renowned, "consecrated" poets. One way she accomplishes this is by tagging the names of famous poets but altering them slightly. Rowe's four cats, all named after some of the most tagged writers (Poe, Dickinson, Woolf, Melville), originally also had their own Instagram profiles.[3] Thus, when #emilydickinsonthecat appears under Instagram's search bar, users may be curious enough to click the playful-sounding link, ready to be captivated by photos of cats snuggling large poetry anthologies. Users may also accidentally click because they are scrolling too quickly through related tags starting with the same phrase; either way, Rowe's profile still gains impressions from indirect views.

Interspersed with images advertising her own books, she also sometimes pairs tags of classical poets with screenshots of their works and her accompanying commentary—though such inclusions do not appear too often, since this could detract from her own poetry. For example, including "Departed to the Judgment" increases traffic from Dickinson fans, which Rowe capitalizes even further through her responses, as with user evanswilliamsauthor. Her statement that "There is no one better than Emily Dickinson," accompanied by copious highlighting, not only exhibits admiration but lends herself authority as a well-read, informed writer. Even the fact that many of her poems externally utilize similar visual effects to those of Dickinson, particularly dashes, bolsters the idea of Rowe as the modern-day Emily.

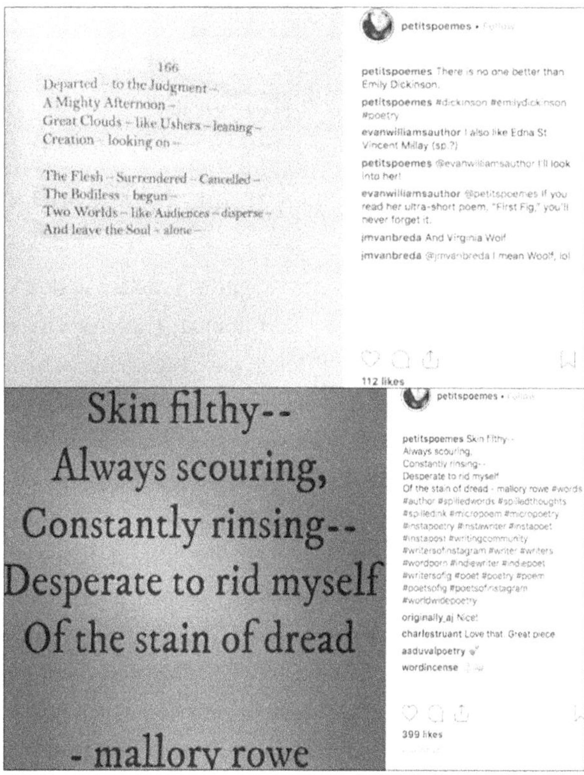

Figure 2.1 Examples of tagging Dickinson by Mallory Rowe, from her original Instagram profile @petitspoemes, posted on July 20, 2018, and August 24, 2018. Accessed September 5, 2018.

The lingerie-merchant Alix Clair (@pointdalencon) goes even further with her literary credits, accompanying each photo of her products, from lacy bralettes to geometric thongs, with detailed textual analysis. One notable example, which has since been deleted, advertised a camisole with embroidered flowers by commenting on floriography's literary role, observing that Shakespeare's Ophelia "offers rosemary for remembrance and pansies for thoughts" not only as a "reflection of popular sentiment, but easily a harbinger of literature to come" (2016). Pointdalencon then backs her claim by referencing several literary allusions, from Louisa May Alcott to Agatha Christie. She even uses rhetorical strategies in the very phrasing of her treatise. The claim that "Flowers could express the sentiments too fragile, daring, or impetuous for speech. / A bouquet, carefully composed, could cajole or entice, flatter or beseech," is itself filled with alliteration, parallelism, and even rhyme (2016). Regardless of their varying analytical aptitudes, however, Rowe and pointdalencon clearly seek the same goal. Privileging an antique aesthetic by tagging poets and poems is not merely a form of nostalgia, but an appeal to the prestigious past as authorization of the present.

Poe(t/m)-tagging Practice 2: A Barely Legible Blue Jumble

A second, even more common poe(t/m)-tagging practice is that of copy-and-pasting long tag-lists of popular poets and poems. These can be automatically generated by apps like All Hashtag, Ritetag, and Tagomatic, which suggest the trendiest options to match selected photos. Readers innocently perusing posts about e.e. cummings or William Wordsworth will suddenly find themselves inundated by completely unrelated posts, connected merely by the extraneous hash-key. For example, after a massive, all-caps post advocating people to gain self-confidence through his health program, the lifestyle guru coach_mantas tags thirty names, from Robert Frost to Carl Jung to Socrates, apparently all related to #meaningful and #purposeliving. The clothing vendor itsok.store makes even less of a pretense of relevance. For example, in one of the store's posts advertising a dress, which has since been deleted, the tag #robe (French for "dress") is followed by twenty-nine other tags, all beginning with the name "Robert." This trick means that anyone searching a famous name, from #robertfrost to #robertdeniro to #robertkennedy, may accidentally be diverted to itsok.store instead.

While hashtags are often inserted into main captions or blurbs, shrewd users hide these giant lists beneath long columns of ellipses, or deep within the comments. This not only conceals the unaesthetic, barely legible blue jumble but ensures that the user is not penalized by Instagram moderators for illegally using the same order of hashtags (Newberry 2020). Taggers who are simultaneously Instapoets also benefit from this strategy in another way, however. By removing the tags so far from the original post that the reader must keep clicking "view more" to even find the hyperlinks, Instapoets can directly feature their own galleries, enjoying 442 percent more engagement if they use at least eleven hashtags (Myers 2023).

Not all Instapoets resort to this clandestine approach, however. The Instapoet Ope K. King, for example, openly inserts large, identical lists of hashtags mixing poets and authors of many styles and periods: #edgarallanpoe, #fridakahlo, and #kurtvonnegut are entangled with #langleav, #christopherpoindexter, and #rmdrake. This strategy is unsurprising—the emotional themes of King's poems are themselves often so universal that identical phrases can be repeated in different posts, simply by having a different background. Regardless of her aesthetic practices, however, her extensive, highly visible amalgamation of tags allows her to boldly connect classical authors, well-known Instapoets, and herself.[4] As she states in the intro of her first published collection, "I may not be as professional or as good in writing poems as the likes of Emily Dickinson, Robert Frost, Edgar Allan Poe, William Blake, and so many more, but what I know, I write as best as I can" (King 2018).

Noticeably, these links between opekingpoetry and the listed canonized poets are usually symbolic rather than linguistic, structural, or rhetorical. However, this principle does not apply to contemporary Instapoets also tagged by opekingpoetry. For example, take the poem by r.h. Sin "let go of what you're used to wait for what you deserve" (@r.h.Sin December 13, 2022) or "It is okay

Figure 2.2 An example list of poet-tags by Ope K. King, from the Instagram account @opekingpoetry on September 10, 2018.

if you are still trying. The goal is to never stop believing in yourself" (@rmdrk March 30, 2021). The poems not only resemble each other in theme, rhetoric, and linguistic brevity, but in their visual layout as well, with 2 to 3 lines of minimalist white font on a plain black background or black font on a white background. The homogeneous tone, length, and language contribute to the ease of propagating these vague aphorisms. In fact, such creations are apparently so effortless that Drake, who had just advertised his new book *The Funny Thing About Healing and Self Love* in March 2021, released a limited bundle entitled *Something Broken, Something Beautiful* in April 2021, and then collaborated with Sin and other poets on *She Fits Inside These Words*, which was released in June 2021. Despite sounding virtually identical, these poets are each followed by approximately 2 to 2.5 million users, so King has a clear potential benefit from linking her poems with theirs. Several of her later pieces are arguably more artistically successful, sometimes containing variations in alliteration, chiasmic metaphors, paratactic apostrophe, and even concrete structure. Yet as a noncommercial, Nigeria-based poet, King does not have the same access as her contemporaries in engaging audiences on a largely Western platform. In order to gain exposure within such a platformized genre, continuously controlled by hidden algorithmic gatekeepers, poets like King must use the hypertext of hashtags to make their poetry visible.

King is certainly not the only user to capitalize on her shared style with current Instapoets. As poets like Kaur continually acquire more visibility, amateur Instapoets increasingly tag them to reterritorialize established microcelebrity for their own advantage. Of the nearly 700,000 tags dedicated to #rupikaur, a vast majority of the posts are neither by Kaur nor feature her actual poetry. In a recent search of the current Top 9 (see Figure 2.3), only the final post promoted an image of Kaur's *milk and honey*; the rest of the posts appear to be a variety of poems produced by amateur Instapoets, some Italian, French, British, and Brazilian, all capitalizing on Kaur's name. On the one hand, this could potentially be viewed as exploitative. Yet Kaur's own poetry resembles that of so many others that the poet Nayyira Waheed has even accused Kaur herself of plagiarism—which Kaur dismissed as a natural occurrence, claiming that many poets, especially women of color, often have "similar experiences and similar ideas about the world" (Kaur, quoted in Carlin 2017). Since Kaur's own poetry is so nebulous, perhaps the hyperlink #rupikuar may have transcended its original use of simple authorial attribution. Instead, it serves as a stand-in for any Instapoet using the same generic, *genre*-ic, confessional tone and language that has come to dominate the form.

Figure 2.3 Collage of Top 9 Posts for #rupikaur taken by the author on May 14, 2021.

With this altered significance, the tag can even appear to work as activism against undemocratic overrepresentation in mass media. Kaur may have initially been a key element in the popularization of Instapoetry. Yet as a millionaire who sells exclusive tickets to performances costing $250 (Roberts 2018), and as an icon who can afford the stylist Christian Classen—also employed by famous actresses like Selena Gomez and Jennifer Lawrence—Kaur cannot be said to personally represent the average Instapoet. By reappropriating her name as a token similar to #igpoetry or #poetryporn to draw more views, amateur Instapoets attempt to reclaim the platform for themselves. The demonstration that their writing could easily be taken for those of other Instapoet microcelebrities counters the ongoing marginalization wielded by those wealthy influencers, with their huge armies of sponsors and resources. Relegating both #edgarallanpoe and #rupikaur into a hyperlink hodgepodge does not merely function to collect impressions. Rather, it serves as a subtle but continual reminder to herself, as well as her readers, that opekingpoetry has just as much right to poetic fame on Instagram's egalitarian digital platform as anyone else.

Poe(t/m)-tagging Practice 3: Pasquinade and Parody

While this method of list-tagging may subtly resist the dominance of branded, high-visible Instapoets, yet another trend, the technique of parody-tagging, even more directly de-territorializes these microcelebrities' elitism. The winking mockery, satire, and humor cultivate a wry intimacy dependent upon the writer and reader's shared knowledge, which in turn allows both participants to shape new meanings from revised tropes. A prime example of this was the now-deleted account "whoopeekaur," whose bio read "Rhymes (not) for troubling times" and featured a rejection letter from Princeton as the profile image. Whoopeekaur's account, which was run by Poorva Navalgundkar, was dedicated to imitating Kaur herself—in tone, style, and even the sketched design of background images. However, where Kaur often featured poems of romantic rejection, Navalgundkar used specific academic and professional allusions to depict the despair of career rejection, as illustrated in Figure 2.4. Even though the tongue-in-cheek poems do not overtly mock Kaur, they clearly subvert her aphoristic outpourings into humorously poignant reflections. The precise order of the hashtags is especially revealing in this case—"fakepoetry," "shitpoetry," and "shitpoem" all come before the source attribution: "rupikaur." Like its namesake, this digital whoopee cushion blew raspberries at Instapoets' typically mystical guru-isms about the universe's harmony, instead reminding us that we live in the real world of acquisitive LinkedIn invitations and perpetual job applications.

Navalgundkar is not alone in her endeavors, as several others on the platform develop creative pastiches, even of canonized poets. The user @naughtyemilydickinson blackouts key lines in Dickinson's poetry with marker just light enough to see the original poem, refashioning them into sexual puns. This invites the amused reader to not only revisit Dickinson's original

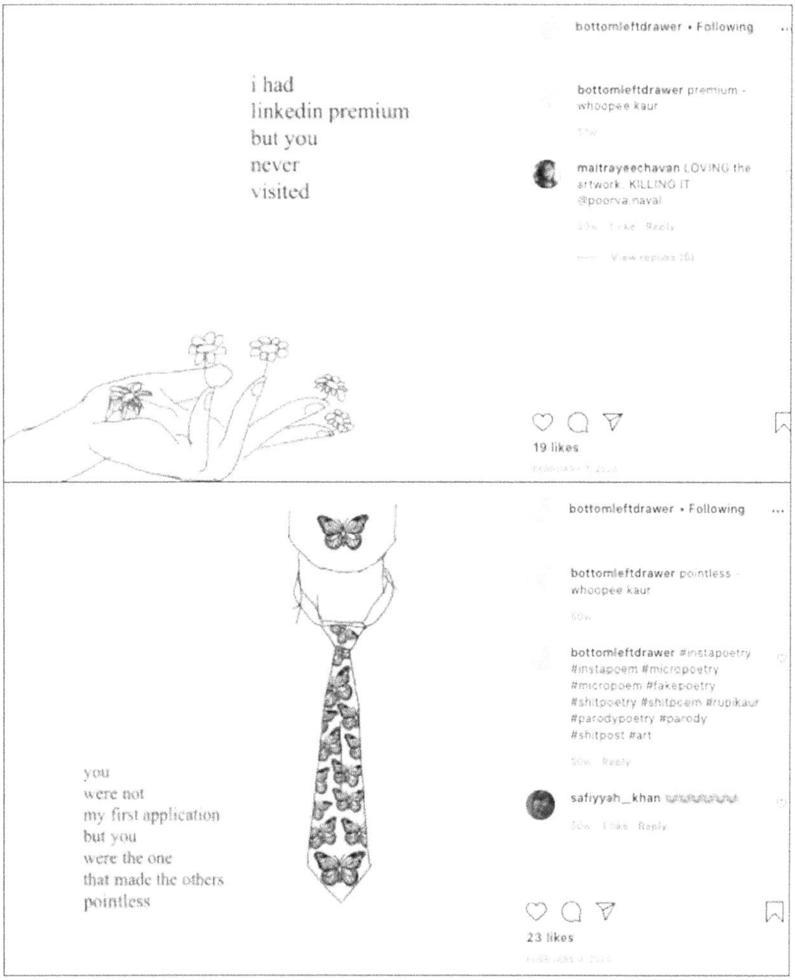

Figure 2.4 Collage exemplifying poetry parodying Kaur. These poems were originally from @whoopeekaur, but have been reposted on February 7, 2020, on Navalgundkar's more recent account, @bottomleftdrawer, which features a wider variety of her artwork.

works—many of which expose her lesser-known, but just as exquisite, poems—but to also more deeply analyze her texts to see if there was more "dick in Dickinson" than previously imagined. Others, like account themotherfaulkner, create "fake news" in the style of modern tabloids. Christopher Carvalho, who writes and owns the account, links past literature with the present in mingled sarcasm and humor. By blending facts and disinformation, Carvalho exhumes forgotten poetic treasures like Byron's satirical "English Bards and Scotch Reviewers," while simultaneously tempering idolization of canonical writers, who have just as many penchants for self-destruction, potentially resulting in "gonorrhea, syphilis, and rockabilly sideburns" (see Figure 2.5). A recent post on themotherfaulkner account (see Figure 2.6) even mocks Rupi Kaur's vague aphoristic style with a tabloid cover entitled, "Art Technically? Rupi Kaur Reads Grocery List" (Carvalho 2023). The tongue-in-cheek commentary paints a scene where "even her most diehard fans" are disconcerted to find that Kaur's

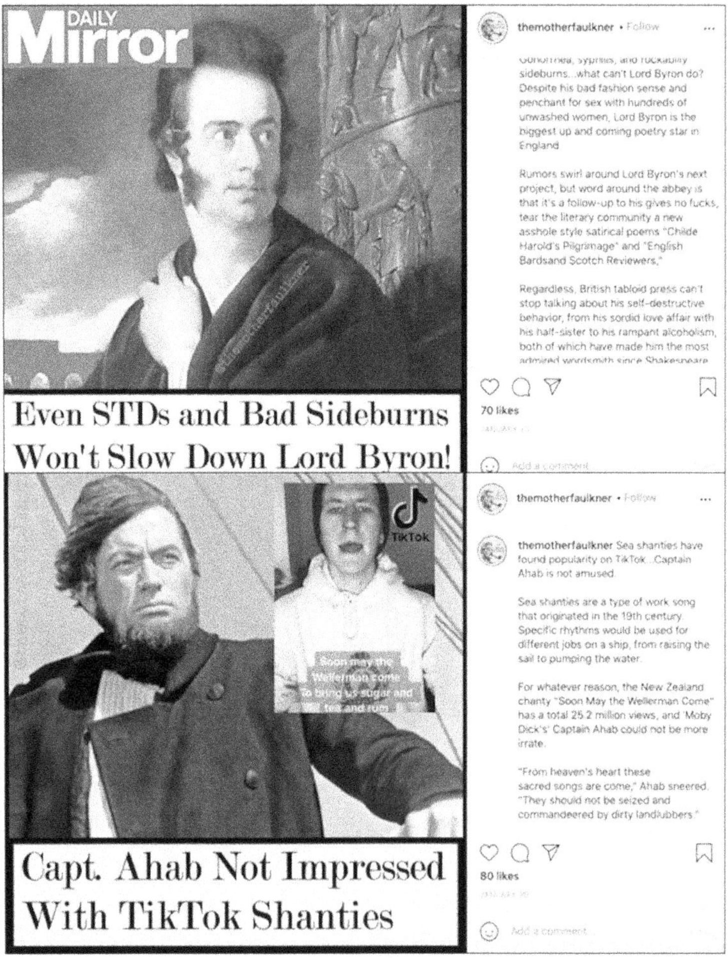

Figure 2.5 Collage of @themotherfaulkner tabloids by Christopher Carvalho, from January 23, 2021, and January 30, 2021. Accessed and compiled by the author on June 2, 2021.

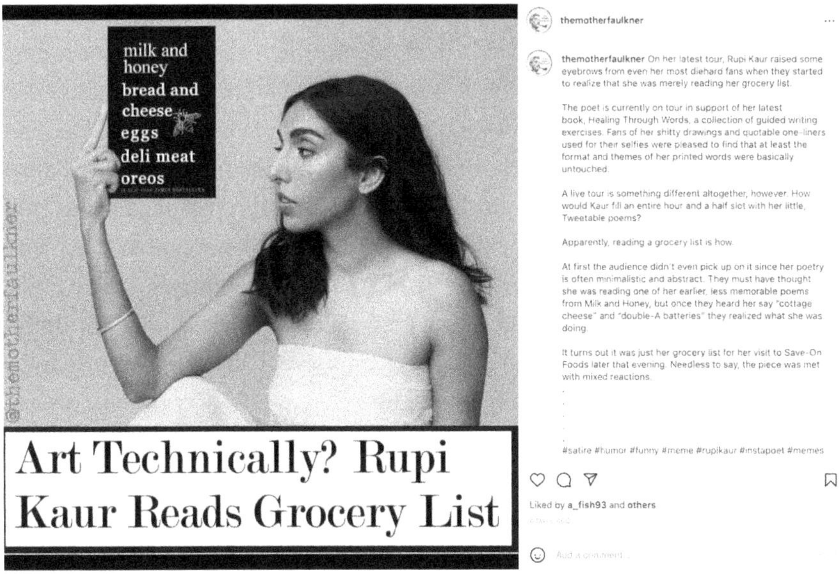

Figure 2.6 "Art Technically? Rupi Kaur Reads Grocery List," by Christopher Carvalho, February 6, 2023. Accessed and screenshot by the author on February 11, 2023.

most recent tour is simply a recitation of her grocery list, the only way that she can "fill an entire hour and a half slot with her little, Tweetable poems" (2023). Despite the mixed reviews of this fictional tour, the post notably mentions that in general, so long as Kaur's "format and themes of her printed words were basically untouched," then the fans of "her shitty drawings and quotable one-liners used for their selfies" would continue to be pleased.

Conclusions and Implications

Despite these notable examples of parodic tags spurring divergent readings, satirical engagement, and even critical politicization, there are still great limitations in using hashtags as sites of resistance. To search these tags in the first place, one must already be aware that #fakepoetry and #shitpoetry exist. Moreover, to maintain visibility in an over-bloated feed, even the most creative Instapoets must inevitably resort to typical crowdsourcing gambits: employing DMs, requesting "follow4follows," and participating in the incessant hustle required to gain Insta-fame. Even if tags could become viral, they can quickly become clogged by artificial wokeness, or even reappropriated by oppositional forces (Omena, Rabello, and Mintz 2020), as seen with the event of Blackout Tuesday, where crucial protest information was obscured by users (including far-right zealots) congesting the feed with millions of empty black squares.

Most importantly, one cannot forget that a digital platform is not a free and open market space, as its name implies. Even though Instagram has halted massive "shadowban" purges, its invisible but omnipresent algorithms still rigidly control the feed, which explains why "Top 9" lists are often filled with the same users, those most consistent and strategic in optimizing their posts. The fact that searchable tags and profiles are ranked by what Instagram thinks is most relevant to you (Canning 2019) demonstrates that hashtag activity is not "equally and meritocratically available" (Gillespie 2017). The tag instead becomes a double-edged sword, superficially allowing "scattered voices to be heard" but simultaneously menacing them by "suppress[ing] their unique, nonexchangeable qualities" (Bernard 2019: 77). Thus, clickbaiting or parodying Kaur, while creative on a personal level, will not ultimately foster equal mediation amongst amateur Instapoets but only further elevate her highvisibility.

So what would it take for poe(t/m)-tagging to have actual cultural efficacy? Sarah Brouillette recalls Russell Keat's theory that linguistic goods are uniquely able to reason and criticize their own faults, eloquent precisely because they can recognize their damage (Brouillette 2014). If writers were willing to expose their own capitalistic participation, they could use these fractured texts as cognizant cultural goods. These meta-goods reveal the potential for increasing cooperative "practices," involving the pursuit of internal rewards and craft excellence rather than only external compensation and prestige. Such practices seek the deeper well-being of consumers and producers, readers, and writers—even the vast, invisible army of those "designing the algorithms or policing away prohibited content" (Gillespie 2017)—who are all being crushed by rationalized labor required to fulfill the market's breakneck demand. Yet this aim is difficult to achieve when consuming literature so easily promotes self-congratulatory, "woke"[5] prop. To prevent Instapoetry writers and readers from falling into yet another privileged echo chamber, the surrounding stage of Instagram must also experience drastic changes. Yet how can such movement take place when the smallest props, from hashtags to @-signs, are manipulated by a vast Deus ex machina wired beneath the platform?

Thus, although the intersecting rods of the hashtag may seemingly afford more opportunities to link backwards, forwards, and across to canonized and contemporary writers, at present, they still enclose even the canniest poe(t/m)-

taggers in a frustratingly tight square space. Unless a major shift occurs to disrupt Instagram's cultural monopoly, these hashed conductors may actually serve as insulative safeguards, forking any lightning of resistance into that bottomless digital night.

Notes

1 In contrast, Tweets with more than one tag decline in engagement, while tagged Facebook posts collect *fewer* impressions than untagged ones (oneupweb 2019).

2 This principle does not apply to obviously non-poetic influencers; Levi's could quote Whitman's "Pioneers" in a commercial without fearing that their normal audience would suddenly turn to buy their jeans from the American Transcendentalist instead.

3 This is not to insinuate that Rowe has named her cats these names for the mere sake of generating likes, nor that she posts images of her feline friends merely for the follows. As a poet, she likely enjoys works by the above authors, and simply shared the adorable images of her pets with her fans. Nevertheless, posting images of her life in this manner certainly helps to more intimately link her with classic poets.

4 This principle would still apply whether she used an automatic tag-generator or constructed the list herself. However, certain phrases are organized in a manner that suggests related thoughtful, human association rather than purely random computerized assemblage: The initialed poets "rmdrake" and "rhsin" are placed side-by-side while the related "poet," "poetry," and "poemporn" indicate clustered linguistic connections. The placement of "nayyirahwaheed" immediately before "rupikaur," the African-American poet who accused her Indian contemporary of appropriating Black narratives is especially insightful, indicating that in this post at least, the distinct hashtag list was likely created by Ope K. King herself.

5 By this term, I am not using it in the sarcastic manner of far-right political groups, but to demonstrate that many social media posts celebrate the importance of being "woke," but do not go further in demonstrating active resistance against harmful marginalizing behaviours.

References

Basile, Lisa. n.d. "How to Create Stunning InstaPoetry Posts." *Little Infinite*. https://www.littleinfinite.com/how-to-create-stunning-instapoetry-posts/. Accessed May 27, 2021.

Bernard, Andreas. 2019. *Theory of the Hashtag*. Cambridge: Polity Press.

Bernes, Jasper. 2017. *The Work of Art in the Age of Deindustrialization*. Redwood City, CA: Stanford University Press.

Bourdieu, Pierre. 1996. *The Rules of Art: Genesis and Structure of the Literary Field*. Maldon, MA: Polity Press.

Brouillette, Sarah. 2014. *Literature and the Creative Economy*. Stanford: Stanford University Press. https://stanford-universitypressscholarship- com.ezproxy.lib.gla.ac.uk/view/10.11126/stanford/9780804789486.001.0001/upso-9780804789486-chapter-2.

Canning, Nikki. 2019. "How to Get Discovered on Instagram Search: 8 Tips for Growing Your Following." *Later*. https://later.com/blog/instagram-search/. Accessed June 6, 2021.

Carlin, Shannon. 2017. "Meet Rupi Kaur, Queen of the 'Instapoets.'" *Rolling Stone*, December 21. https://www.rollingstone.com/culture/culture-features/meet-rupi-kaur-queen-of-the-instapoets-129262/. Accessed May 27, 2021.

Carvalho, Christopher. [@themotherfaulkner]. 2021. [Instagram profile]. "Art Technically? Rupi Kaur Reads Grocery List." *Instagram*, February 6, 2023. https://www.instagram.com/p/CoVWIGivHNp/. Accessed March 17, 2023.

Carvalho, Christopher. [@themotherfaulkner]. 2021. [Instagram profile]. "Capt. Ahab Not Impressed with TikTok Shanties." *Instagram*, January 30, 2021. https://www.instagram.com/p/CKr8dkKhQzG/. Accessed March 17, 2023.

Carvalho, Christopher. [@themotherfaulkner]. 2021. [Instagram profile]. "Even STDS and Bad Sideburns Won't Slow Down Lord Byron!" *Instagram*, January 23, 2021. https://www.instagram.com/p/CKZ661PhzxH/. Accessed February 11, 2023.

Carvalho, Christopher. [@themotherfaulkner]. 2021. [Instagram profile]. *Instagram*. https://www.instagram.com/themotherfaulkner/. Accessed February 11, 2023.

Chakraborty, Sujay. 2020. "Cristiano Ronaldo Is Highest-paid Athlete on Instagram, Raking in $889K Per Post." *Republic World*, October 12. https://www.republicworld.com/sports-news/football-news/cristiano-ronaldo-is-highest-paid-athlete-on-instagram.html. Accessed June 5, 2021.

Craig, Ailsa. 2007. "Sustainability, Reciprocity, and the Shared Good(s) of Poetry." *The Journal of Arts Management, Law, and Society*, 37 (3): 259–68. DOI: 10.3200/JAML.37.3.

Edwards, Samantha. 2017. "How Instapoetry Is Changing the Way We Read Look at Poems." *Fashion*. https://fashionmagazine.com/culture/instapoetry/. Accessed May 27, 2021.

Foucault, Michel. 1972. *The Archaeology of Knowledge*. New York: Tavistock Publications Limited, Pantheon Books.

Gillespie, Tarleton. 2017. "The Platform Metaphor, Revisited." *Digital Society Blog*, August 24. https://www.hiig.de/en/the-platform-metaphor-revisited/. Accessed June 6, 2021.

Gleim, Mark, Catherine Johnson, and Stephanie Lawson. 2019. "Sharers and Sellers: A Multi-Group Examination of Gig Economy Workers' Perceptions." *Journal of Business Research*, Elsevier, 98 (C): 142–3. https://www.sciencedirect.com/science/article/abs/pii/S0148296319300591. Accessed June 5, 2021.

Gregson, Tyler. 2020. [Instagram profile]. *Instagram*. https://www.instagram.com/tylerknott/. Accessed May 28, 2021.

Kaur, Rupi. 2020. [Instagram profile]. *Instagram*. https://www.instagram.com/rupikaur_/. Accessed May 28, 2021.

King, Ope. 2019. [Instagram profile]. *Instagram*. https://www.instagram.com/opekingpoetry/. Accessed June 6, 2021.

King, Ope. 2018. *YOU WILL FIND FREEDOM HERE: Penned Thoughts and Poems*. Amazon Kindle Edition.

lassenl. [Instagram profile]. *Instagram*. May 12, 2020. https://www.instagram.com/p/CAFIy40l1Xk/. Accessed March 17, 2023.

Maslow, Abraham. 1965. *Eupsychian Management: A Journal*. Homewood, IL: Richard D. Irwin and the Dorsey Press.

Morgan, George and Pariece Nelligan. 2018. *The Creativity Hoax: Precarious Work and the Gig Economy*. London: Anthem Press.

Myers, Louise. 2023. "How to Use Hashtags on Instagram for Amazing Growth in 2024." *Louise Myers Visual Social Media*. https://louisem.com/7198/how-to-use-hashtags-on-instagram.

naughtyemilydickinson. 2018. [Instagram profile]. *Instagram*. https://www.instagram.com/naughtyemilydickinson/. Accessed May 28, 2021.

Navalgundkar, Poorva. [@bottomleftdrawer, previously @whoopeekaur]. 2020. [Instagram profile]. *Instagram*. https://www.instagram.com/bottomleftdrawer/. Accessed June 6, 2021.

Newberry, Christina. 2020. "The 2020 Instagram Hashtag Guide – How to Use Them and Get Results." *Hootsuite*. https://blog.hootsuite.com/instagram-hashtags/#:~:text=It%20might%20be%20tempting%20to,be%20penalized%20by%20the%20algorithm. Accessed May 27, 2021.

Omena, Janna, Elaine Rabello, and André Mintz. 2020. "Digital Methods for Hashtag Engagement Research." *Social Media + Society*, 6 (3): 2–3. DOI:10.1177/2056305120940697.

Oneupweb. 2019. "On Which Social Media Platforms Do Hashtags Work?" Available online: https://www.oneupweb.com/blog/hashtags-social-media/. Accessed June 5, 2021.

petitspoemes. 2018. "You Can Break My Heart in the Best Way Possible." *Instagram*. https://www.instagram.com/malloryroweauthor/.

Petriglieri, Gianpiero, Susan Ashford, and Amy Wrzesniewski. 2018. "Agony and Ecstasy in the Gig Economy: Cultivating Holding Environments for Precarious and Personalized Work Identities." *Administrative Science Quarterly*, 64 (1): 132, 134–5. https://doi-org.ezproxy.lib.gla.ac.uk/10.1177/0001839218759646. Accessed June 5, 2021.

Pointadelencon. 2016. [Instagram profile]. *Instagram*, September 19. https://www.instagram.com/pointadelencon/. Accessed June 6, 2021.

Pointadelencon. 2016. "Ophelia Offers Rosemary for Remembrance, Pansies for Thought." *Instagram*. https://www.instagram.com/pointdalencon/.

Prassl, Jeremias. 2018. *Humans as a Service: The Promise and Perils of Work in the Gig Economy*. New York: Oxford University Press. https://oxford-universitypressscholarship- com.ezproxy.lib.gla.ac.uk/view/10.1093/oso/9780198797012.001.0001/oso- 9780198797012. Accessed June 5, 2021.

Reeves, Richard. 2001. *Happy Mondays: Putting the Pleasure Back into Work*. Cambridge: Perseus.

R. M. Drake. 2021. [Instagram profile]. *Instagram*. https://www.instagram.com/rmdrk/. Accessed May 28, 2021.

Roberts, Soraya. 2018. "No Filter." *The Baffler*. https://thebaffler.com/latest/instapoetry-roberts. Accessed May 27, 2021.

Rowe, Mallory. 2018. [Instagram profile]. *Instagram*. https://www.instagram.com/petitespoems/. Accessed September 5, 2018.

Sin, r.h. 2021. [Instagram profile]. *Instagram*. https://www.instagram.com/r.h.sin/. Accessed May 28, 2021.

Sinicki, Adam. 2019. *Thriving in the Gig Economy*. Berkeley: Apress. DOI:10.1007/978-1-4842-4090-8.

Tylerknott. 2020. "You Are the Poem I Never Knew How to Write." *Instagram*. https://www.instagram.com/tylerknott/.

Wallach, Omri. 2021. "The World's Top 50 Influencers across Social Media Platforms." *Visual Capitalist*, May 14. Available online: https://www.visualcapitalist.com/worlds-top-50-influencers-across-social-media-platforms/. Accessed June 5, 2021.

Warren, Jillian. 2021. "This Is How the Instagram Algorithm Works in 2021." *Later*. https://later.com/blog/how-instagram-algorithm-works/. Accessed June 5, 2021.

3

Missed Possibilities from Unobtainable Data: The Case of Instapoetry and a Wish to Go beyond Rupi Kaur

Camilla Holm Soelseth
Oslo Metropolitan University

Eleonora Natalia Ravizza
University of Catania

Introduction

Whenever new literary movements, genres, subgenres, or simply trends begin to establish themselves, one question researchers are inevitably faced with concerns their access points: How do we select, assess, describe, analyze, and criticize? Should we consider certain authors/works more relevant or representative than others, and why? What constitutes their specific value? Of course, finding access points is not simply a matter of constructing perspectives, gaining knowledge, and elaborating methodological or theoretical tools, but also a matter of paving the way for the diffusion of literary works, as well as for future research. Academia is one of the many cogs in the literary machine, but it plays a fundamental role in the dissemination, popularization, and consolidation of canons. Research, differently put, is a highly self-referential enterprise. While it creates new pathways into the intricate tangle of the new works produced and published yearly, it also ossifies them by directing public attention toward certain questions, aspects, and literary endeavors.

Digital approaches may offer new gateways, as they may address corpora of texts without operating pre-selective choices based on criteria such as aesthetic judgment, critical consent, or the success or fortune of certain authors and works. Corpora, in other words, may allow researchers to elaborate ways to investigate not only the contribution of some "elected few" but rather wider interconnections and affiliations. They would establish new access points to allow researchers (and readers) to move beyond the idea of canon. Processes of canon formation, after all, have been at the center of widespread scrutiny and criticism for several decades because of the strong limitations they impose on the way literature is recognized (i.e., received, sold, taught, published, and circulated) (Herrnstein Smith 1988; Graff 1992; Gullroy 1994; Bona and Maini 2006). They are a form of conscious, arbitrary gatekeeping resulting from a complex entanglement of ecological patterns, power relationships, and processes working differently at different times and scales. Besides, as Tangerlini and Leonard remind us, even when digitalization seems to have brought down the physical barrier that did not allow researchers to get hold of difficult-to-get books (what Cohen [1999: 23] calls "The Great Unread"), canon still seems to act as a selective principle when there exist far too many works in the target corpus to be able to read all of them carefully (2013: 726).

The emergence of the recent phenomenon of Instapoetry—a type of literature that is not "digitized" but rather the product of a digital environment—has undoubtedly opened new horizons of humanistic inquiry. As researchers in the field of the humanities, we are faced with new modes of production and circulation of literary works and a substantial remodulation of the traditional roles and functions of the many agents in what we have termed the "literary machine." The democratization of publishing brought about by social media, the shortening of the distance between authors and readers, and the very redefinition of "text"—a concept that is becoming ever more fluid as it travels across our screens and is freely shared, copied, pasted, or modified—force us researchers to address Instapoetry from a new transdisciplinary perspective, one which is able to integrate literary criticism with digital humanities, and raise new questions about the nature of literary interactions. The new modes of production and circulation also add another layer to the who and how we select works for further academic inquiry.

As we construct our research questions regarding Instapoetry, we need to consider the epistemological and deontological dimensions of doing research. We need to reflect on how we may produce and circulate knowledge on a cultural and literary phenomenon, the methods and theories we may develop, and the possibilities of inquiries we may have, are allowed to ask, or are foreclosed to us. With digital humanities, new computational methods emerge, capable of reading patterns on different scales, which also means creating different contexts for the choice of works for inquiry, as well as providing information about phenomena, genres, and the like, which was unavailable to us before. For the sake of humanistic research, this is invaluable. But what happens when we have the tools but suddenly not the data? What do we lose?

For example, following in the footsteps of traditional literary classifications and periodization, most research on Instapoetry focuses on individual authors rather than Instapoetry as the product of a digital environment, with specific forms of intertextual organization and interconnections, and characterized by specific linguistic features, such as the hashtag, which function not only as signs but also as aggregators. Despite Barthesian claims of its death (Barthes 1984 [1967]), the idea of "author" is very much present in the mind of scholars. Often, for reasons that, as we shall see, are both cultural and methodological, it represents the most immediate access point to the phenomenon of Instapoetry as a whole, determining the very ways we interact with Instapoetry on Instagram. The social media's interface allows users to access content through the accounts of the authors and, as our attempts to delve into the possibilities of carrying out research in the digital environment of Instapoetry show, it determines how we can collect, as it is much easier to scrape by user account than by a more extensive corpus. One direct consequence of this is the early construction and stiffening of canons—i.e., the choice of works considered more significant than others, often at the expense of experiences that are marginalized or even overlooked. Let us mention, for example, the fact that many seem to identify Instapoetry mainly with Rupi Kaur and a few others and that, as a consequence, the works of this (primarily anglophone) "selected minority" seem to be used as a privileged gateway to understand something which is much more complex and diversified.

In this chapter, we address some of the difficulties we faced while attempting to wander off the beaten track and address Instapoetry from a digital humanities perspective. We relate how our search for new entry points has been frustrated by the company behind Instagram itself and what data are available to us, and how concepts that we were trying to leave behind, such as "canon" and "author," constantly came back with a vengeance to haunt our research.

The Initial Research Project

The research question from which this project started concerns how social media interferes with the very nature of the literary text. We are not just dealing with a digitized phenomenon, but a digitally situated phenomenon, where the logics of social media shape production, distribution, and consumption. Dealing with Instapoetry requires developing a series of methodological approaches which allow us to analyze poems not simply in light of their semantic, ideological, or aesthetic qualities but also as products of digital/social interactions. The paratext (Genette 1987), and most specifically the metadata which describes, manages, and structures posts, plays a central role in the understanding of the poem not only as an artifact but also as regards its production, circulation, and reception within a collaborative digital environment.

When we set out to write this article, we planned to create images showing visual networks of co-occurrences of hashtags used when publishing Instapoetry on Instagram. We aspired to examine something containing roughly 300,000 Instagram posts tagged as Instapoems. We hoped to contribute to a distant reading of a phenomenon like Instapoetry by comparing the Norwegian and Italian spheres of Instapoetry on Instagram. Suddenly the data became unobtainable through the usual method. Below follows a quick walk-through of this initial plan and why it suddenly became impossible to execute.

Based on the preliminary findings from the distant reading of metadata of Scandinavian Instapoetry of researcher Camilla Holm Soelseth, we wanted to see if the Norwegian and Italian practices of Instapoetry were similar or different. Here, we would employ the same method of scraping Instagram, as Holm had done, and further on, do an initial analysis of the data regarding users' posting practices. The second and main part of the analysis would focus on a hashtag co-occurrence analysis of the two hashtag networks, comparing their visual makeup by focusing on distribution, centrality density, size, clusters, and structural holes.

Findings from the distant reading of metadata connected to Scandinavian Instapoetry had revealed many interesting patterns. The general topics and themes showed a heavy focus on emotions, social relations, and mental health, but also with different sub-spheres (i.e., mental illnesses). In addition, users employed hashtags differently, with some focusing on displaying themes and content of the poems and others using metalinguistic tags, such as "writing" and "writer," and morphological variations of these. From these findings, it was possible to say something about how poetry was used and how the people behind the works described their work through hashtags, as well as how certain types of hashtag use created communities, or ambient affiliations. These findings were based on a set of 30,000 Instagram posts from almost 1,400 unique users in the period of January 2015–May 2019 (Soelseth 2023).

Based on these initial findings, the questions we wanted to answer in our new and comparative study were (1) what types of hashtags were used and how, (2) what could they tell us about the themes and topics of Instapoetry, and (3) did use and themes differ from the Norwegian to the Italian context? To answer these questions, our sample data set was set to be a collection of Instapoetry from 2019 and 2020. This gave us the added possibility to see if there was an impact from COVID-19 on the poetry posted.

However, the data we planned to collect, available publicly on Instagram, suddenly became unobtainable through automated collection. A manual collection would take months.

Running into Unforeseen Problems

While Instagram closed its API in 2018 following the *Cambridge Analytica* scandal, it was still possible for researchers to scrape social media for public data for a long time. In some ways, this was even better than accessing data through the API, as what you get through an API is always decided by the company behind it, and this shapes what type of analyses can be conducted (Weller and Kinder-Kurlanda 2021). At the same time, relying only on companies' willingness to provide (limited) APIs to researchers can be dangerous (Freelon 2018: 666).

Some, therefore, argue that the closing of the API has been a good thing for researchers as it offers advantages like working from the context of production and encourages digital fieldwork over detached standardized data, especially when the APIs are developed for commercial and not for research purposes (Rogers 2018; Venturini and Rogers 2019). Instead of ready-made formatted data, scraping offers "a way to extract structured information from heterogeneously formatted data online" (Marres and Weltevrede 2013: 322). A caveat is that scraping does limit the amount of information that can be collected and processed, as you may collect only what is visible through the interface.

However, scraping involves breaking the Terms of Service (ToS). This means that scraping is also an ethical issue because, as a researcher, you need to argue for how research on something is more important than following a company's terms of use, which you agree to when creating an account on the platform. But foregrounding research as free and not controlled by corporations will lead to arguing for yes.

Another part of an ethical evaluation means looking at the ramification of scraping. Currently, breaking ToS only means the possibility of your account being closed or frozen, as legally, you, as a researcher, are not breaking any law when doing it (at least not in the EU, Norway, or the United States). A third part involves ethically reflecting on what to collect and how to handle and store data.

However, our main problem suddenly was not ethically arguing for scraping but executing the scraping itself. The ToS suddenly became enforced through means of hindering the automated collection of data. While this has been foreshadowed by academics in the field of internet research (Freelon 2018; Bruns 2019), it is and will continue to be a problem because it means that we are steering toward a system of having to apply and pay for data at the mercy of private corporations, which will undoubtedly create a "have" versus "have-not" system (Walker, Demercea and Bastos 2019: 1538).

Running into Data Collection Trouble

In early 2021, the open-source Instagram-scraper script (*Instagram-Scraper [Version 1.6.1]*) was employed to do the new data collections. The script, however, continuously failed whenever we tried to run it. After initial investigations, the reason was that Instagram had implemented the detection and freezing of accounts scraping data from its *graphql API*. This does not mean that it is now impossible to scrape, but that time and effort into creating a new script was needed,[1] which is not always the forte of every researcher in the digital humanities.

When the scraping proved impossible, we were suddenly left without data. We were now experiencing the limitations of research against powerful corporations and were thrown back into a more traditional paradigm when looking for other options. What did this mean for our possibility of understanding Instapoetry as a phenomenon? To be able to say something about this, we first have to shed light on text selection processes of examples of phenomena, canonization, and the researcher's part in these processes.

Is the Author Really Dead? Authorship, Canonization, and the Limits of Current Research

Our quantitative investigation of hashtags had a particular objective: an analysis of the "visible" scaffold of an accelerated intertext, in which connections between different texts are organized in ways that follow new patterns of aggregation and dialogical interactions. Differently put, what we set out to achieve was an investigation of the way intertextual relations go even beyond the vertical, diachronic structure of what Gérard Genette called the "palimpsest" (1982). By selecting specific themes and allowing users to connect around these, hashtags contribute to building horizontal, synchronic connections, thus fostering what Michele Zappavigna calls "ambient affiliation" (2013). Differently put, by displaying their alignment around common values or interests, sharing patterns of evaluation, or using aggregators as hashtags, users become part of larger, abstract communities in which they may interact directly (e.g., by responding or linking and sharing content) or indirectly (i.e., simply by signaling their presence and/or ideological positioning). Our research would have allowed us to gain insights into the fluidity of an ever-expanding intertext, constantly enriched by new inputs and contributions which may establish new contextual and interpretative dimensions to previously published/shared content. Besides, it would have allowed us to follow the way the literary text becomes part of a variety of intercommunicative acts involving not just individuals but also newly formed communities (or, to use Zappavigna's terminology, "ambients") of poets/readers.

As the possibility of carrying out this kind of analysis was foreclosed to us, we realized that another option would have still been viable: we could have analyzed hashtags by manually choosing the profile of Instapoets. Nevertheless, the necessity of orienting our research according to the principle of pre-selecting authors would constitute precisely the limit of our findings. First, it would have required us to change our focus from the intertext as a site of polysemous, multidirectional interactions to a return to the very idea of "author." The practice of addressing literary phenomena through the lens of this concept has been the object of widespread criticism since the publication of Roland Barthes' essay *La mort de l'auteur* (1984[1967]), but, as a matter of fact, in traditional literary scholarship, "authorship" remains a fundamental criterion around which critical studies, essays, and anthologies are organized. The challenge that digital humanities are facing is precisely that of finding new methodological and theoretical tools that would allow researchers to approach textual interactions and dissemination. Understanding how the new digital environment works is essential not only to understand the text as an artifact but also specific cultural and communicative dynamics. Second, an author-based approach would have necessarily entailed a loss of data: if a poem is not published by a selected author but maybe by someone who is overlooked—whether because they publish less, have fewer followers, or, in general, do not enjoy enough visibility—we would not be able to access it. Third, as a corollary to this, we would have to establish criteria for which specific authors would be included while others would not. We would have contributed to the creation of a canon of Instapoets, around which our research would have revolved.

One of the factors which make Instagram a particularly innovative, highly democratic platform for the publication of digital poetry is that it seems to offer the possibility to establish direct relationships between readers and writers without the mediation of the usual apparatus of pre-selection, promotion, and distribution. Nevertheless, this apparatus is not entirely disconnected from the fruition of Instapoetry: Rupi Kaur, Nikita Gill, Atticus, Amanda Lovelace, Tyler Knott Gregson, Yesika Salgado, Hollie McNish, Lang Leave, Nayyirah Waheed, and many other successful Instapoets are publishing their poetry collections in the traditional channels, often by prestigious publishing houses (Andrew McMeel Publishing, Simon and Shuster, MacMillan, etc.) and are receiving widespread media attention from internationally renowned newspapers (*The Guardian*, *New York Times*). Attention from the publishing industry, and subsequently from the world of academia and education, further contributes to the expansion of their social media profile. This secondary mediation (alongside the issues of visibility connected with the way algorithms are shaping the environment in which Instapoetry circulates) is allowing a new canon to emerge, on which current research is mainly focusing.

The association of Instapoetry and "canon" is, nevertheless, a controversial one. Until the 1970s, most widely accepted definitions of "canon" focused mainly on the aesthetic value of literary works, projecting them onto a pure, disinterested sphere (Bloom 1994). The necessity to decenter a mainly Western, white, and masculine canon in order to include more women, non-White and non-Western authors has been affirmed ever more vigorously in the past decades (Herrnstein Smith 1988; Graff 1992; Gullroy 1994; Bona and Maini 2006), especially in consideration of the fact that the very idea of canon has a profound impact onto the transmission of specific cultural values. The fact that so-called canonical works are deemed as "essential" in most academic reading lists goes to the detriment of the inclusiveness of educational programs. Social media seem to offer the most inclusive platform for the publication and fruition of poetry: theoretically, no pre-selection, preventive evaluation of the aesthetic quality of a poem, or discriminatory patterns alongside the lines of gender, class, or ethnicity should hinder the reception/dissemination of Instapoetry.

Paradoxically, the fact that Instapoetry seems to offer the privileged platform to reach that decentralization of the canon that many have been wishing for seems to have become the very foundation on which new Instapoetry canons are being built, providing apparently easy points of access for readers, orienting cultural debates, and directing research that the academia is producing. A significant share of the research on Instapoetry focuses on Rupi Kaur (Cox 2020; Manning 2020; Oliveira and Fazano 2020). In the majority of these studies, Kaur, along with a few others, seems to be used as the gateway to understand the main features of the much more complex Instapoetry phenomenon. There seems to be a clear underlying premise in these analyses: if we can understand Rupi Kaur, we can understand Instapoetry. This leads to Instapoetry mainly being seen as a genre created by young women of minority or immigrant backgrounds expressing themselves and their experiences (Khilnani 2021: 136). It is also described as a genre consisting of "simple one-liners presented in colorful formats" (Roy 2020: 269) or "minimalist in form, made up of brief lines" (Bucknell 2020), or even as a type of "self-help poetry" (Pâquet 2019). As associate professor in English Stephen Ramsay so bluntly states: "arguments from the standpoint of popularity satisfy neither the canoniclast nor the historian" (Ramsay 2013: 4).

Whenever we analyze canons, the first thing that we should consider is that they are usually connected with specific communities and/or nation-building endeavors. Julia Staub, for example, defines canons as "a corpus of secular literary texts deemed valuable and fit for preservation by certain social groups. 'Canon' implies cultural and political distinctiveness" (2011). As this volume shows, Instapoetry has to be understood along the lines of both the national and the transnational. The transnational is particularly tricky to pinpoint, as it is very easy to fall into the trap of identifying it simply with the metropolitan dimension of poets living across cultures, but mainly choosing a dominant language such as English to mediate and/or sell their perspective as an advantaged one. Especially if we want to approach Instapoetry as a border-crossing, constantly expanding phenomenon which challenges our understanding of the literary text, we should be aware of its instability and focus on how newly formed internet communities constantly redefine themselves, influencing the very structure of the text.

Algorithmic Influence on Canonization

Circulation and reception are today touched by algorithms and computational processes, especially on social media. What we consume comes to us shaped by nonhuman algorithmic decision-making, influencing circulation, distribution, and what becomes visible. Instagram as a platform is more than just an intermediary. This means that "the Great Unread" today is unread because of other reasons. Algorithms play a part in what gets read and talked about or which

Instapoets get published and written about. In other words, the choice of works and authors examined by researchers to say something about a phenomenon like Instapoetry is being influenced by the infrastructure of Instagram.

Accessing Instapoetry on Instagram is either by way of accounts you follow posting to your feed, through what shows up on your search page or through search results for a specific hashtag. This involves algorithms that work in ways influencers constantly try to manipulate to their benefit to "play the visibility game" (Cotter 2019). This includes using the right hashtags and creating content that will elicit types of interactions favored by the algorithm. The act of becoming a representative author of Instapoetry, of being visible for being chosen as someone to be studied, is directed not only by the usual cogs in the literary machine but by algorithms on Instagram and how well Instapoets are able to play these, either intentionally or unintentionally, their literacy in the use of the platform vernacular (Gibbs et al. 2015), and also by how readers interact with the posts. This can be referred to as a hybrid media system, where the publishing of a poetry collection through the more traditional route in the literary field also affects chances of being chosen, and visibility is "built upon interactions among older and newer media logics" (Chadwick 2017: xi). This means that visibility is amplified by both primary and secondary mediation, feeding back into each other.

However, looking specifically at who and what becomes visible through Instagram, what we are seeing is a different form of selection, which is something that should possibly be called a vernacular-algorithmic selection. Selection is, in many ways, being made by authors and readers partaking in the visibility game and interacting with the algorithms in ways that push something to the forefront and others to the back. The more bound to a social medium, the more critical the vernacular-algorithmic logic is in who becomes visible. By employing digital methods for distant reading, we not only bypass this but also form our corpus selection based on other metrics than traditionally used, such as book sales or reviews, or archival metadata such as genre or decade of publication.

Distant Reading of Culture as Data as a Starting Point for Objects of Study, Corpus-Creation, and Canonization. Reflections and Concluding Remarks

The turn to digitally produced or digitalized cultural expressions has meant the possibility of applying digital methods and quantitatively distant readings of large corpora. This has had a significant effect on literature research: instead of privileging the canonized, the sea of the unknown can be accessed, and methods can be employed to discover greater patterns, re-adjust genre or author ideas, or re-discover forgotten works which, for different reasons, could reveal new insights into literary knowledge.

A distant reading of something, be it metadata of a corpus, or the content of the corpus itself, means doing literary criticism with the aid and the use of data and data sets, with the premise that data and data sets help us see something new and help us do better work as literary critics. Through distant reading, we create our own infrastructures for the sifting of material while still being reflective in that this is still not "objective" or exhaustive. The entry point is still a specific one, just as with the selection of works and authors by the number of sales, reviews by literary critics, or the general renown of the author. However, new entry points also mean giving more attention to selection criteria.

This new entry point, through conducting a distant reading before selecting samples, has already been employed for the digitized collection of literature with interesting results. Berglund and colleagues did thematic comparisons of contemporary Swedish popular and literary fiction, concluding that the latter is, in fact, a genre of the textual-thematic (Berglund et al. 2019: 237). Another study is Tangherlini and Leonard's *Trawling in the Sea of the Great Unread* (2013). It shows that through trawling the great corpus of a specific period, it is possible to show that "although the polarizations of 'movements' might apply thematically or even stylistically to those 'defining members' of a school or a movement, the vast majority of artistic expressions falls somewhere in between" (Tangherlini and Leonard 2013: 745). Both findings come from distant reading of corpora *after* the canonization of literary movements, genres, and the like.

However, with these methods available, we can now employ them for contemporary digital, literary, and artistic phenomena, which to a great extent, also exist as forms of data scrapable and initially accessible to researchers. This also means we can possibly reconfigure the canonization processes—perhaps for the better. While we should be careful to believe that products of computational analysis are produced by objective procedures, as long as such methods are used for critically scholarly ends and not instrumentally (Dobson 2019: 46), it should be possible to approach unexplored angles. In the case of Instapoetry, this means also having entry points tied to the metadata made by the users' part of publication and circulation of Instapoetry, adding a new layer to the distant reading of the data sets.

This chapter started with a reflection on a failed attempt to apply methods from the digital humanities to investigate how hashtags connect a variety of Instapoems and what these hashtags, in combination with other metadata, could tell us of Instapoetry as a greater phenomenon. The failure determined a falling-back, but it helped us detect some of the criticism that is orienting current Instapoetry research. The problems we faced were of two orders: (1) canonization, authorship, algorithmic interference, and the kind of questions we are used to asking when researching cultural and artistic expressions, which determine the framework of studies; (2) the fact that, when implementing new methodologies, there may be limitations put in place by new agents within the ecosystem of cultural production.

The first order considers how digital methods can be used to bypass traditional modes of canonization, where digital methods can be seen as a solution to problems faced earlier. Corpora belonging to different domains are much larger than the few chosen as representatives.

Regarding Instapoetry, how can we argue for Rupi Kaur, Atticus, Tylor Knott Gregson, Yesika Delgado, and Yrsa Daley-Ward being representative of the whole of Instapoetry when the corpus of Instapoetry is so large, expanding so much more than what a single researcher could ever read? While Rupi Kaur can be researched as Rupi Kaur, it is faulty when she is brought to stand as the example of the phenomenon she is a part of. She might be the best-known Instapoet, but she is certainly not paradigmatic for the whole genre.

Recalling Staub's definition of canon as a specific corpus of texts deemed valuable and fit for preservation by a certain group (2011), we have to ask questions about how these texts came to be discovered in the first place and why they are deemed valuable for preservation. In the case of Instapoetry, as the algorithmic selection and visibility game shows, we see only those texts and authors favored by algorithms going through a whole different selection process than previously, with another type of bias attached to it: metrical bias. Algorithmic inference forms a new selection of texts and authors for canonization by different criteria. We need to acknowledge that the reason why we choose Nikita Gill or Rupi Kaur is of algorithmic influence, and its feedback loop with the secondary mediation, as a result of a hybrid media system. These are not the result of freely trawling the greater corpus of Instapoetry to find both examples of greater patterns or the overlooked authors and works who have disappeared in the great noise of algorithmically circulated Instagram content. Instapoetry, which is perhaps hailed as a democratizing art form, is becoming a demagogically canonized enterprise, with authors who will be chosen time and time again as objects of inquiry simply for the fact of being visible.

If we are to make a claim on what Instapoetry is, we need to read the phenomenon from a distance at first. We need the patterns to become visible. As DH researchers Le-Khac and Hao write, DH methods can help fields "be more rigorous in examining their own corpus-building practices," working against an anecdotal and unsystematic scholarly landscape (2021). With scraping data from Instagram, we have the possibility of examining thousands upon thousands of texts across different spheres, finding smaller and larger patterns and interesting cases, authors, and posts that bring the phenomenon in new directions.

In addition, what is also a very important aspect of a distant reading of Instapoetry is the possibility of analyzing something which is digital in its materiality, which means that looking at hashtag co-occurrences can not only give us information on the themes and topics of Instapoetry, but also make it possible to say something about how new modes of intertextuality are part of the circulation and reception. As a matter of fact, the publication of literary texts on social media casts new light on intertextuality, as it favors connections that are not only vertical but also horizontal as a result of spontaneous affiliations.

The second-order problem is not having access to the material. The research of Tangherlini and Leonard (2013) and Berglund et al. (2019) has shown how important it is to investigate larger corpora. Data offers insights about cultural phenomena and movements we could not otherwise see. As stated in the introduction to the special edition of *Post45 x Journal of Cultural Analytics*, "to reject data is to risk alienating ourselves from the ontological and sociological grounding of the works we study" (Richard 2021). But what if it is not *us* rejecting the data, but instead the platform where these data are created which rejects us?

Facebook, the corporation, is now plugging all holes in an effort to monopolize the data, taking bigger ownership of the digital culture we are part of. As cultural critics and researchers, we are being amputated and forced to go by way of more traditional entry points, even when scraping. Choosing authors and scraping their accounts would mean doing precisely what we wanted *not* to do.

When dealing with digitally situated cultural phenomena, research is materially conditioned by the rules that social media establish. ToS are made, and we agree to them passively when creating accounts. But even when there are ethical reasons for breaking them, we are still being stopped. The access to data is being withheld, and researchers are not part of the decision-making process. Instead, it is only available to a select few.

This means that we must still hold on to the moral argument that supersedes the commercial interests of platforms like Facebook; "the need for independent, critical, public-interest scrutiny of social media spaces that are now critical to public communication" (Bruns 2019: 17). Lacking data also hinders us as researchers from contributing valuable knowledge and insight. Instead of trawling the great sea of Instapoetry, we are stuck with what we see. And what we see are the vernacular-algorithmically produced waves hitting us, blocking our view. There are different ways of gaining attention, and a researcher's job, or a disseminator of culture, has an ethical obligation to make sure different texts gain attention. We are also part of the circulation of texts.

We will therefore conclude this chapter with the appeal to prevent the destruction of the Carthage of our times. Furthermore, we demand that social media platforms provide transparent data access to critical, independent, public-interest research.

Note

1 In the last stages of writing this chapter, a new script appeared on GitHub promising the possibility of being able to scrape by a new technique (Ahouzi 2021). However, one wonders how long this will work. As Axel Bruns states, the closing of APIs has likely kick-started an "unsustainable arms race" (Bruns 2019: 17). Bruns suggests that keeping the pressure on platform providers is essential. He advocates that social media researchers should conclude all their articles, papers, and presentations with this sentence (Bruns 2019: 18).

References

Ahouzi, Anas. 2021. Instagram-Scraper-2021 [Github Repository]. https://github.com/aahouzi/Instagram-Scraper-2021

Barthes, Roland. [1967] 1984. "La mort de l'auteur." In *Le bruissement de la langue*, edited by Roland Barthes, 61–7. Paris: Éditions du Seuil.

Berglund, Karl, Mats Dahllöf, and Jerry Määttä. 2019. "Apples and Oranges? Large-Scale Thematic Comparisons of Contemporary Swedish Popular and Literary Fiction." *Samlaren*, 140: 228–60.

Bloom, Harold. 1994. *The Western Canon. The Books and School of the Ages*. San Diego, CA: Harcourt.

Bona, Mary Jo and Irma Maini. 2006. *Multiethnic Literature and Canon Debates.* Albany: State University of New York Press.

Bruns, Axel. 2019. "After the 'APIcalypse': Social Media Platforms and Their Fight against Critical Scholarly Research." *Information, Communication & Society*, 22 (11): 1544–66.

Bucknell, Clare. 2020. "Instapoetry." *London Review of Books*, 42 (10). https://www.lrb.co.uk/the-paper/v42/n10/clare-bucknell/instapoetry

Chadwick, Andrew. 2017. *The Hybrid Media System: Politics and Power*. Oxford: Oxford University Press.

Cohen, Margaret. 1999. *The Sentimental Education of the Novel*. Princeton, NJ: Princeton University Press.

Cotter, Kelly. 2019. "Playing the Visibility Game: How Digital Influencers and Algorithms Negotiate Influence on Instagram." *New Media & Society*, 21 (4): 895–913.

Cox, George. 2020. "Archived Bards?" *C21 Literature*, 8 (1): 1–21.

Dobson, James E. 2019. *Critical Digital Humanities: The Search for a Methodology*. Champaign: University of Illinois Press.

Freelon, Dean. 2018. "Computational Research in the Post-API Age." *Political Communication*, 35 (4): 665–8.

Genette, Gerald. 1982. *Palimpsestes. La littérature au second degré (Poétique)*. Paris: Éditions du Seuil.

Genette, Gerald. 1987. *Seuils (Poétique)*. Paris: Éditions du Seuil.

Gibbs, Martin, James Meese, Michael Arnold, Bjorn Nansen, and Marcus Carter. 2015. "#Funeral and Instagram: Death, Social Media, and Platform Vernacular." *Information, Communication & Society*, 18 (3): 255–68. DOI: 10.1080/1369118X.2014.987152.

Graff, Gerald. 1992. *Beyond the Culture Wars. How Teaching the Conflicts Can Revitalize American Education*. New York and London: Norton.

Guillory, John. 1994. *Cultural Capital. The Problem of Literary Canon Formation.* Chicago and London: The University of Chicago Press.

Herrnstein Smith, Barbara. 1988. *Contingencies of Value. Alternative Perspectives for Critical Theory*. Cambridge, MA and London: Harvard University Press.

Khilnani, Shweta. 2021. "'Moving' Poetry: Affect and Aesthetic in Instapoetry." In *Inhabiting Cyberspace in India: Theory, Perspectives, and Challenges*, edited by Simi Malhotra, Kanika Sharma and Sakshi Dogra, 135–42. Singapore: Springer. DOI: 10.1007/978-981-15-9934-7_14.

Le-Khac, Long, and Kate Hao. 2021. "The Asian-American Literature We've Constructed." *Post 45 x Journal of Cultural Analytics*, 7: 108–41.

Manning, Maria. 2020. "Crafting Authenticity: Reality, Storytelling, and Female Self-Representation through Instapoetry." *Storytelling, Self, Society*, 16 (2): 263–79.

Marres, Noortje and Esther Weltevrede. 2013. "SCRAPING THE SOCIAL?" *Journal of Cultural Economy*, 6 (3): 313–35. DOI: 10.1080/17530350.2013.772070.

Oliveira, Ulisses, and Bruna Fazano. 2020. "O Gênero Instapoetry e a Inteligência Coletiva/The Instapoetry Genre and the Collective Intelligence." *Revista de Estudos Da Linguagem*, 28 (3): 1161–90. DOI: 10.17851/2237-2083.28.3.1161-1190.

Pâquet, Lili. 2019. "Selfie-Help: The Multimodal Appeal of Instagram Poetry." *The Journal of Popular Culture*, 52 (2): 296–314.

Ramsay, Stephen. 2013. "The Hermeneutics of Screwing Around; or What You Do with a Million Books." In *Pastplay: Teaching and Learning History with Technology*, edited by Kevin Kee, 111–20. Ann Arbor: University of Michigan Press.

Rogers, Richard. 2018. "Social Media Research after the Fake News Debacle." *The Open Journal of Sociopolitical Studies*, 11 (2): 557–70.

Roy, Sreejata 2020. "Wellbeing, Nature and Insta-Poetry: Rhetoric of Healing in the Poetry of Rupi Kaur." *SSM Journal of English Literature and Culture*, 9 (1): 267–82.

So, Richard Jean. 2021. "Introduction: Contemporary Culture after Data Science." *Post45 x Journal of Cultural Analytics*, 7: 1–10. https://post45.org/2021/04/introduction-contemporary-culture-after-data-science/

Soelseth, Camilla Holm. 2022. "When Is a Poet an Instapoet?: The Effect of Platformization on the Practice of Being a Poet, and Instapoets as Examples of Poetry Content Creators in the Social Media Entertainment Ecosystem." *Baltic Screen Media Review*, 10 (1): 96–120.

Soelseth, Camilla Holm. 2023. "The Relational Hashtag Patterns of Scandinavian Instapoetry: An Exploratory Metadata Analysis of the Poetry Phenomenon, Focusing on Community Practices and Thematical Patterns in the Instapoetry Ecology." *First Monday*, 28 (6). DOI: 10.5210/fm.v28i6.12714.

Tangherlini, Timothy R., and Peter Leonard. 2013. "Trawling in the Sea of the Great Unread: Sub-corpus Topic Modeling and Humanities Research." *Poetics*, 41 (6): 725–49.

Venturini, Tommaso and Richard Rogers. 2019. "'API-Based Research' or How Can Digital Sociology and Journalism Studies Learn from the Facebook and Cambridge Analytica Data Breach." *Digital Journalism*, 7 (4): 532–40. DOI: 10.1080/21670811.2019.1591927.

Walker, Shawn, Dan Mercea, and Marco Bastos. 2019. "The Disinformation Landscape and the Lockdown of Social Platforms." *Information, Communication & Society*, 22 (11): 1531–43. DOI: 10.1080/1369118X.2019.1648536.

Weller, Katrin, and Katharina Kinder-Kurlanda. 2021. "Uncovering the Challenges in Collection, Sharing and Documentation: The Hidden Data of Social Media Research?" *Proceedings of the International AAAI Conference on Web and Social Media (Standards and Practices in Large-Scale Social Media Research)*, 9 (4): 28–37. DOI: 10.1609/icwsm.v9i4.14687.

Zappavigna, Michele. 2013. *Discourse of Twitter and Social Media. How We Use Language to Create Affiliation on the Web*. London: Bloomsbury Publishing.

Authors' Contributions

This article is the result of joint research. Both authors were involved in devising the project, discussing the outline, and reviewing the final manuscript. CSH is mainly responsible for the designing of the computational framework and data collection. ENR contributed to the theoretical framework regarding literary canonization. Both authors were involved in the analysis and discussion of data. The sections "The Initial Research Project," "Running into Unforeseen Problems," "Running Into Data Collection Trouble' and "Algorithmic Influence on Canonization" were written by CSH. The sections "Introduction" and "Is the Author Really Dead? Authorship, Canonization, and the Limits of Current Research" were written by ENR. "Distant Reading of Culture as Data as a Starting Point for Objects of Study, Corpus-Creation, and Canonization. Reflections and Concluding Remarks" was written jointly.

4

"Poetry Is about People Seeing Themselves": An Interview with Kirsty Melville

James Mackay
European University Cyprus

JuEunhae Knox
University of Sheffield

Kirsty Melville has a good claim to being the Sylvia Beach of the Instagram generation. The Australian publisher, working with Andrews McMeel in Kansas City, has spotted most of the writers who have gone on to be the breakout English language poets in the last decade, and in the process has taken her company from nowhere (poetically speaking) to being the predominant force in poetry sales. We interviewed her over Zoom.

Reading #Instapoetry editors (RI): Your company has gone in a decade from a highly commercial publisher of titles largely aimed at the gifts trade to being one of the largest publishers of new poetry in the world. How did this happen?

Kirsty Melville (KM): Andrews McMeel has always been known as a publisher of humor and gift books, best known for comic strip publishing in syndication. Our products have always been short form, with relatable content, humor, warmth, and kindness messages. As newspapers—which had always been a marketing platform for our comic strips—started to decline, we looked to evolve and it became evident that a lot of people were experimenting creatively outside the normal traditional publishing routes.

We've always been a little outside of the mainstream in the way we've published because we've acquired content through syndication or worked directly with creators and artists. So we noticed that some poets were starting to self-publish. One of them was Lang Leav, who's based out of Australia. She had self-published some poetry, and was an artist as well, and was getting a lot of interest from booksellers around the world, but she couldn't meet the demand. There's been a long tradition of self-publishing in poetry, of course, and new technology meant that Lang could do one off print-on-demand editions of her book, but she couldn't get the scale of distribution.

Her agent called me and said, "I've got this young poet with a fan base, but I don't know anything about Tumblr—would you be interested?" I took one look at the work that Lang was publishing and her readership, the complete involvement that her readers were having with her work, and said, "Yes, I know exactly what to do with this." So we published Lang, paying a very big advance (which was unusual for us at the time), and sold this globally.

This was a time before Instagram, when these artists and creative people were experimenting in places like Tumblr, and sharing their work in a way that traditional publishers were not reaching. So we started to look for other poets on Tumblr, and then later on Instagram, who'd self-published their work. One of the early poets we reached out to was Rupi Kaur, who had self-published *milk and honey* while she was a student in Toronto. She was a visual artist who was trying to express her own work through poetry and art and spoken word performances.

There was a whole underground movement of these artist-poets who were sharing their work with each other, and as social media took off, it helped to expand those direct relationships. All we really did was enable those books to find their way into the mainstream, because it was there already, being read and circulated amongst smaller groups, in pockets of university students, and at that time, most mainstream publishers didn't even know what was going on. We saw this social poetry emerging.

Rupi led the way. She broke down the doors of publishing, broke with the establishment, and enabled young people to publish and write for each other without the gatekeepers of traditional publishing.

RI: How do you go about finding and selecting poets?

KM: Social media has definitely provided an opportunity for young people to write and to see themselves represented in the work that's been published. So we seek out authors we hear about, we get recommendations from other poets. We have a website, Read Poetry, which celebrates poets and writing poetry, and sometimes we get people contacting us directly.

There was a trend a while ago, when Rupi was very successful, where agents for celebrities would suddenly think, "Oh, I can have my client write or ghostwrite a poetry book." We acquired a couple of rights to those initially, but they didn't sell well. What that tells you is it isn't a case of "I have a profile. I have a platform. I'm interested in poetry, I'll do it." Because they weren't poets, and they didn't get engagement for their poetry. That's the distinction between them and a Rupi or a Lang or an Iain S. Thomas, or a Courtney Peppernell. Our poets write the feelings and experiences that they have, and their readers respond to that—it's not like you can just say "I'm going to be a poet."

So we look for those poets with really responsive audiences, but sometimes it's also a matter of timing. For instance, Rupi's just started a world tour, and part of her approach is that in all the cities she's been to she's reached out to local poets and asked for submissions, and then invited new young poets up on the stage to perform their work as an opening act. Last night in Kansas City she had a young woman that she'd found from Missouri performing this incredibly beautiful work, and I hope we'll sign her. You see, there's a community of support and sharing of their life experiences through poetry.

I think we've become where they want to be published because we've been so successful with writers who express feelings about their world being in such flux, and about writing about everyday experiences of mental health and depression. These are relatable topics that maybe the old white guys don't understand and certainly are not writing about.

We also try actively to find representatives of communities of interest. Just the other day a young Christian poet submitted to us, and we realized that we didn't really have anyone who spoke to that audience. Generally, it has been a really remarkable opportunity for us as a company to explore and be in the world where young people are, to enter the conversation about the topics being discussed in the world. It has enabled us as a publisher to really embrace diversity and representation.

RI: You talked before about Andrews McMeel's history as a "publisher of kindness." And yet what you're talking about is almost a revolutionary literary movement. We normally talk about literary movements that are "revolutionary" as being like punks or anarchists—this seems to be the opposite.

KM: The very first cartoonist we ever published at Andrews McMeel was Gary Trudeau, who was a student at Yale and had created this comic strip Doonesbury, which was political commentary. Trudeau's been syndicating his work with us for fifty years, and he's beloved because he challenges orthodoxies. There's many presidents in the United States who hate Gary Trudeau, because he makes fun of their policies. Then there's Gary Larson, whose humor was also very irreverent and provocative, and Calvin and Hobbes, which really exudes warmth, affection, and wisdom. The poetry we publish is a natural evolution.

But it was a big decision, because Lang writes poetry about love and relationships, and Rupi goes into sexual trauma, abuse, the patriarchy, misogyny, and all those things that form an identity. With Rupi, particularly she speaks to young women who haven't felt like they had a voice. Now we have all these issues in the United States around abortion and women's rights, and she stands for women who don't feel like they're being heard. All of our poets, particularly the poets of color, are making a way in the world, in the United States, where women of color have typically not had a voice. That's also been really important to us as a company, where we've got a big commitment to equity, inclusion, and belonging.

Poetry is helping us evolve in other ways. You can't have all our poets of color edited by white, young men. It doesn't work. And so we are very intentional about how we publish, who we work with, so that we're sensitive to those issues. It means we as a company are evolving with the work we're publishing as well.

RI: You've got this catalog that's very diverse, with many young women, first generation-immigrants, international voices represented. You've spoken about the idealistic reasons for doing that, but how has it been on the commercial side?

KM: The decision to publish Lang Leav was easy. But when it came to Rupi—well, we're a privately held family-friendly company, mostly publishing comic strips for general consumption on the funny pages. Rupi's subject matter and the expression of it in *milk and honey* was a real stretch for some people here. When I think about decisions I've made that have had a big impact, the one that sticks out was that decision to publish *milk and honey*, because it went so outside what we'd typically published.

But there's nothing like success to change people's minds, or perhaps their comfort level with certain content. *milk and honey* sold 4 million copies, and suddenly everyone thought this poetry thing wasn't so bad! Some of the poetry submissions that we've received have definitely been challenging for some people within our organization, and so we've had to really think hard about that.

From a practical perspective, poetry is not very expensive—nowhere near as pricey as, for example, a full color cookbook. We've always done full color production, and our margins were always tight because of the costs. But with poetry, the costs are not that great, and you can print them anywhere in the world. This commercial success, of bestselling books that did not cost too much to print, was phenomenal, and that also fueled interest and expansion. But then the other real interest was that we created a new category within poetry publishing. I was very intentional in trying to dominate this category and take market share from other publishers, because I wanted us to be the home and to be the leader. At one point, we had around 48 percent market share of all poetry titles sold, and we continue to be the leader on Bookscan. Rupi is the bestselling poet of all time. Keeping Andrews McMeel as the market leader is one of my strategic priorities.

A lot of other publishers thought to jump on this trend, but they weren't committed because it just didn't seem logical to them. Typically, publishers make their money on more commercial fiction and then they invest in poetry as a commitment to literature, but it's not seen as profitable. We just turned that on its head. I've had a number of colleagues tell me they didn't realize that anyone could be a successful poetry publisher.

I think what's challenging as a publisher of our size is larger publishers: Penguin Random House, HarperCollins … the big ones. That means we are very focused on staying in certain categories that we're good at, not trying to be all things to all people. That gives us an edge. And we can be nimble, because we don't have the large mouth to feed that these bigger companies do. We're more thoughtful and we want to publish people we can do a good job with as well.

RI: Why do you think poetry has specifically flourished on Instagram, much more than other platforms?

KM: That little square sits perfectly for short form poetry. It wouldn't for ballads, but if you have a short few lines with some art that you want to post, it's easy to do it. Part of the phenomenon is that the experience of reading poetry on Instagram or Tumblr is not the same as the experience of reading a book. The very nature of poetry is reflective, and thoughtful, and you can have that small bite of emotional impact with a short poem on Instagram that's very shareable. You can have people themselves performing certain poems and then sharing them on TikTok.

Poetry's about people seeing themselves and reflecting on their lives through the words of the poet. And while we do sell ebooks, and we've done audio books of the performances, in the end, the book that you hold in your hand and read and reflect on is still the most powerful medium for poetry. Something we discovered when we first started publishing was that young people were going into bookstores to buy the physical book they'd seen on Instagram. Our sales were not on Amazon, they were in Barnes & Noble. They were at Indigo bookstores, they're at Waterstones. *milk and honey*, I remember was at the cash register at Waterstones, they had tables full of poetry. Social media was the platform for raising awareness, but for the experience audiences still wanted to buy the physical book.

James Daunt, the CEO of Barnes & Noble and Waterstones, talks about how YA fiction is driving revenue by getting young people going into bookstores and buying books. But poetry got there first, to be honest. Young people were finding themselves in the work. This is a group that grew up on Harry Potter, they've grown up on books, and they see the value of the experience of reading. There's nothing like being published in book form, people still want that prestige, the timeless nature of poetry in books. But it's all augmented by social media.

RI: What design decisions do you make to enhance that prestige quality?

KM: Depends on the author. Part of the shift to poetry is that it's very personal, both how you express yourself and how you want your books to look and feel. So we collaborate very closely with our authors on the design, often giving them creative freedom.

My first experience with that was with Lang Leav, who designed her second book with blue cover with a young girl's face. We took it to the buyer at Barnes and Noble, and he said that book will never sell. That it looked like a dead girl on a book. We went back to Lang, and she said, "He doesn't I know my audience. This book will sell." And it did! Lang had been an artist who done fashion labels in Japan, and she had a real feel for young women's sensibilities, particularly in Asia. That's why we trusted her, with that aesthetic background.

We have another author, Atticus, who was one of the original, big authors, who is bringing out a book this fall. The title is written as *LVOE*. So we had a call, again, and I said, "I don't think it works. Help me understand why this LVOE." "Well," he said, "It's because love is imperfect." I asked him to write a note about that at the front of the book, to explain this intention.

Another example is Courtney Peppernell, the author of *Pillow Thoughts*. When she first submitted her ideas for design, she had a jellyfish on the cover. I, being Australian, am not that fond of jellyfish—I did not see that the jellyfish could be evocative. But I said, "Let's have a call so I can understand where she's coming from." Courtney's reason was "Jellyfish float in the world, and you can identify with that in whatever way you want—it's very fluid. we know that my audience loves jellyfish." Clearly, I was not the core audience, but I trusted her. And she was right. She understood the representation that people were looking for, how they read her work, and why the jellyfish actually made sense.

That's the other difference between a traditional poet and these artists. They've grown up in a visual world. Visual representation of their ideas is a part of what they're trying to do. They're artists, a lot of them, and their creative expression is achieved through design, through feel. They're very thoughtful. I've learned always to trust them, because they understand what they're doing. That makes us a different type of publisher, because we're willing to trust our authors. We're investing in them, saying, "We believe in you and your work. How can we best support you?"

RI: Who are the audiences for your live readings, and how do they react?

KM: Different poets have different comfort levels. There are certain writers who are quite shy. There's Atticus who hides with the mask, and who's got a whole new crazy concept for hiding himself for the launch of this new book that I can't share with you because it's still under wraps.

A few years ago, pre-COVID, we had a special panel at the Book Expo (a bookselling trade industry event), with several different poets. Some of them were really shy and uncomfortable, and nervous to be up in front of other people. Sometimes writers are introverts that don't actually naturally perform. Amanda Lovelace, who's the author of *the princess saves herself in this one* and numerous other feminist retellings of fairy tales, was very shy to do events at the beginning. Now she's posting on Instagram, and she's found her tribe, if you will, of witches who follow her. Courtney Peppernell's work is very accessible and easy, but she was not a very good reader, and she was very shy, but her work stood for itself. So some poets almost hide behind social media, where it's more about what they write and how that resonates.

And then you have Lang, who will go and do a reading in Kuala Lumpur, and be treated like a rock star by all these young women who show up to hear her read, thanks to her expression and her style. You have performers like Valerie June Hockett and Tarriona Ball, both musicians who moved from writing lyrics into poetry and spoken word. That's a completely different audience again.

Think how many different types of people there are in the world, how many communities each with their own feelings and ideas. Some of these ideas are universal, and speak to everyone. Some speak mainly to their core audience.

RI: How does the brevity of the poetry translate into performance?

KM: I think it's a confidence thing. Poets go on stage and talk, explaining the genesis of the poem, or the themes it's exploring. Then … pause. Three lines of poetry. The young woman I mentioned earlier who opened for Rupi had two poems. The second one was the one that made Rupi choose her. She began with a trigger warning about childhood trauma, letting the audience get oriented with the idea. Only then did she read it, and it was so powerfully moving.

Many poets have very short poems, but longer spoken word pieces. It's more about the meaning than the length. We've experimented with poetry on Spotify, where you've got single tracks of poetry, and we've put music to poetry, and used high production values to enhance the reading.

RI: What do you think of the term "Instapoetry"?

KM: I don't like it. I think it diminishes the work. At the time when these poets were becoming popular, people started using it mainly to denigrate them.

If Rumi or Kahlil Gibran were writing today, we wouldn't call them Instapoets. We would talk about their work and its meaning and the words they use. The problem with "Instapoetry" is that it's caught up in the platform, as opposed to the shared experience that these social media platforms have facilitated. That's why I prefer to call it "social poetry" because it's *shared* poetry. I understand that Instapoetry is an easier marketing term for people who want to write about the style and the origins of the work, but it belittles young women who are expressing themselves in that way. It's a way of saying this isn't real. This is not proper poetry. This is Instapoetry. I don't like it because it's denying the real power of the work.

RI: Have you seen a shift with newer poets attitude to the term?

KM: I think what's interesting is that we don't even talk about it anymore. It's more hashtag poetry, really, as opposed to Instapoetry, but, again, that's just a mechanism for sharing, recognizing that there's a very supportive group of people who want to share their work and that of others. It's a new form of publishing, really, their own self-publishing on a social medium using hashtags.

In the United States, right now, there are several poets on the bestseller list. There's Amanda Gorman, who came to prominence when she performed at the inauguration of Joe Biden. She's become a voice for young black women. And there's Ocean Vuong, who's a Vietnamese immigrant literary writer, a beautiful poet. I love his work. And there's Warsan Shire, also another poet who was one of the original Instapoets who's recently published another book. These writers show the way poetry is heading.

The other thing I'd say is that some of the earlier poets are older. Rupi's turning thirty. When we published *milk and honey* it was seven years ago. She's evolved into writing about new themes. I think there's a group that's going to grow with her.

There's no shortage of people who want to write and express themselves. TikTok is evolving and creating possibilities for creative expression in a completely new way. I still love Instagram myself, even though the problem with it is the algorithms are really mucking up the ability to share. That's why people are going to TikTok—and there'll be something else after that, I'm sure.

RI: Particularly at the start of the movement, there were many dismissive pieces in the press. They attack Instapoetry as being simplistic, unliterary, or as always sounding the same. How do you respond?

KM: There's a combination of feelings that are going into those opinions. One is envy. Jealousy by the critics that their work isn't being seen as widely. I mean, it must be very hard for a poet who's slaved away, studied, and then sells maybe a thousand copies of a small chapbook, to see an Amanda Gorman or a Najwa Zebian suddenly selling tens of thousands, even millions, of books.

I am not a fan of judgmental people, really, because I think that it's important to appreciate that the world is a diverse world, and that different types of people express themselves in different ways. It's clinging to a particular frame of reference, not being very open or curious. Also, it sometimes shows ignorance. For instance, Rupi's way writing with simplicity, not simplistically, comes from her Sikh tradition. It's very clear when you look that her style of writing follows her own cultural traditions. To judge her work from a Western colonial perspective is deeply unfair.

Taking this smugly intellectual perspective on these writers is superior and condescending.

RI: How much do you see the writers who you work with as compromising to write for a marketplace?

KM: I think that writing poetry is extremely personal. OK, so on social media some people get blinded by the fame aspect, but the good poets aren't doing it for that. They're expressing themselves, and their feelings. These are very heartfelt stories, often with people writing about their lives and their experiences. They're using writing and poetry as a form of healing, to try and understand and work through questions that they have about their lives. They're vulnerable and they're human. The "look at me" aspect of social media masks the reality of that vulnerability in the subject matters that these young people are writing about. It's so brave of them to put out poems that are lyrical and well written, and also about childhood trauma. It's a different way of being out in the world. The discomfort that some introverts might have about splashing your face all over social media, I understand that, but mostly it's just discomfort with a different way of being in the world.

RI: Of all the many poems that you've published, is there one that holds a special place?

KM: I have one framed on my wall in my office, a Rupi Kaur canvas from *milk and honey*. On International Women's Day, to have an inclusive global marketing push, we had this poem recorded in fifteen different languages, with different women reading it. We edited the clips together so that people had this sense of what this poem meant to these women around the world. It begins

> *i want to apologize to all the women i've called pretty*
> *before I've called them intelligent or brave*

I love that poem because it's talking about the resilience of women, how women are so much more than how they look. That's a universal message that speaks to women around the world. And that's what so much of our poetry represents.

5

Instant Confessions

Yara Gawrieh Ekmark, Poet

I was twenty-three years old when I wrote my first line on my Instapoetry account @cinnamonbunpuns: "I want to live in a city that loves its people." Accompanied by the hashtags #poetry#city#love#people#world#humanity#art #creativewriting#quote, this poetic line suited the emotions I was trying to address at a time when I was moving between countries, trying to find a sense of home or belonging, and starting over after fleeing the war in Syria. Getting 105 likes and a few comments from Instagram users who expressed their interest in my writing, and one comment which dubbed my line with the word "Humanity <3," was exactly the essence I was looking for on this new platform. I was living in a country where I did not speak the language very well, while simultaneously watching my parents struggle to start over and trying to find my own way in this new part of the world. I craved a cosmopolitan connection where I did not have to learn a certain language, nor worry about any legal documents, papers, or any other bureaucratic details. I felt welcomed by multiple users on Instagram from all over the world, of different ages and genders, who seemed willing to encourage me and engage with what I was posting/creating. I felt like I could do what I loved most (writing poetry) without any barriers or serious considerations. With every single post that followed, it felt like I was attempting to make sense of my emotions and my days. I wrote about love, belonging, home, boredom, and existential confusion in general. The combination of photography, visual effects, and the instant feedback I got from my followers created an ultimately inspiring process for me. Writing each Instapoetry post offered a confession to the world. It felt freeing and comforting to know that other people related to what I was feeling and even applied my words to their own experiences. This fusion of the personal with the public or universal has been a major part of the Instapoetry experience for me.

I studied English Literature at Stockholm University, and my Instagram account inspired me to write my graduation paper about "The Confessional Voice of The Female Poet and The Rise of Instapoetry," in which I used the term "over-confession" to describe the poetic process of writing poetry on Instagram. I have found that the feeling of emotional association allowed by Instagram goes hand in hand with the desire and need to write. This desire to find meaning, intimacy, emotional catharsis, and an understanding of the "self" in relation to the world, which is often the reason why writers write, is one of the therapeutic features of Instagram and Instapoetry in particular. The experience of sharing, producing, and receiving is certainly empowering when it comes to artistic production.

I write in a poetic-diary style of writing, and I wasn't entirely sure when I started my Instagram account whether I was writing prose or poetry as my writing blended elements of both genres. Instagram was a way for me to figure out my writing style, which is both poetic prose and prose poetry, and it made me realize that I do not necessarily need to strictly define it. Instagram was a way for me to find an eerie territory in my writing which belonged to me only, but was also universal. My writing was eventually freed from the constraints of traditional narrative, conventional verse, and categorization, allowing me to focus on subjective impressions and synthesis in my writing and expressing my thoughts and experiences in a way that felt authentic to me. When I write Instapoetry, I often experience an elliptical feeling of being spread out over the world since I often approach the writing in a scattered way, paying little attention to chronology or spatial elements. This scattered approach allows me to capture my thoughts and emotions in a more spontaneous and unfiltered way, although my writing is often very interior, focusing on emotional introspection rather than physical substance and experiences. Nevertheless, due to the public nature of Instagram, this introspection paradoxically results in an atmosphere of blurring the personal with the public/universal and the interior with the exterior in my writing, creating an effect of sfumato; a softening of sharp edges to make my posts bleed into each other. This sensual relationship and overall flow of continuity is limitless on the Instagram platform. I start from a point of perceptual unity and then transcribe it on the page using visual techniques such as typography, layout, line breaks, visual illustrations, and format.

I attempt to evolve my style every time I post a new poem, and the techniques I use throughout my poems are often very different stylistically. My main concern when writing a deeply personal poem is making it resonate with a wider audience, though I usually trust that the emotional resonance of the poem will naturally facilitate its connection with a universal audience. Due to the limited space on Instagram, I rely on emotional resonance when writing a poem. This is why I carefully incorporate imagery and musicality, so that the short verses of my Instapoems have a longer impact on readers' minds. That is essentially how I try to balance the deeply personal with the universal on such a global platform. Subjective reality is extremely complex and sometimes difficult to convey, but by attempting to depict that complexity in an Instapoem, I always hope that the emotional resonance of the Instapoem will capture the reality for other people too. The recognition of shared emotions and complexities through Instapoems is what makes the platform experience worth it. Therefore, I would suggest that Instapoems should be read with instinct rather than intellect. The emotional urgency and resonance of Instapoems result in an immediate stream of responses from readers on Instagram. Another aspect of Instapoetry that contributes to its over-confessional nature is that the poems are shared instantly, so I do not have the chance to be an objective reader when editing my poems. Each Instapoem I post remains a work in progress since I can go back to it whenever I want and edit it before reposting it.

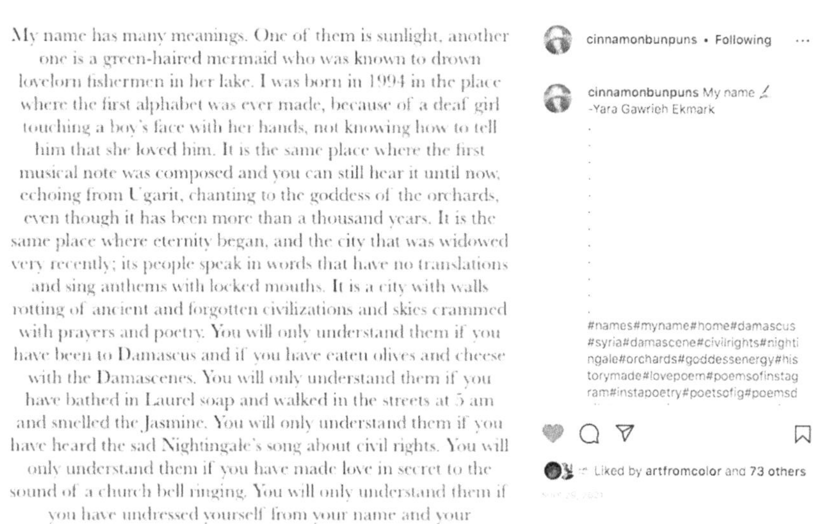

Figure 5.1 "My Name." 2021. Author's own image from @cinnamonbunpuns. https://www.instagram.com/p/CPcvqzSlq2t/

I rely on allegory, metaphors, persona, and identity throughout most of my poems. The speaker is often me, or my Instagram persona. However, I moved from persona to autobiography with the poem "My Name" (shown in Figure 5.1), in which I explore the transformative nature of names and how they often have subjective implications for each person, despite their universal ties. This poem suggests that society's response to our names, which often have rich histories, political associations, and geographical ties, also has an impact on our selfhood and how we perceive our place in the world. I used a lot of sensory imagery in the prose poem to bring the setting of the poem to life. The emotional ending allows the idea of the transformative power of names to strongly resonate. The politically charged ending captivates the reader, who can sympathize with the feeling of leaving one's home and crossing a border. The oblique view of names implied by the poem generates endless interpretations of each line. However, since the last line is the last thing the reader reads, I always try to make it resonate. The afterlife of the poem begins in the last line, and it is the last note that is revealed before the reader scrolls down to the next post on the Instagram feed. I tried to let the last line in this poem transform everything that came before to encourage a reappraisal of the emotionally transformative power of names. This poetic metamorphosis is what gives the poem its resonance.

Considering the restricted length of Instapoems, they often feel compulsive. The driving force of the language in an Instapoem is the emotional urgency that comes with the emotions one experiences on a shared platform such as Instagram. When creating an Instapoem, there is always an elliptical presence of all the online readers who will read it instantly when it is posted. I have also found that to be able to write about myself, I needed to create what feels like a personal mythology, a mythology constantly being reshaped with every post on my Instapoetry account. The inspiration behind the poem in Figure 5.1 is derived from the various meanings of the name "Yara," blended with the history of my home country and the experiences of Syrian refugees. Although I do not explicitly mention my own name "Yara," the autobiographical nature of the prose-poem certainly suggests to my readers on Instagram that I am introducing myself to them with the poem. This unique and intimate depiction of my identity through my name, which connects personal and historical elements, contributes to the poetic identity on my Instapoetry account in an individual yet widely undefined and expansive way.

In the process of writing an Instapoem, I often imagine that my readers will be individuals who share a similar intensity about their feelings and perceptions of reality. I also think about other Instapoets such as Rupi Kaur, Alicia Cook,

Trista Mateer, and many others, who drew me to Instapoetry because of how effortlessly I connected with their writings. The shared artistic and poetic experience on Instagram allows me to constantly respond to these poets 'works, and this connection has even led me to buy print books by these Instapoets. I often feel like I want to keep writing whenever I read other Instapoets' posts. It is undeniable, however, that at times one might feel overwhelmed by the need to constantly share new things on the platform of Instagram, but it is important to keep in mind that creativity comes in waves; one must have faith that it will return eventually. Nevertheless, promoting oneself on Instagram is crucial, so one has to be constantly active and present for one's readers. This aspect is part of the whole over-confessional poet/reader immersion experience. I noticed that when I was less present for my readers, my following decreased. Both readers and Instapoets are craving this connectedness offered by the platform. However, in the context of the immediacy and dominance of social media platforms in our daily lives, it is essential to be understanding and accepting of oneself when one is not constantly producing new work. This inconsistency is part of the creative process.

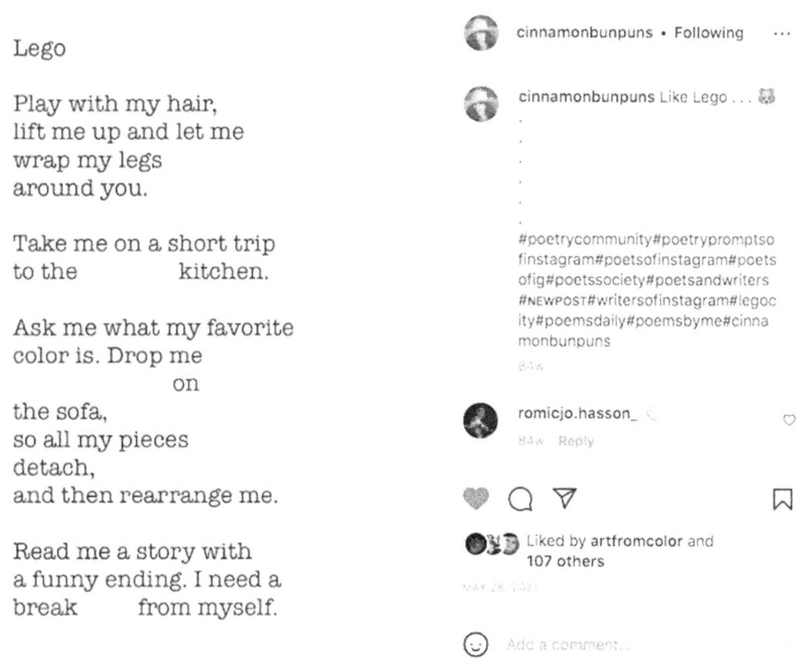

Figure 5.2 "Lego." 2021. Author's own image from @cinnamonbunpuns. https://www.instagram.com/p/CPZTHkYF4mt/

In Figure 5.2, the Instapoem "Lego" is visually presented on the white space in a disconnected manner, with individual words or word fragments appearing to be placed together almost randomly. The title "Lego" represents the structure of the poem, with the individual lines and line breaks functioning like interlocking blocks of Lego. In addition to tying the words of the poem together, the title adds another layer of meaning and a sense of urgency, but also a sense of childishness which reflects the state of emotional vulnerability in the poem. I have attempted to use the white space in a way that invites the reader to resonate with the thought process of the narrative voice and enhances the overall atmosphere of the poem. The form and the structure of the poem create a visual representation of the movement from one place to another within it. There is a sense of intimacy and familiarity created by the narrative voice and the eye-catching compression throughout the lines, which emphasizes the central theme of needing to take a break from one's own self and the desire for distractions. The poem depicts a moment of warm and friendly interaction which invites the reader to envision themselves in it and to contemplate the thoughts suggested by the narrative voice. The form of the poem reflects the poem's message and draws the reader in, leaving little room for the reader to feel disconnected from the poem. As a result of its reflective few words, the enigmatic message has a larger, more abstract presence than the physical poem itself. This effect allows the poem to overcome the spatial restrictions and limitations of the Instagram platform. In this poem, the poetic persona has taken a friendly tone, leaving little distance from the reader, which could be interpreted as a plea or an invitation for connection. Perhaps Instagram was the blissful distraction or escapism that I needed in the moment of writing this poem.

I frequently use a prominent, expressive voice and incorporate musical elements such as slant rhymes in my Instapoetry. The poem titled "Strawberries and Yogurt" (shown in Figure 5.3) uses white space to convey a flow of movement and to maintain continuity in the line structure. The repetition of certain sounds and patterns adds a musical and rhythmic quality. The repetition highlights the immediacy of the process of writing Instapoetry and depicts the narrative voice trying to make sense of complex things such as love or life choices. The poem, therefore, serves as a medium for the narrative voice to try to explain something that seems inexplicable. Due to Instagram's immediacy and ability to instantly publish content, my writing in this poem has an instinctive feel, with very little artifice. I often strive to minimize the

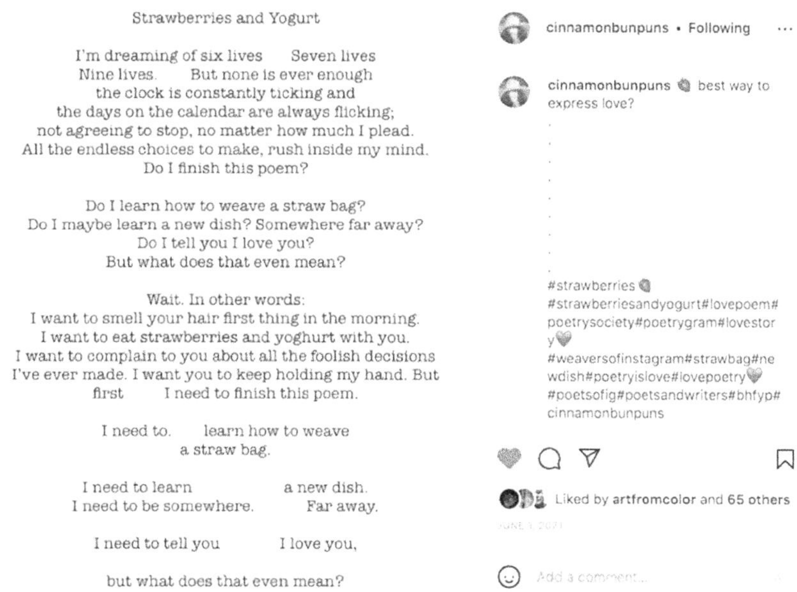

Figure 5.3 "Strawberries and Yogurt." 2021. Author's own image from @cinnamonbunpuns. https://www.instagram.com/p/CPl9ZvwFPVc/

use of committed adjectives in my Instapoems for a more concise and effective writing style and to focus the reader's attention on specific ideas and themes. "Foolish" is the most committed adjective in the poem, but it is used for its emotional resonance rather than its functional meaning, such as in the phrase "new dish." The lack of adjectives gives the poem a cleanliness and lack of clutter that works with Instagram's atmosphere, where readers are introduced to a work of art instantaneously. I have noticed that my shorter poems are more attention-grabbing, but I haven't let that stop me from writing or posting longer works. I find that there are times when I feel like posting a one-liner, and other times when I enjoy sharing a longer piece or perhaps adding the longer text in the caption of my Instagram post which contains a snippet of the full work. This broadly depends on what emotions or themes I want to express each time and since Instagram allows a great deal of freedom, I tend to take liberty mixing things up and getting creative. The most important thing for me when it comes to my Instapoetry account is that it enriches my creative process, provides a public platform for me to voice my thoughts and my poetry, and connects me with other readers and poets.

Reference

Gawrieh Ekmark, Yara. 2021. [Instagram profile]. *Instagram*. Available online: https://www.instagram.com/cinnamonbunpuns/. Accessed March 17, 2023.

6

"Former Contours": Posts, (Post) Pregnancy and Re/turning to Creative Processes

Dr. Laura Tansley
University of Glasgow

In *A Life's Work*, Rachel Cusk writes, "[B]irth is not merely that which divides women from themselves, so that a woman's understanding of what it is to exist is profoundly changed. Another person has existed in her, and after their birth they live within the jurisdiction of her consciousness. When she is with them she is not herself; when she is without them she is not herself" (2001: 12). In late 2017, pregnant with my first child, I have an increasing awareness of the rent that may open up between who I am, and who I might be after birth. Related to this, and of particular concern, are the ways my writing practice might be affected by this. There is work I am in the middle of that I would like to finish. I would like the writing I produce to maintain the quality and qualities I'd fostered for it and myself. But when Cusk describes the wrench between work and mothering as "[succeeding] in one means to fail at being the other," becoming a parent suddenly becomes an anathema to creativity and productivity, and vice versa (2001: 62). Of course Cusk's experience might be different to my own; but the concern of how these two facets of a person, the mother and the writer, and how they may or may not be able to coexist is not a new idea (see, for example, Literary Hub's guide, "14 Famous Writers on Whether or Not to Have Kids," which covers a century's worth of discussion on the topic by western authors). During my first pregnancy it felt impossible to know how to succeed at either, and so in the manner of a person looking to exert some kind of agency over the unknowable, I chose to make some predictions, and perhaps some assumptions too. I preempted the experience of splitting myself from myself, as Cusk suggests, of being someone else even in the presence of myself, by looking to Instagram to support a new creative process: one specifically designed to accommodate what

I imagined my new parent reality might entail, illustrated and informed by an exploration of Instapoetry as a self-(re)generating hybrid form.

When devising this process, I considered the way this new writing could support the management of expectations—my own mainly—on my time, my capacity to create or contribute to a conversation, and my sustained interest in anything. I wanted the process to respond to a feeling I'd begun to foster, and that other parents had mentioned, about how easy it would be to have everything shrink to the size and shape of me and a newborn, in a room, in a flat; how easy it might be to untether toward loneliness and isolation, and how detrimental this might be for what would become a shared sense of well-being between me and my child. This assumption was a way of troubleshooting, of attempting to know an unknown quantity, but an assumption based on what I already knew about myself and what I might need during a period of potential vulnerability. So, this creative process would involve small, rapidly produced pieces of writing with a more process-orientated (as opposed to product-orientated and therefore keenly edited) structure in place, all performed outdoors, or at the very least in spaces outside of my home. These felt like practical and logistical choices as well as an opportunity to embed notions of well-being into each act. I was also cementing the place creative practice holds for me as not only part of my professional life, but also a significant aspect of my personal life—as a source of self-care, and of creative and critical expression and exploration. This writing was going to keep me engaged as opposed to adrift, as well as challenge me as a writer. The shape of my practice up to this point had been driven by an attraction to, and an exploration of, short(er) forms of prose and prose-poetry, so to continue to experiment with how restricting length (both in time and literal space) might open up creative possibilities felt like a way to not only extend my practice, but to tether myself to myself: the former to the latter, pre-and post-birth.

From early 2018 I was almost entirely unemployed; to save money, and to ease my ever-expanding body, I walked absolutely everywhere. Walking in this way, for a reason, but often for no reason, I permitted myself to be less urgent. The walk itself became a productive act, as opposed to only a means to an end—be it to a shop, a meeting, or a more comfortable way to feel in my hips and my back. I looked around, noticing contrast or context, as opposed to traffic and people, buildings and structures. Mostly there was unremarkable litter. But occasionally there was what I interpreted as incongruity: an onion blossoming by the side of the road; a shiny red Christmas bauble abandoned in dark, pavement mud; a brown paper bag in a pile of fallen leaves. I carried specific items with me

Figure 6.1 My Instapoetry toolkit, 2021. Author's own image.

everywhere: a pen; a slim, A6 size notebook; a pack of three pads of mini, neon-colored, small Post-it notes; my phone—all items that would fit inside a coat pocket, that were light and took up little space. Words or phrases that sprang to mind whilst paused were jotted in the notebook, played with, then extracted on to a Post-it—filling just one square (at first)—and placed beside the scene. I took a photo with my phone, picked the Post-it note back up, and kept walking, knowing that if I tried to return to attempt a second draft, the paper bag would have blown away, the bauble would have been broken by footfall, the onion cleared away or disintegrated by winter rain.

I posted each picture on Instagram because I wanted to keep a record, and because I wanted other people to see these pieces. This form invited viewing as much as they were for reading which is why I chose to post them on Instagram, it being a platform that supports the collaboration of the visual and the textual. But I also wanted to be seen / to be productive / to be still writing / to be a writer, and to evidence this work and explore its impact by posting, or publishing, these pieces for others to engage with. The Post-it pieces became Instapoetry then, because of the nature of the platform itself but also because Instagram supports the manifestation of a desired self. Claudia Dey writes in "Mothers as Makers of Death" that there is an expectation that "the mother's body, after birth, is to

Figure 6.2 "Sympathetic Camouflage," 2021. Author's own image. Published in the collection, *Notes to Self*, Trickhouse Press, 2021.

be returned as quickly as possible to its former contours. This is true for her mind as well" (2020). Looking back at the choices I made to establish a creative process—to continue my practice but in a transformed way, and to evidence this practice on Instagram—I am aware that by creating these Post-it pieces I was quite possibly attempting to shape myself into something recognizably productive after the birth; that I was attempting to re/turn to myself as quickly as possible and using Instagram to propel this process. Perhaps these Instapoems were a way to meet this expectation. When I posted these pieces I was attempting to manifest the self I had predicted when designing the process using Instagram, a platform of aspirational curation where what we would like to be is more forthcoming at times than our reality.

Instapoets who directly address the experience of parenthood often explore an aspirational output by committing to a confessional and frank honesty in their work, seeking out the kind of authenticity that drove the success of 2016's

Figure 6.3 "After Birth," 2021. Author's own image. Published in the collection, *Notes to Self*, Trickhouse Press, 2021.

Nobody Told Me, the memoir-collection hybrid by writer and performance poet Hollie McNish about her experience of pregnancy and early motherhood. McNish, who found a significant following for her work via social media and is on Instagram as @holliepoetry, posts both new and existing poems as well as so-called sketches which often center around unfair gender expectations springing from her experience of motherhood and her own daughter's childhood. Defiant and straight-talking, these poems often feel as if they are coming from a place that demands acknowledgment by evidencing the very existence of the poet. In "No Stones In Her Stomach," McNish describes a crawling baby's attempts to swallow everything within reach, and the reason the narrator gives when asked why they haven't "got any / work done," is because they "have saved the baby's

Figure 6.4 "Weight," 2021. Author's own image. Published in the collection, *Notes to Self*, Trickhouse Press, 2021.

life / at least a hundred fucking times" by ensuring they haven't swallowed any "stones; / no dog shit; not one fucking / jigsaw piece" (2020). In the poem, the narrator hasn't produced anything, no work, "no fresh cookies in the / oven," instead the productive act is care which goes unrecognized (McNish 2020). Yet by posting the poem, McNish is highlighting her productivity, having produced something from the experience of not being able to get anything done: a post of white text on a duck-egg blue square that received 1,320 likes. Using Instagram to explore the challenges of writing whilst simultaneously producing writing feels like an odd contradiction, but one that would fit with the narrative around Instapoets and the kind of writing produced and/or posted there: both authentic and curated, in-progress and published.

In "The Cult of the Noble Amateur," Rebecca Watts writes about McNish that the effect of her poems "is limited to recognition, which merely reinforces the reader or audience member's sense of selfhood" (2018). McNish, in response to Watts, says about her use of Instagram: "Some poems I do write quickly and for years I only shared the poems I spent a long time on or thought were alright. But I don't want to do that anymore. It's fun sharing 'sketches' too. And it's fun sharing poems on different platforms with different people using them in all sorts of ways" (2018). Instagram seems to encourage an in-progress practice, perhaps because this, in turn, means the constant need to add to, to update, to maintain the motion of progression—something key for the growth and investment in a social media platform that thrives on a kind of attention to continual diversion. In regard to my own choice to engage with Instapoetry, and whether I should consider these pieces as in-progress and therefore somehow less rigorous examples of my writing in comparison to traditionally published work, I feel conflicted. The quality of the Post-it poems is tied to the purposeful qualities I embedded in the process, and so I find it difficult to evaluate them in the way that Watts proposes for poetry—that affective poetry should be challenging as opposed to recognizable. Attempting to evaluate the product of a process that I had purposefully embedded with a lack of evaluation, for my own sake, for creative exploration, would suggest that after the fact they are valuable and valueless and everything in-between depending on the context, and on the reader. Perhaps these pieces are also artifacts; illustrative and enquiring examples of the constant present tense experience of new parenthood, as explored by Mei-Mei Berssenbrugge in "85 Notes." In this hybrid essay, Berssenbrugge considers her experience of the changes in, and changes to, meaning after the birth of her daughter. Under a section headed "Days," time, its relationality, its fragmentation as well as its tidaling (as a consequence of, or reaction to, having a child and the impact this has on acts of thought, understanding and experience) is enacted and explored in eighty-five fragments.

> 33. You try for a coherent tension between the accidental appearing and clearly organized passages within a day. Everything is a field or a maze you get through serially, from point to point. You follow, and you're left with a network of points, and these points may be able to become your thought. (Berssenbrugge 2003: 213)

I feel like I understand this viscerally; that with very young children there is no traveling, only immediacy, only the right now, and then the next right now, and the pressing present is constant. My choice to create Instapoetry during this time of pregnancy and new parenthood seems less pragmatic within this frame, and more fundamental, more reflexive. Instagram records a series of un/related instances, an assemblage of experiences focused into a single profile. The next experience repeatedly replaces the last as a new present, as a mode to enact selfhood through acts of self-curation. Each post is, or has, a point to be followed, in amongst a network of points that build and articulate selfhood. In this way, both the process by which I produced these Post-it note pieces and the act of posting itself reflected and enhanced, created and affirmed, the experience of motherhood, and the capacity Instagram has to manifest a (manufactured) selfhood.

If Instagram is a platform that captures our ongoingness, re/presenting our ever-present, then the work we share on the platform should be considered within that frame. As Don Paterson, editor of Hollie McNish's work suggests, "You measure it against its own ambitions," as opposed to demanding it meet a set of rules around writing that it intentionally and explicitly wasn't produced for (2018). Despite this, the contradiction exists that when we record this in-progress-ness, when we capture and record and hold still a moment by posting a piece of Instapoetry on our profiles, we create a product, and in every sense that word entails. In relation to motherhood, the experience of immediacy and the next pressing present it creates, which demands a lack of stable conclusion, means that the Post-it pieces I produced are both a record of ongoingness and the death after death after death of previous iterations of self; a manifestation, and a reflection of, the struggle to maintain myself/selves, amplified by the pressure to build myself/selves in the context of new motherhood as both a writer and a person.

Whilst pregnant I experienced feelings that were like a small grief. A mourning process in reverse, I acknowledged the losses I anticipated after the birth as the space for a child opened up: a loss of time for thinking, writing, and a loss of being in numerous inexplicable and inexpressible ways. My due date became the signifier of a fundamental end. Claudia Dey writes, "No one had warned me that with a child comes death. Death slinks into your mind. It circles your growing body, and once your child has left it, death circles him too" (2018). The Instapoems I produced at this time were in response to these feelings but were also an attempt to create a continuum by manifesting a self that I could predict emerging as a new mother. In this way I could establish consistency, some uninterruptable thing that could continue on and beyond the utterly unknowable dark tunnel of life after birth. This could be interpreted as an attempt to cheat death, to keep myself, or a part of my self, alive; cleaving an element of myself as a way to retain something recognizable about my creative practice and therefore myself. At the same time it may also have been a way to bring about the death of self that to me seemed unavoidable, and that inspired the shift in practice. In an interview with *The New Yorker*, the writer Samantha Hunt says, "When I became a mom, no one ever said, 'Hey, you made a death. You made your children's deaths.' Meanwhile, I could think of little else. It's scary to think of mothers as makers of death, but it sure gives them more power and complexity than one usually finds" (Leyshon 2017). I see this literal death and the more metaphorical kind in motherhood-focused Instapoetry—in the grief experienced by parents for former lives, in the fear they have for the safety of their child, in the deaths that are all around us that are suddenly so apparent and that prompt shielding. @themumpoems writes in a post from July 2020 that has since been removed about singing a lullaby to her child while dreaming of the last holiday before the baby arrived, the sleep that was had, the seven course meal, and the special amendments made to the food in order to keep the baby safe from the potential listeria in blue cheese; an acknowledgment of the danger that lurks in innocuous, usually care-free spaces.

In this short piece there is a sense of the loss of a former self and their escapades, the threat of loss that looms in every pregnant mouthful, and the loss that is to come when the baby ceases to be part of a person's body. It is a narrative of death, but as we await the next imminent post, it is also a narrative of becoming.

References

Berssenbrugge, Mei-Mei 2003. "Eighty-Five Notes." In *The Grand Permission: New Writings of Poetics and Motherhood*, edited by Patricia Dienstfrey and Brenda Hillman, 211–16. Connecticut: Wesleyan University Press.

Cusk, Rachel 2001. *A Life's Work*. London: Fourth Estate.

Dey, Claudia 2018. "Mothers as Makers of Death." *The Paris Review*, August 14. Available online: https://www.theparisreview.org/blog/2018/08/14/mothers-as-makers-of-death/. Accessed June 4, 2021.

Flood, Alison and Sian Cain. 2018. "Poetry World Split over Polemic Attacking 'Amateur' Work by 'Young Female Poets.'" *The Guardian*, Tuesday, January 23, 2018. Available online: https://www.theguardian.com/books/2018/jan/23/poetry-world-split-over-polemic-attacking-amateur-work-by-young-female-poets. Accessed June 4, 2021.

Leyshon, Cressida 2017. "This Week in Fiction: Samantha Hunt on the Unspoken Terrors of Being a New Mother." *The New Yorker*, May 15. Available online https://www.newyorker.com/books/page-turner/fiction-this-week-samantha-hunt-2017-05-23. Accessed June 4, 2021.

McNish, Hollie 2018. "PN Review." *Hollie Poetry*, January 21. Available online https://holliepoetry.com/2018/01/21/pn-review/. Accessed June 4, 2021.

McNish, Hollie. 2020. "No Stones in Her Stomach." *Instagram*, April 20, 2020. https://www.instagram.com/p/B_N7zEkBg8Y/.

Tansley, Laura. 2021. "Sympathetic Camouflage," "After Birth," "Weight." In *Notes to Self.* Lancaster/Dundee: Trickhouse Press.

Temple, Emily 2018. "14 Famous Writer's on Whether or Not to Have Kids." *Literary Hub*, June 6. Available online https://lithub.com/14-famous-writers-on-whether-or-not-to-have-kids/. Accessed June 4, 2021.

Watts, R. 2018. "The Cult of the Noble Amateur." *PN Review*, 44 (3): 13–17. Available online: https://www.pnreview.co.uk/cgi-bin/scribe?item_id=10090. Accessed June 4, 2021.

7

"The Floodgates Have Been Opened": Instapoetry and the Recentering of Marginalized Poets

Laura Gallon
Research Associate at the University of Sussex, UK

In "The Cult of the Noble Amateur," white British poet Rebecca Watts condemns the state of the contemporary poetry scene and its "invasion by those intent on bringing down all barriers on the grounds of fairness" (2018: 16). The "floodgates," she writes, "have been opened"; "[i]t is the job of poets to safeguard language" (14, 17). Writing in the aftermath of the Brexit vote, the xenophobic and classist underpinnings of her metaphor are striking. Like recent debates around the death of the novel which reflect anxieties about changes in the literary landscape and in society (Cosslett 2020), the issue here is not so much the disappearance of a literary form, but the dethroning of a particular and privileged image of the author and poet.

Accusing the literary establishment of belittling "intellectual engagement and [...] craft" by praising the accessible work of popular contemporary poets, Watts (who has an English degree from Cambridge and a master's from Oxford) gives voice to the concerns of many other traditionally educated poets and critics (2018: 13). Though her article pays comparatively little attention to Instapoetry and concentrates more on the print spoken-word poetry of Hollie McNish, it has come to embody the voice of the genre's detractors since its publication in *PN Review* in December 2017. Unsurprisingly, the prestigious literary magazine received many supportive responses for featuring the essay. Its editor, Michael Schmidt, reported to *The Guardian* that "[m]any of our readers seem relieved that literary criticism is at last being applied to writing that has, hitherto, been welcomed with open arms by journalists because it is easy to read, contains few challenges [...] to insist that it can stand on a sure footing beside poetry in what I have now too often seen described as 'dusty old books'" (Flood and

Cain 2018). Not all reactions were as positive, however, and the public outcry from literary magazines and fellow poets Lemn Sissay and Anthony Anaxagorou prompted *PN Review* to publish a statement on Twitter defending the article. The statement in question goes on to deplore "ad feminam attacks" (2018)—a somewhat incongruous comment, given the very gendered language that Watts's essay deploys and its targeted attack on a "cohort of young female poets" (2018: 13). Significantly, male Instapoets (including r.h. Sin, Atticus, and Tyler Knott Gregson) have much less been subject to criticism and viral online trolling than their female counterparts (Miller 2018). They are also less likely to attract the types of online sexual harassment and death threats that bestselling Irish Indian Instapoet Nikita Gill and Salvadoran American Instapoet Yesika Salgado confront on their respective Instagram pages. In an interview, Watts defended her arguments by stating that "women have an awful lot to lose from the denigration of critical culture" (qtd. in Chandler and Mitchell 2018), voicing the reasonable insecurities of women poets who have historically been excluded from the canon. Having long been "reviewed based on their gender and less on their literary qualities" (Ostriker 1986: 2), women poets continue to be acutely aware of their awkward positioning in what is considered by many to be the most prestigious literary form.

This territorial dispute is critical because it represents one of the first academic engagements with Instapoetry, because it is indicative of the changing face of poetry and literary criticism in the age of the internet, and because it reveals the threat that Instapoetry poses to more traditional understandings of poetry. What is taking place here is a battle over *what* gets defined as poetry and craft, *who* gets defined as a poet, and who can claim the *authority* to make such decisions. It is certainly no coincidence that these debates are emerging at a time when the publishing world is seeking to remedy its structural racism and as writers of color and/or from working-class backgrounds are increasingly being heard. As British poet Momtaza Mehri notes, "These 'debates' are often poorly disguised attacks against poets who are seen to have monopolized on a kind of literary affirmative action" (2018). Indeed, "Watts, and many others, are not members of an embattled class [; t]heir anxieties are echoed everywhere from *The Times Literary Supplement* to *Private Eye*" (2018), and, even more recently, *The London Review of Books*. These anxieties also partly explain the slow academic response to the phenomenon: despite Instapoetry's emergence in 2014, at the start of my research in 2018 there were only a handful of publications on the subject. The situation has visibly improved since, but debates about the genre's literary legitimacy, the threat it may pose to "real" and "deserving" poetry, and its highly commercial nature often dominate the discussion. While these are important considerations, they risk overshadowing the real-world impact of Instapoetry on sales of works by poets who have been stereotypically marginalized on account of their gender, ethnicity, and social standing. It is now widely acknowledged that women and writers of color and/or of migrant descent dominate the form. These include Rupi Kaur, Lang Leav, Yrsa Daley-Ward, Nayyirah Waheed, Cleo Wade, Upile Chisala, Najwa Zebian, Orion Carloto, Isha Loona, Komal Kapoor, Key Ballah, and Samantha King Holmes, among many others. They engage with issues often considered non-universal by documenting their experience of marginality, discussing female sexual desire, and they experiment with language, rhetoric, and form in innovative ways that deserve to be examined. Locating the new genre within a wider context of postcolonial and women's poetry, I argue that Instapoetry as a form emerged precisely as a consequence of the lack of publishing opportunities for writers of color and women, with significant transformational repercussions on the publishing industry. In what follows, I consider the cultural value of the genre for its writers and readers. I highlight its creative and aesthetic possibilities, while calling for a more inclusive form of poetry criticism which decenters the Western canon and considers the influence of other visual, linguistic, and cultural backgrounds.

In Search of a "Space of Their Own"

Since its development in the eighteenth century, the Western publishing world has been almost exclusively white (Cottenet 2014). A survey released in 2019 by the children's book publisher Lee & Low Books shows that the North American publishing work force is still more than three-quarters white. Similar results were reached in 2015 by the British development agency Spread the Word, which drew attention to how white and middle-class the British publishing industry remains. All this, of course, carries powerful implications at every stage of the publishing process, in terms of which stories and writers get published, how texts are marketed and read, and how well they sell. The recent wave of protests by Black Lives Matter activists across the globe, sparked by the killing of George Floyd, shone a spotlight on institutional racism in publishing. In June 2020, hundreds of authors highlighted the pay inequality between black and nonblack writers by sharing their book advance payments on Twitter under the hashtag #PublishingPaidMe, which was initiated by African American writer L.L. McKinney. #PublishingPaidMe exposed the racial disparity as white authors with no track record reported very high advances on their debuts, whereas well-established black writers revealed that they earned comparatively small ones that grew slowly over time. As Gill insightfully reveals, this creates a vicious circle where "[s]maller advances to authors of colour means less marketing for our books which means our books aren't featured titles which means less books in stores which means fewer sales which leads to publishing's favorite myth 'POC books just don't sell' which leads to smaller advances" (2021). As the British "Rethinking 'Diversity' in Publishing" (2020) report reveals, such pay inequality is buttressed by the assumption that minorities do not read, with the target reader being a 50-year-old white middle-class woman with time and resources on her hands (Saha 2020: 20). Consequently, books by writers of color tend to be marginalized, pigeonholed, or exoticized for this reader (Saha 2020: 4). To counter Watts's color-blind allegation that "there is no expectation that the output of novelists or playwrights should reflect their personalities" (14) then, the reality is that writers of foreign or less privileged backgrounds are constantly read and marketed as native informants and valued on their "authenticity"—i.e., their conforming to stereotypical views of their communities (Huggan 2020).

The poetry world fares no better. As Dorothy Wang reveals in her study of contemporary Asian American poetry, "[T]here exists a double standard in discussing the work of poets of color and those who are supposedly 'unmarked'" (2014: xx). Literary critics look to the work of white poets as "contributing to 'universal' questions of subjectivity and poetics" (i.e., poetic tone, syntax, etymology, prosody, and form). By contrast, when discussing the work of black or ethnic writers, they tend to concentrate on "political or 'black' content" and reductively read it as "an ethnographic window into another culture" (Wang 2014: xx). In other words, marginalized poets are often left out of the questions of form, poetic tone, and syntax that are discussed by "hard-core" or "real" literary critics, and therefore, these are "assumed to be the provenance of a literary acumen and culture that is unmarked but assumed to be white" (17–20). Assumptions that marginalized poetry lacks "universalism" and that engagement with politics is strictly opposed to literary craft, permeate the ways we view, review, and reward poetry. A 2018 study commissioned by the University of Liverpool reveals that the reviews published in UK and Irish poetry magazines are primarily written by white men, and that male critics are more than twice as likely to review other men. This accounts for the strikingly small amount of poetry by women and people of color in prestigious poetry magazines and poetry prizes. Between 2011 and 2018, for example, all the critics at *London Review of Books* were white, 83 percent of them were men, and all the books reviewed were written by white poets, the majority of whom (70.6 percent to be precise) were men, with four of them accounting for 24.7 percent of all the poems published in the magazine (Ledbury Critics 2018). Efforts have been made to improve the situation, with, most notably, the founding of the Ledbury Critics Programme in 2017, a UK mentorship program for poetry reviewers to encourage diversity in the poetry reviewing culture. Its positive impact was already noticeable in the 2018 study referred to above, but there is still a lot of work needed to remedy the structural marginalization of poets of color.

In this hostile context, the turn to self-publishing on Instagram in 2014 provided an outlet for writers who had no print prospects. Gill turned to Instagram after her poetry was rejected for publication 137 times, for instance. Unlike traditional forms of self-publishing, Instagram offers the advantage of sharing work more widely to a more international and popular audience. Instapoetry is more financially accessible for authors, who are not required to pay submission fees to literary journals or contests, or even to purchase an individual ISBN for their self-published book (which, in the UK, costs a prohibitive £89) to get their writing in the market (Johnson 2017: 144). It is also more financially accessible for readers, who are not required to purchase books in order to read. And unlike conventional publishing, Instagram self-publishing accrues power to the writers instead of the publishers and enables "minority" authors to transcend the burden of representation by targeting the audience of their choice. Turning to Tumblr and/or Instagram in order to eventually obtain a book contract with a publisher, some, including the successful Cambodian-Australian Instapoet Lang Leav, use typefaces traditionally associated with print and adopt relatively conventional rhyme schemes and forms. Others, such as Kaur, who shared her writing on Instagram before self-publishing *milk and honey* on Amazon's CreateSpace in November 2014, make comparatively more experimental use of Instagram's visual possibilities by incorporating hand-drawn illustrations to their texts, and straightforwardly take to task the publishing industry.

One such example is Kaur's "Women of Color," a short six-line and eleven-word-long poem accompanied by a simple drawing of a naked woman's back, from her hips to the top of her head where she sports a messy bun. The poem features in Kaur's first book and fascinatingly juxtaposes a critique of the print publishing industry with a political message about female solidarity and a discussion on ethnic female identity. The absence of punctuation and upper-case letters in the poem is characteristic of her style, a homage to the Punjabi Gurmukhi script, where "letters are treated the same," and where the only punctuation is a period (Kaur 2021). Through a play on words ("our backs / tell sorties / no books have / the spine to / carry") and form (with the line breaks making the poem curvy and reminiscent of the drawn woman's body), Kaur highlights the vulnerability of women's bodies to trauma, but also suggests that the book as material object is both too fragile and limited to carry the stories women do across generations, time, history, and space. Having initially published this poem online, Kaur contrasts the ongoing nature of Instagram and the infinite capacity of the internet to the small space of the book. By extension, she also implies that the book industry does not have the courage to publish stories they presume to be unsellable until proved otherwise. The text is ultimately a call for more voices and stories to be heard, testimonies of the kind found on Instagram pages such as *@brownhistory*. Like all her other black-and-white and voluntarily racially unmarked doodles of women, Kaur's rather simplistic outline of a faceless woman's back enable all women to identify and relate, for, in the words of comic book theorist Scott McCloud, "the more cartoony a face [or body] is [...] the more people it could be said to describe" (1994: 31). In addition to her pared-down and accessible use of English (the international lingua franca), Kaur's deliberate decision to use an inclusive "our" and a racially unmarked female body before announcing her allegiance to "women of color" is an expression of the transnational female solidarity that occurs online.

Carving out a new literary space on the "low brow" yet highly popular platform enabled Kaur and others to bypass literary gatekeepers while simultaneously creating a new genre which accommodates experiences of unbelonging identities and challenges cultural, social, and political marginality. It is now evident that Instapoetry participated in a bottom-up movement which required publishers to recognize the market for traditionally marginalized women's poetry. Kaur's highly unusual success story epitomizes the popular success of Instapoetry. Her meteoric rise to prominence in 2015 was followed by her book being picked up by Andrews McMeel Publishing in 2016, eventually unseating Homer's *The Odyssey* by selling more than 3.5 million copies worldwide and being translated in over forty-two languages. As a testament to her success, her latest book *Home Body* was published by the much more prestigious publisher Simon and Schuster. Instapoetry's pivotal role in the spectacular rise in poetry sales in the past ten years, the diversification of the poetry readership, and the rise in the demand in bookshops for poetry by female African American poets is now widely documented. According to US book-sales monitor NPD Bookscan, in 2017, 12 of the top 20 bestselling poets were Instapoets. That same year, a report by the National Endowment of the Arts (the largest survey of American adults' participation in the arts) and UK statistics from book-sales monitor Nielsen BookScan showed that the number of poetry readers had nearly doubled in the past five years with a 21 percent annual growth in sales of poetry books in the United States (where the share of adults reading poetry rose by 76 percent) and a 12 percent annual increase in the UK, "making it one of the fastest-growing categories in publishing" (Brodie 2021). The largest increase was among young adults; the percentage of poetry readers between the ages of eighteen and twenty-four doubled during that period, from 8.2 percent in 2012 to 17.5 percent in 2017 (Charles 2018; Garber 2018). More importantly still, "it was women and people of color, in particular, who helped drive the expansion" (Garber 2018): 15 percent of African Americans and 13 percent of Asian Americans reported reading poetry in 2017, against 7 percent and 5 percent in 2012 (Ross 2019). Similarly, UK statistics show that in 2018, women under 35 represented 40 percent of poetry buyers, a move away from 2014, when "27% of poetry buyers were young women and another 27% were middle-aged or elderly men" (Ferguson 2019). As Donna Ferguson revealed, young women were instrumental in driving up sales of texts by women of all backgrounds, including contemporary poets Wendy Cope, Pam Ayres, Helen Dunmore, and Carol Ann Duffy and works such as Audre Lorde's 2017 posthumous *Your Silence Will Not Protect You*, and therefore pushing British poetry publishers to diversify their repertoire (2019). Jill Bialosky, poet and executive editor at Norton, saw a similar trend in the United States, with a dramatic increase for traditional verse, including that of Lorde and Rita Dove (Maher 2018). Instapoetry is operating as a gateway and has offered renewed attention to voices which usually trail behind white classics.

Criticism, Craft, and Gatekeeping

While detractors of contemporary poetry bemoan its "rejection of craft" (Watts 2018: 13) and suggest that Instapoets do little more than "rolling out some pastry-coloured prose, adding a sprinkling of white space, then cutting it up into little shapelets" (Tremain 2018), it is our duty, as critics, to consider our potential role in further silencing already marginalized voices under the authoritative guise of craft. Although Wang, cited above, reminds us that failing to pay attention to craft in poetry by "minority" writers contributes to their marginalization, it is crucial also to note that references to formal tradition and aesthetic standards have long been deployed to diminish and silence these voices. This "framing of work by poets of color as unliterary, 'light verse,' 'performance poetry,'" is often, as British poet Sandeep Parmar suggests, a form of dog whistle (2019).

Gill makes a similar argument in a thought-provoking Twitter thread taking to task a blog post by a white female Ph.D. student who described her work as "inextricably superficial." Accusing academic criticism of being inconsiderate of her linguistic and cultural background, Gill also stresses its arrogance in "demand[ing] that what we ['black and brown' Instapoets] cater to them in ways we never agreed to" (2020) by measuring Instapoetry against Western literary standards which Instapoets possibly never subscribed to in the first place. Like Kaur before her, who argued that her poems were "for that [...] 17-year-old brown woman in Brampton who is [...] just trying to live, survive, get through her day" (Brown 2018), Gill appears to shun criticism by taking refuge in stating that she "write[s] for young girls (teenagers)" (2020). The dubious implications that one's female identity, race, or social background excuses "lack of craft" play into the narratives that have long been used to dismiss a certain class of readers or writers. But problematic as these claims are, not all books have to be works of art. True equality in publishing includes the right for minorities to pen more widely read "commercial" texts at the same unquestioned rate as privileged writers do. Ultimately, Gill's thread challenges the pretense and elitism of high art. It calls for a more respectful form of literary criticism which does away with preestablished and condescending interpretative readings, is considerate of authorial intention, and engages with the specificities of texts *on their own terms.*

This thread inevitably brings up uncomfortable questions for early-career white female academics researching Instapoetry, who, wanting to be taken seriously in the academic world, frequently find compelled to distance themselves from the traditional Instapoetry audience (which they are nonetheless part of) by performing a hostile form of critical detachment. All too often, as Watts's essay illustrates, membership to the scholarly community is affirmed or granted through the safeguarding of its literary borders. This is but another example of the pervasiveness of what Sarah Mesle describes as "the circular logic by which a piece of art becomes serious because a serious critic attends to it, and a critic becomes serious by tending to serious art" (2019). Exploiting a consensus according to which Instapoetry is of little value, while building our academic careers on the back of a genre established by marginalized authors, carries a heavy cost. I am, of course, not suggesting that we leave behind critical rigor, but that we let our guard down and practice a more hospitable, generous, and collegial form of criticism that takes its lead from the contextual, thematic, formal, and linguistic concerns of this new writing. This approach constitutes a type of "reparative reading" as advocated by Eve Kosofsky Sedgwick in 1995. Critiquing the well-established "hermeneutics of suspicion" as defined by Paul Ricoeur (or what she refers to as "paranoid reading") that underpin much of literary criticism, Sedgwick called instead for a way of reading which engages with "the many ways in which selves and communities succeed in extracting sustenance from the objects of a culture—even of a culture whose avowed desire has often been not to sustain them" (Sedgwick 2003: 150). Instead of approaching the form with the intent of taking issue with its literariness, to read Instapoetry reparatively is to leave room for surprise. It is to accentuate the genre's formal qualities, its empowering and healing potential, and its capacity to enable social change.

It is crucial, then, that we reevaluate our critical tools. Although craft principles are understood to be universal and objective, they are culture specific and "account for some artistic producers, some communities of readers, while dismissing and marginalizing others" (Adsit 2017: 50). Craft, as it is often identified by Western critics and creative writing programs, is an established taste which "still often remains coded to privilege the white, educated, non-disabled, middle-class participant" (Ibid). To regulate it, then, is to attempt to police literary borders by ensuring that the figure of the literary author remains a position that is difficult to access. Postcolonial and "minority" writers have subversively challenged the presumed opposition between craft and politics to highlight how it normalizes the experience of poets who are exempt from child-care concerns, economic worries, and issues of social injustice, and how it excludes the voices of poets who are not. An illustrative example is the provocatively entitled "Fuck Your Lecture on Craft, My People Are Dying" poem by the Palestinian American poet Noor Hindi, which was featured in *Poetry* in December 2020 and openly confronts the authority of Western craft-based readings. Through her title and lines such as "I want to be like those poets who care about the moon" and "Metaphors about death are for poets who think ghosts care about sound," Hindi contrasts the questions of poetics and form central to the canon of Western poetry with the more urgent political concerns of postcolonial and "minority" poets. Refusing flowery language and conventional poetic subject matter, the poem is composed of accessible, simple words and images, and straightforward sentences. Built on contrasting statements such as the one in the title and "Colonizers write about flowers / I tell you about children throwing rocks at Israeli tanks / seconds before becoming daisies," the poem highlights the comparatively stable material conditions that inspired and produced much of Western poetry. In contrast, she writes, "Palestinians don't see the moon from jail cells and prisons." The text resonates with the opening lines of another poem written in 1972 by the black South African poet James Matthews during apartheid (a context frequently compared to contemporary Israel) before his work was censured and he was thrown into prison:

> It is said
> that poets write of beauty
> of form, of flowers and of love
> but the words I write
> are of pain and of rage

Like Matthews's, Hindi's poem does not, in fact, reject craft altogether. It ironically reappropriates the Western form of the sonnet (traditionally associated with romantic love) and uses the imagery of flowers throughout as a symbol of death and empire. By doing so, it further emphasizes the complete disconnection between the concerns of privileged literary critics and poets worried about form and the future of poetry, and those of truly oppressed people. Rather than implying a problematic binary opposition between "committed" and "aesthetic" poetry, or even suggesting that writing about "hard political realities" does not require the poet to consider form, Hindi invites us to question the white Western literary establishment's self-entitled authority over definitions of literariness and poetry.

The term "Instapoetry" itself is miles away from the time-consuming principles of craft associated with high-culture literature and is therefore somewhat of an oxymoron. Though coined by the media "to make 'the new poetry' sound exciting" (Leszkiewicz 2019), its resonance with instant coffee and instant food, i.e., quick, make-do, inferior, unsatisfying, and innutritious meals prepared by people lacking the skills, time, or experience to make "the real thing," contributes to its being considered unliterary. As Janelle Adsit notes, "With terms like 'craft' and the 'workshop,' creative writing associates itself with the unalienated labor of the artisan," i.e., a person who "produces something with skill," is fully devoted to their work and removes all distractions (2017: 27). Ann Leszkiewicz insightfully exposes how the term "variously refers to the platform on which a work is published, the style of writing, the poem's level of popularity, the poet's path to publication, or the work's artistic value" (2019). In other words, it not only indiscriminately lumps together different poetic forms under a single title, but it also sometimes includes the work of traditionally published poets who occasionally share their work on social media such as McNish, and writers who disagree with the label altogether. It does not take into consideration the critical distinctions between poems from different cultures and languages, whether Japanese haikus, Urdu poems or even the ghazals which have inspired some of Kaur's writing. Although over time, Instapoetry has become associated with a particular type of self-help aesthetic embodied by Kaur's and r.h. Sin's work, defining this body of poetry simply by reference to Instagram, its original place of publication, enables us to envision the wider possibilities offered by the form.

Unlike traditional poetic forms in print, the aesthetic constraints of Instapoetry are sometimes less reliant on syllables, lines, feet, or even rhymes, and more on size, space, font, shapes, and visuals. Whether they use a typewriter or handwritten font, present themselves as calligrams, appear in front of a colored background, or incorporate illustrations, their visual appeal on a platform that is dedicated to picture-sharing and where they have to compete with others for audiences' attention, is crucial. As Sarah Rosenthal suggests, graphic novel theory might therefore be a more adequate framework to approach the work of Instapoets (2019). Instapoetry is not the first poetic form to experiment with visuals; it follows in the footsteps of William Blake's illustrated poems, Guillaume Apollinaire's 1918 *Calligrammes*, and Stevie Smith's interweaved poems and doodles. That said, McCloud's claim, in his influential *Understanding Comics*, that "words and pictures *together* are considered, at best, a diversion for the masses, and at worst, a product of crass commercialism" (McCloud 1994: 140), applies well to the criticism which equates Instapoetry's accessibility with lack of depth. While Instapoems generally differ from comics by standing alone as opposed to creating sequential narratives, they are a similarly popular form which creates meaning from the interaction between content and form, text, and visuals. Graphic narratives, like Instapoetry, have been instrumental in representing issues including trauma, and/or marginalized voices that have historically been censored or relegated to silence (Chute 2010: 2). Furthermore, according to Hillary Chute (another leading voice in comics criticism), the hybrid form brings together "high-" and "mass-" culture, private and public elements. It is handmade but mass-produced, and the common use of handwriting "underscores the subjective positionality of the author" and creates an impression of intimacy that stands in tension with the graphic novel's public character (2010: 10). While this goes beyond the scope of this chapter, the handwritten Instapoetry of Wade, Daley-Ward, and Kaur's famous hand-drawn doodles have a similar effect on the reader and contribute to the public performance of intimate "authenticity" that is Instagram's trademark (Maares et al. 2021). Graphic novel theory is all the more necessary given the critical tendency to omit the visual aspects of Instapoetry when reproducing or analyzing it, as Watts (2018: 13) and many others do. To leave out visuals (whether font or illustrations) is to not do full justice to the form's cross-discursive nature.

Looking Forward

In "Amateur Creativity," Aarthi Vadde rightly claims that it is impossible to "make a blanket case for or against the emancipatory potential of participatory culture on the Internet" (2017: 29). On the one hand, the circulation of free culture has the potential to "democratize the monopoly of culture by professionals" by transferring power from institutions to the public as illustrated above (2017: 28). Yet on the other, it enables privately owned platforms and corporations to exploit and appropriate the work of unremunerated creators, thereby removing power from the hands of regulated public institutions and organized workers, for private enterprise. Instapoetry, even more so than traditional publishing, is embedded in capitalist commercial mechanisms, where the drive for profit largely outweighs the drive for literary excellence and/or originality. Changes in algorithm protocols following Kaur's success story have, for instance, contributed to the form's association with an inspirational self-help aesthetic as numerous creators adopt and repeat the winning formula to increase user interaction and consequently gain a wider audience (Bronson and Steele 2021). Significantly also, Instagram does not offer any protection to Instapoets as they create in an unregulated framework. In 2016, it implemented an algorithm change which made it less likely for users to view Instapoems in their feed and implicitly encouraged Instapoets to pay to promote their content. Previously, the feed had been chronological. The new algorithm puts forward content from accounts the user has engaged with, alongside advertisements and posts by celebrities, and pushes down the rest, rendering it much less accessible. To quote Jonathan Ford, "the result, even if unintended, has been that a medium once celebrated as democratic and giving marginalized writers a voice, has become more selective and controlled" (2019). While it is therefore highly unlikely that new Instapoets will reach the same type of success experienced by Kaur or r.h. Sin, this ought not to detract from the fact that the form has been instrumental in transforming the publishing landscape for women and people of color. And while criticism has accurately drawn attention to Instapoets' frequent capitalizing on trauma, instrumentalizing feminist values, and exoticizing their ethnicity for personal gain rather than collective social improvement (Huggan 2020; Lovelock 2021), they have also opened up a more democratic space for "minority" women to write, publish, associate, and be heard. They have created a literary form which fuels fascinating discussions about critical approaches and contemporary literature. With publishers performatively engaging with marginalized authors in the Black Lives Matter era to capitalize on contemporary issues, sometimes without questioning their own complicit behavior, only time will tell how transformative Instapoetry's effects are on the long term. In the meantime, though, through free writing clinics on Instagram and the curation of a collection of poems by unpublished "minority" authors, writers such as Gill and Chisala are seizing the moment and building on their success to open the door to many others.

References

Adsit, Janelle. 2017. *Toward an Inclusive Creative Writing: Threshold Concepts to Guide the Literary Writing Curriculum*. London: Bloomsbury.

Brodie, Jessica. 2021. "Instapoetry: Redefining Genre for Millennials, or Art Form Going from Bad to Verse?" *Sunday Times*, March 14, 2021. https://www.timeslive.co.za/sunday-times/lifestyle/2021-03-14-instapoetry-redefining-genre-for-gen-ys-or-an-art-form-going-from-bad-to-verse/.

Bronson, Zac and Warren Steele. 2021. "Algorithmic Poetics: Self-Branding & Identity in Instapoetry." Presentation at the Digital British Association for American Studies Conference, April 6–11, 2021.

Brown, Jeffrey. 2018. "How Poet Rupi Kaur Became a Hero to Millions of Young Women." *PBS NewsHour*, January 2, 2018. https://www.pbs.org/newshour/show/poet-rupi-kaur-reaches-new-audiences-in-a-new-way.

Chandler, Eleanor and Josie Mitchell. 2018. "T.S. Eliot Was a Terrible Hip-Hop Artist." *Granta*, January 26, 2018. https://granta.com/discoveries-34/.

Charles, Ron. 2018. “Poetry Reading by Young People Has Doubled since 2012.” *The Washington Post*, September 12, 2018. https://www.washingtonpost.com/entertainment/books/poetry-reading-by-young-people-has-doubled-since-2012/2018/09/12/a5724954-b6bd-11e8-94eb-3bd52dfe917b_story.html.

Chute, Hillary. 2010. *Graphic Women*. New York: Columbia University Press.

Cosslett, Rhiannon Lucy. 2020. “The Novel Is Dead—Again. And This Time, It’s Women Who Have Murdered It.” *The Guardian*, July 10, 2020. https://www.theguardian.com/commentisfree/2020/jul/10/novel-dead-again-women-murdered-it-sally-rooney.

Cottenet, Cécile. 2014. *Race, Ethnicity and Publishing in America*. London: Palgrave Macmillan.

Ferguson, Donna. 2019. “‘Keats Is dead … ’: How Young Women Are Changing the Rules of Poetry.” *The Guardian*, January 1, 2019. https://www.theguardian.com/books/2019/jan/26/new-generation-young-women-poets.

Flood, Alison and Sian Cain. 2018. “Poetry World Split over Polemic Attacking ‘Amateur’ Work by ‘Young Female Poets.’” *The Guardian*, January 23, 2018. https://www.theguardian.com/books/2018/jan/23/poetry-world-split-over-polemic-attacking-amateur-work-by-young-female-poets#:~:text=3%20years%20old-,Poetry%20world%20split%20over%20polemic%20a-ttacking%20%27amateur,work%20by%20%27young%20female%20poets%27&text=According%20to%20Nielsen%20data%2C%20these,for%20new%20work%20in%20poetry.

Ford, Jonathan. 2019. “How Instagram Could Stifle a New Generation of Poets.” *OZY*, June 10, 2019. https://www.ozy.com/the-new-and-the-next/how-instagram-could-stifle-a-new-generation-of-poets/94620/.

Garber, Megan. 2018. “Poetry Is Everywhere.” *Atlantic*, August 20, 2018. https://www.theatlantic.com/entertainment/archive/2018/08/when-poetry-isnt-poetry/567571/.

Gill, Nikita [@nktgill]. 2020. “It’s a Weird af Thing to 1. Not Be Taken Seriously ….” *Twitter*, July 17, 2020. https://twitter.com/nktgill/status/1284094344857870336.

Gill, Nikita [@nktgill]. 2021. “Smaller Advances to Authors of Colour Means Less Marketing for our Books Which Means ….” *Twitter*, April 25, 2021. https://twitter.com/nktgill/status/1386309714334605313.

Hindi, Noor. 2020. “Fuck Your Lecture on Craft, My People Are Dying.” *Poetry Foundation*, December 2020. https://www.poetryfoundation.org/poetrymagazine/poems/154658/fuck-your-lecture-on-craft-my-people-are-dying.

Huggan, Graham. 2020. “Re-evaluating the Postcolonial Exotic.” *Interventions*, 22 (7): 808–24.

Johnson, Miriam. 2017. “The Rise of the Citizen Author: Writing within Social Media.” *Publishing Research Quarterly*, 33 (2): 131–46.

Kaur, Rupi. “F.A.Q.” *Rupi Kaur*. https://rupikaur.com/pages/about-me. Accessed April 15, 2021.

Kean, Danuta. 2015. *Writing the Future: Black and Asian Writers in the UK Marketplace*. London: Spread the Word.

Ledbury Critics. 2018. *The State of Poetry and Poetry Criticism*. Liverpool: University of Liverpool.

Lee and Low Books. 2020. "Where Is the Diversity in Publishing? The 2019 Diversity Baseline Survey Results." *The Lee & Low Books Open Book Blog*, January 28, 2020. https://blog.leeandlow.com/2020/01/28/2019diversitybaselinesurvey/.

Leszkiewicz, Anna. 2019. "Why Are We So Worried about 'Instapoetry'"? *New Statesman*, March 6, 2019. https://www.newstatesman.com/culture/books/2019/03/instapoetry-rupi-kaur-genre-rm-drake-rh-sin-atticus-hollie-mcnish.

Lovelock, Millicent. 2021. "Rupi Kaur and the Promise of Transformation." Presentation at the Digital British Association for American Studies Conference, April 6–11, 2021.

Maares, Phoebe, Sandra Banjac, and Folker Hanusch. 2021. "The Labour of Visual Authenticity on Social Media: Exploring Producers' and Audiences' Perceptions on Instagram." *Poetics* 84 (2): 1–10.

Maher, John. 2018. "Can Instagram Make Poems Sell Again?" *Publishers Weekly*, February 2, 2018. https://www.publishersweekly.com/pw/by-topic/industry-news/publisher-news/article/75976-can-instagram-make-poems-sell-again.html.

Manning, Maria. 2021. "Crafting Authenticity: Reality, Storytelling, and Female Self-Representation through Instapoetry." *Storytelling, Self, Society*, 16 (2): 263–79.

Matthews, James and Gladys Thomas. 1972. *Cry Rage!* Johannesburg: Spro-cas Publications.

McCloud, Scott. 1994. *Understanding Comics*. New York: Harper Perennial.

Mehri, Momtaza. 2018. "Letters from a Young (Female) Poet." *The Millions*, January 31, 2018. https://themillions.com/2018/01/letters-from-a-young-female-poet.html.

Mesle, Sarah. 2019. "A Television of Her Own: On Emily Nussbaum." *L.A. Review of Books*, August 30, 2019. https://v2.lareviewofbooks.org/article/television-emily-nussbaum

Miller, E. Ce. 2018. "Are 'InstaPoets' Destroying the Art Form or Reviving It? A Defense of Social Media Poetry." *Bustle*, March 21, 2018. https://www.bustle.com/p/are-instapoets-destroying-the-art-form-reviving-it-a-defense-of-social-media-poetry-8530426.

NPD. 2018. "Instapoets Rekindling U.S. Poetry Book Sales, The NPD Group Says." *NPD.com*, April 5, 2018. https://www.npd.com/wps/portal/npd/us/news/press-releases/2018/instapoets-rekindling-u-s–poetry-book-sales–the-npd-group-says/.

Ostriker, Alicia Suskin. 1986. *Stealing the Language*. Boston: Beacon Press.

Parmar, Sandeep. 2019. "A Q&A with Sandeep Parmar: Supporting Emerging Critics of Color." *Poets.org*, January 24, 2019. https://poets.org/text/qa-sandeep-parmar-supporting-emerging-critics-color.

PN Review [@PN_Review]. 2018. "Regarding 'The Cult of the Noble Amateur' published …." *Twitter*, January 23, 2018. https://twitter.com/PN_Review/status/955742549368623104.

Rosenthal, Sarah. 2019. "What Scott McCloud Taught Us about Internet Storytelling." *Literary Hub*, February 25, 2019. https://lithub.com/what-scott-mccloud-taught-us-about-internet-storytelling/.

Ross, Jenna. 2019. "For a Diverse New Generation, Poetry Is a 'Growth Industry.'" *Star Tribune*, January 14, 2019. https://www.startribune.com/for-a-diverse-new-generation-poetry-is-a-growth-industry/504180842/.

Saha, Anamik and Sandra van Lente. 2020. *Rethinking Diversity in Publishing*. London: Goldsmiths Press.

Sedgwick, Eve Kosofsky. 2003. *Touching Feeling: Affect, Pedagogy, Performativity*. Durham: Duke University Press.

Tremain, Rose. 2018. "Twenty Questions with Rose Tremain." *Times Literary Supplement*, November 19, 2018. https://www.the-tls.co.uk/articles/twenty-questions-rose-tremain/.

Vadde, Aarthi. 2017. "Amateur Creativity: Contemporary Literature and the Digital Publishing Scene." *New Literary History*, 48 (1): 27–51.

Wang, Dorothy. 2014. *Thinking Its Presence*. Palo Alto: Stanford University Press.

Watts, Rebecca. 2018. "The Cult of the Noble Amateur." *PN Review*, 239 (44): 13–17.

8

"Fat, Fly, Brown Poet": Yesika Salgado, Instapoetry, and Politics in the Undergraduate Classroom

María Carla Sánchez
University of North Carolina, Greensboro

Can Instapoetry nurture a nuanced critique of institutional gatekeeping and cultural hierarchies? This chapter, which foregrounds experiences in the undergraduate classroom, proposes that the answer to this question is a resounding "yes." My focus here is the work of the Salvadoran-Californian writer Yesika Salgado, a self-proclaimed "fat, fly, brown poet" and a growing star in US poetry. Since discovering Salgado as part of the self-proclaimed "Latina Feminist poetry collective" Chingona Fire (along with fellow poet Angela Aguirre), I have taught her work in several undergraduate courses.[1] She is invariably one of the most popular authors I teach, with students expressing admiration for her work and even gratefulness for it. Their esteem for Salgado, often phrased in glowing terms, stands in stark contrast to the sneering contempt for Instapoetry as a genre demonstrated by an ever-growing body of critics. In this chapter, I analyze selections of Salgado's work alongside my students' written responses to it, as a means of addressing three subjects often identified by critics as problematic: "relatability" as a desirable literary trait; the demographics of Instapoetry and its readers; and the subversion of poetry's status as an art form with long-established forms, venues, and credentialed arbiters. My purpose in joining my students' views to a discussion of Salgado's work is to interrogate common, dismissive ideas about who writes poetry, who reads it, and what that writing and reading amount to. Underlying much of the current Instapoetry critique are sexist, racist, and class-biased ideas regarding poetry's place in the world—and who gets a say in determining that place. Both Yesika Salgado and her readers—among them my students—are already engaged in "claiming their own space," and making it a home for poetry. They do so as part of an ardently feminist, body positive, and antiracist practice, and they are waiting for the rest of the poetry world to catch up.

"I am a brown woman who writes poetry about her brown life"

Yesika Salgado's success has developed steadily since she first began sharing her poetry on Instagram. The native Californian spent the early 2000s honing her poetic skills in the Los Angeles slam poetry circuit, and releasing zines of her work. Since that time, her popularity has increased through mutually constitutive factors: the publication of three collections of poetry, *Corazón* (2017), *Tesoro* (2018), and *Hermosa* (2019) on Not a Cult Press; her use of social media, including YouTube videos created by the Latinx media site Mitú as well as a TEDx talk on body positivity; and of course, the arrival of Instapoetry. While some poets maintain an Instagram page, Salgado truly can be called an Instapoet. She posts several poems each week, either in whole or as excerpts from longer pieces. Some can be found in her books, and are photographed so as to show the edge of a physical page, or to feature her trademark stiletto nails. Others are taken from her digital zines and copy their distinctive design. The rest exist on Instagram, interwoven in her feed alongside the typical content of the platform: selfies, brief videos, music recommendations. For Salgado, that ordinary fare is embellished with endorsements of PoC-owned businesses, as well as screen shots of the lewd, sometimes hapless sexual offers she receives via direct message. The result is a lively curation that one student praised as "not only giving you accessibility [but also] giving you authenticity."[2]

Salgado's social media foregrounds her status as a poet. Both her Instagram and Twitter profiles identify her as a "poet" and "fat activist," while her YouTube/Mitú videos introduce her as "a fat, fly, brown poet." Dozens of her Instagram posts feature the work of fellow writers of color, especially women; a recent online information campaign, "So Your Friend Just Published a Book?" offered advice on amplifying the literary efforts of "Black, Indigenous & WOC writers," and was developed by Salgado. While the self-identification as poet may not strike all as a particularly notable decision, its quiet audacity is discernible when viewed against the backdrop of "establishment" poetic networks. As recent data demonstrate, the US publishing industry remains overwhelmingly white, in terms of both its employees and its products.[3] Similarly, US periodicals publish more male authors than female or nonbinary, again skewing toward a dominant whiteness, as tracked yearly by the organization VIDA: Women in Literary Arts.[4] Salgado herself describes her mindset when writing her first book, *Corazón*, as defensive: "I was someone who was still trying to prove a lot to the world … that I deserved to be published, that I deserved a career, that I deserved to be listened to." For many readers, then, as well as publishers, editors, and fellow writers, it seems clear that outside of social media and non-establishment forums such as spoken word, slam poetry, and Instapoetry, the term "poet" does not initially conjure the image of someone who is "fat, fly, [and] brown."

In an extensive interview for the *Los Angeles Times*, reporter Vera Castaneda characterizes Salgado as "think[ing] of herself as outside of the literary world, particularly when she receives backhanded compliments using the term 'Instapoet' in contempt." Salgado tells Castaneda, "I want my work to be in unconventional places … you write in poetry journals to get fellowships and grants, not for an audience … My readers don't read journals." This interview, along with her Instagram commentary, bluntly positions Salgado as an outsider in the worlds of academia and *belles lettres*: she does not have an MFA or a post-secondary degree of any kind, being a high school dropout; she has never held prestigious creative writing fellowships; and as she herself states, does not publish in poetry journals, themselves often associated with collegiate creative writing programs. Referring to the many speaking engagements she enjoyed on college campuses before the pandemic, she says, "I take pride in saying that I created something where institutions have to come to me. I don't get you, you have to get me." That forthright statement of positionality and status encapsulates the potential power of Instapoetry and of social media's reach. Even as scholars in multiple disciplines demonstrate social media's ability to form its own de facto institutional barriers, at this historical moment it still enables some individuals to circumvent and thus subvert older powers: to make "institutions have to come to" Salgado, wooing the woman who lacks academia's basic entry-level certification of a high school diploma. With 136,000 followers on Instagram and 28,000 on Twitter, Salgado's reach on these platforms far exceeds that of recent US poet laureate and of the latest Nobel Prize for Literature winner, poet Louise Glück.[5] Thus in Julia Barajas's words, "Salgado is part of a new generation of artists established on the stage—through the spoken word and slam tradition—and magnified on the internet." As with many such artists, forays into those verboten worlds of academia and *belles lettres* remain circumscribed. While she has spoken on many college campuses, no scholarly study of Salgado yet exists. The MLA Bibliography, which tracks and catalogues scholarly publications for the US market, lists three peer-reviewed journal essays on Instapoetry as of spring 2021, and none include Salgado.

A sense of being on the outside of powerful institutions is one shared by many of my students at UNC Greensboro. The university is "one of the original three UNC system institutions," but has altered much since its days as the Women's College of North Carolina. With a student enrollment of roughly 20,000, the university is classified as an MSI, with significant African American and Latinx populations; and as a Title III school, with the majority of students hailing from the working and middle classes.[6] UNCG boasts large numbers of adult and returning students, as well as many who are "first gen"—the first members of their families to attend college.[7] Though officially coeducational for decades now, the school remains majority female at 68 percent of enrollment. Combined with a reputed friendliness toward LGBTQ persons that is citywide, the campus as a whole touts impressive achievements: racially and ethnically diverse, an engine for social mobility and economic advancement, and generally welcoming toward gender nonconformity.[8] This picture was mirrored in the undergraduate courses in which I assigned Salgado's work. The classes ran under the auspices of the English department and were cross-listed with the Program in Women's, Gender, and Sexuality Studies; the majority of the students came from those two majors, alongside significant representation from other humanities and social science disciplines; most identified as female or nonbinary, and the classes were nearly evenly divided amongst students identifying primarily as white, black, and Latinx.[9] In other words, the students in my classes did not share much, demographically speaking, with the publishing industry in their homeland. But they have much in common with Yesika Salgado.

"We have all experienced this"

The terms that students use most often to describe their experience of reading Salgado's poetry are precisely those singled out for derision by Instapoetry critics: "relatable" and "accessible," intermixed with common synonyms and with descriptors like "raw" and "authentic." For the students however, these terms connote their highest praise, and are often embedded in their own sharp critiques of institutional gatekeeping and the bias rooted in classist, sexist, and racial animosities. Salgado's lauded "relatability" is typically identified as the effect of her rendering of emotional states, her focus on common and often deeply gendered experiences, and a shared "underdog" worldview rooted in working-class and underprivileged socioeconomic status. The poem "Good Love," excerpted on Instagram, included in *Corazón* and also performed in a Mitú video, exemplifies Salgado's resonant conjuring of romantic love experienced, ended, and recollected: "what about the happy love? all that good love that tells you it's okay to stay in the house and watch Martin reruns" (Salgado 2017d: 32). Salgado's speaker indulges in poignant moments of nostalgia, recalling the happy oblivion of love: "and you're not wondering where anyone else is because/ all you ever wanted is there in that room on the couch/with you …."

"Good Love" follows its speaker through mundane yet evocative markers of a relationship's progress: sharing the simplest activities like "watch[ing] … reruns" and cocooning at home ("it's okay to stay in the house"). The unremarkable nature of the poem's action throws the affective state into relief: this "happy love" causes the speaker to lose track of others and of a world outside, as "[they're] not wondering where anyone else is." Indeed, so all-consuming is this phase of romance that it condenses both yearning and time for the speaker: "all you ever wanted is there in that room on that couch." That conflation is mirrored by the use of the second person "you," which evokes both a writer/speaker producing the poem and an invited reader with similarly marked memories of a "happy love." Just as the beginning of the poem gleefully shrank to one imagined room, the middle expands actively, as the speaker pictures "this/ love that's got you glowing. this new name that you say/ over and over. that's got you running around smiling at/ strangers. looking at the world like it's an answer." As the poem approaches its end, the speaker exhorts herself and the reader to concentrate on the good, and "forget the after: the part where it ends, or when it got quiet." Indeed, the final words of "Good Love"—the question "remember?" posed twice—send both speaker and reader back to its beginning, where the ominous "quiet" has yet to invade the cozy TV-couch-living room scenario.

"I think that grief plays a huge role in her poems," notes one student, pointing out that Salgado writes not only of death (losing family members, enduring miscarriages), but also the "loss of relationships [and] dreams." "Yesika beautifully explores the coming back into oneself after ending a relationship. The messy, complicated reintegration of the self." "Salgado seems to use her poems like many of us might," writes another, "which is to process pain, trauma, our sense of selves, etc." Others stated that they felt an age-old stereotype remains in place, but admired Salgado's "owning" of it: "Women are too often criticized for being emotional. The acknowledgement of her emotions while still being confident is … a clear example of Salgado's progression in healing from her past trauma … [She] is slowly, through every poem, freeing herself." These comments praise the poet's exploration of love and loss, while also recognizing its gendered dimension. One student characterized their response as both appreciative and sobering: "What I find most appealing about Yesika's work is how sadly relatable it is. She touches on so many things like negative body image, bulimia, shyness, shame[,] among other experiences that some girls have." Ultimately, a classmate succinctly expressed the "relatability" that so many were naming: "We have all experienced this."

Class members have not "all experienced" romantic love in the same way, however, and pointed to Salgado's descriptive detail as means of both "relating" to and "learning" from a skilled poet. Salgado employs sensual, tactile imagery, such as mango juice sliding down fingers while eating, or "eyes watering between bites" of a potent homemade salsa ("Molcajete"). She evokes a ruthless physical and mental wearing down in "My Depression Has Questions" and "Ansiedad" ("Anxiety"), picturing speakers too overwhelmed to move, speak, or seek help. Throughout her poetry, she recalls a variety of common events, like a "First Kiss" ("he said my friends were pretty but I was funny/I nodded/I knew I couldn't be both"), learning to swim in "1995" ("but I just floated there/crying"), going on a "Blind Date," and taking stock "After Another Bad Date" ("it isn't that I like him/I like the idea of being wanted"). In response, students lauded Salgado's "authenticity" and "honesty," conveying appreciation that she "[shares] herself so wholly" and that this sharing enabled them to understand common experiences in a more nuanced, enlightened, and even mature way. "I was just thinking I could learn a lot from Yesika!" confides one student. "I think most of us are REALLY hard on ourselves and sometimes we take that pain in and don't process it very well." "The raw honesty of her emotions creates trust within the reader that Salgado has experienced the same things that she or he has," says another. The students' sense of a "trust" being established between author and audience inspired some to label her "a role model" and ruminate on what her work as a whole helped them to see. "I think Yesika's message is that she isn't one thing or another and her emotions aren't one or another," wrote one student, determining that "her raw authenticity" acted as "a beacon of example for genuine, messy acceptance." "Her work teaches the normalcy in being conflicted in our feelings," stated a classmate.

The students' commentary is permeated by the language of self-care, itself frequently echoed by Salgado's poetry and in her Instagram feed. However, where critics of Instapoetry portray these topics as markers of the form's superficiality and narcissism, students figure it very differently as a necessary response to pervasive institutional sexism, racism, classism, and fatphobia. "Her poems are a brilliant window," writes one student, "into seeing the struggles she faced to accept herself in a fatphobic and xenophobic world." Class discussions of these struggles coalesced around poems such as "Gorda," whose speaker uses second person with visceral effect: "you take the word. the one that sliced through you like a/knife through pan fresco" (Salgado 2017e: 76). Here the speaker reveals the painful connection between her struggles and the behavior of others, both family and foe. The word "gorda" is "the one your Tío called you de/cariño. the one the boys in school hissed as you walked/by." Thus our speaker begins the process of retaking and remaking the word, a process that is far from easy: "you take the word and write it down. one time. Two/times. say it in English. Fat. it hurts that way too … "

Salgado typically uses capitalization sparingly, and here her stylistic choice pays dividends. "Fat," one of only two words capitalized in these opening lines, stands alone, as does the speaker facing the plural "hissing" boys. Our poet often chooses italics to differentiate her Spanish from English, but not this time, as she leaves "de cariño" (affectionately) unemphasized. Rather, "Tío" (uncle) is capitalized, foregrounding instead the sting of hearing "gorda" from a familial voice. As with "Good Love," "Gorda" follows its speaker through a process, and in this one she reveals how poetry can indeed transform. Writing the words "gorda" and "fat" repeatedly, she alters them: "you are a bruja when you write it down./look at that magic, Gorda. mira que bella. Gorda. your/body answers: *hello. I'm here. thank you.*" The poet as bruja, or witch, turns pain into pride and beauty ("bella"), ending in simple confidence. "*I'm here.*"

Several students commented on the "raw" quality of these lines, comparing the pain and anger revealed in them with the body positive self-representation of Salgado's Mitú and TEDx videos. "Many people feel a sense of rejection when someone else says something about their body," observed a student. "People like to crack jokes but they don't realize how that can hurt feelings … " Another described reading this poem as "special, almost sacred for me," given that "fat people rarely get to see themselves represented in a way that isn't comical or just outright depressing, and [Salgado] is changing that with her writing." Several students expressed views aligning with those of fat studies scholars Esther Rothblum and Sondra Solovay, who posit that "[e]very person who lives in a fat-hating culture inevitably absorbs anti-fat beliefs, assumptions, and stereotypes, and also inevitably comes to occupy a position in relation to power arrangements that are based on weight" (Rothblum and Solovay 2010: xi). Working against this socialization, and "claiming one's embodiment," as Salgado does and as my students wish to, constitutes "a form of political resistance" (xv). Easier said than done: one student confided that "feeling bad about my body image when I am considered a smaller size makes me seem silly or conceited," so they are caught in a tautology of feeling bad about feeling bad. Many testified to anger and disgust with things said in online comments sections, where they found "so much negativity about [Salgado's] body size and how she needs to change." These sentiments were nearly universal in my classes, where regardless of size, students lamented feeling continually judged and found wanting in their physical appearance—hence Salgado's much-mentioned relatability.

"I don't like gatekeeping"

In the numerous diatribes against Instapoetry easily found through a simple Google search, derogatory judgment of the poetry often blurs with judgment of the poet, alongside only slightly less snide implications regarding those who choose to read them. As witnessed with previous female-identified cultural trends such as chick lit, purportedly objective critique turns hyperbolic when it comes to this subject. "'Instapoetry' may be popular, but most of it is terrible," stands as both title and verdict from Thomas Hodgkinson in *The Spectator*. An opinion piece by Talah Bakdash on the women's media site *The Tempest* ups the ante with its title/announcement: "Those Instagram poets are ruining everything good in this world—this is why I'm against them." (The equally restrained sub-header opines, "Every time someone posts a bad poem and says it's magical, a piece of me dies.") Even the comparatively subtle, now oft-cited takedown essay by Rebecca Watts, "The Cult of the Noble Amateur," casts aspersions in its word choice. If Instapoets and their readers represent a "cult," then they cannot be acting in a thoughtful or admirable manner. From whence all this handwringing?

My students read all three of the essays cited, and were quick to discern ingrained biases in all, particularly regarding class and its educational markers. "I feel like critics of Instapoetry are really struggling with the fact that instapoets lack a writing education," remarked one class member, noting that Salgado, like many Instapoets, does not possess an MFA—or indeed, any degree at all. Referring to Watts, another student wrote: "I think that she finds this concerning because she fallaciously believes that the poets creating Instapoetry are undereducated and not giving poetry the scholarly attention ... or reverence it deserves." Reverence is in short supply though, among this generation, one of whom speculated that "the attack on Instapoetry is from conservative authors who inevitably would attack many progressive movements that sound anything closely related to millennials." Regardless of what any critic's actual politics are, the upturned noses toward Instapoetry and its accessibility coincide with deeply conservative "gate-keeping." After all, the barriers to Instapoetry are relatively low—internet access—compared to admission to a graduate program. Students were quick to identify the latent snobbishness in critiques of accessibility: "One thing I have always appreciated in many art forms is accessibility," said one. "The fact that poetry, an often white, academic, and elitist art form, can be seen and shared to anyone and allows anyone to express themselves is hugely important." Referencing Watts once more, this same student determined "that she thinks she can understand poetry better than 'the masses' ..., which I think [is] extremely egotistical. The fact that any demographic, whether it's [*sic*] age, economic, ethnic, etc. can be exposed to poetry through social media is really exciting to me." Another sensed that Watts "is attacking the audience that is accessing these works. Almost to say that there are certain 'kinds' of people that shouldn't be reading poetry." (Another classmate evinced a wry sense that critics might find their turf threatened by Instapoetry: "These poets are rewriting the narrative of poetry in and of itself. Which I get can be earth-shattering for poets aiming to be 'professional' by set parameters.")

Even while finding the critiques of Instapoetry "elitist" and "unwarranted," the students retained their awareness of the larger stakes involved: "I view expensive, elite college education [as] a symptom of capitalism and white supremacy," wrote another, "and while Instagram may be a by-product that fuels a capitalistic agenda, using it to amplify queer and POC and black minorities' art, work, and voices is a great way to counteract that." In other words, students grasp Instagram's place in a commercialized world. Indeed, they demonstrate a nuanced understanding of how the platform functions and how any individual might levy its workings to gain followers, sponsors, and funds. But these workings were obvious to them, transparent and seemingly easily navigated in a way that higher education and the publishing industry are not. (Given the high percentage of first-generation students at UNCG, it should not surprise anyone that many would find college a mystifying institution, even when they're in it.) Another student addressed the issue of accessibility as obscuring an old binary: "This focus on substance over feeling (as if Yesika and Rupi [Kaur] have no substance) is part of a larger historical cycle of suppressing the voices and thought of women of color all over the world by likening their work to emotional work, which is seen as not intellectual." Academia and the publishing industry remain worlds that the students perceive as at best difficult to enter, and hostile to their very existence at worst—sexist, racist, homophobic, and all around "elitist." A poet who writes of shared experiences, uses media they already know, and has circumvented the institutions that they and their families have struggled to access? No wonder that reading Salgado meant "I am enjoying something I never thought I would."

"I fully support #instapoetry"

Throughout the pandemic, Yesika Salgado has offered poetry workshops for her social media followers. The latest, Florecer ("to flower," "to bloom"), entices participants with a simple, enjoyable premise: "let's write poems together." The guise is that of companion rather than instructor or critic, and poetry writing—the creation of art—is presented as something that a group of women, persons of color, and socioeconomically nonelite people might do in an egalitarian, collaborative way. Instapoetry, as practiced by Salgado, conveys a potent and coherent message: this is for you. My students' reactions to this sentiment suggest that other forms of poetry have much work to do in articulating a similar sense of community.

"I should start off by saying that I have a dislike for poetry," confided one student, "because I was never able to understand it in the way teachers wanted me to … I've avoided taking an English class for the last three years." For this student, however, reading Salgado led not only to "an appreciation" of her work, but also to a sense of an "aesthetic" that they "understood … and could relate to." "I almost dreaded poetry before this," admitted another, vocalizing a sentiment that unfortunately was not uncommon among the students. But the experience of reading Salgado's poetry, and particularly of encountering it on Instagram alongside other formats, banished the dread. "Her page made me realize that Instagram can actually add layers of contextualization to poetry readers' experience," observed one student, with others remarking on how Salgado's feed allowed them to see her as "family-oriented," a lover of memes, "approachable," "vulnerable," "joyful," "supportive," and in sum, someone they could imagine befriending. "I love Yesika Salgado's Instagram page!" declared another, noting that among many other valuable traits, the page seemed to offer "a community." "I am not going to lie … I cannot stand poetry," said yet another student. "However, when I began to read Salgado's work, I felt something different … it touches me and my experiences." In celebrating Salgado and Instapoetry, the students cannily identified the meanings of "relatability" and "accessibility": a sense of belonging in a community where one is understood, valued, and respected. As long as Instapoets continue to foster such communal feeling, the form will prosper, gatekeeping or no. One student's summation distilled their connection to poetry's new forms in a digital age: "I fully support #Instapoetry."

On October 21, 2020, Yesika Salgado commemorated an important anniversary on Instagram: "4 yrs ago today I worked my last shift at CVS. Being a full time artist has been a wild rollercoaster. It hasn't been easy but it's been beautiful. Thank you for your love and support all this time." Thirty-nine words and reference to a common, predominantly low-wage business endeared Salgado to her IG followers, who were full of congratulations, and it performed the same task for my students. There is a CVS pharmacy store less than one block from UNCG's campus; hundreds, perhaps thousands of students pass it every day on their commute, and those students, their friends or their family members might work there or at another of the chain's nearly 10, 000 locations nationwide. Those thirty-nine words offer encouragement that someone who has indeed "made it," and for whom creative work is now the economic mainstay of her existence, started where they started. This is the relatability and accessibility students consistently identify when speaking of Salgado and of Instapoetry as a form, and especially because these values and those who cherish them are belittled by establishment voices, as it were, the virtual communities that Instapoetry establishes will be hard to challenge. Their appeal is too fundamental: as one student put it, "Who knows, we may be in class with another Salgado in the making?" For good or ill, I have never encountered a student who said as much about Shakespeare, Milton, or a poet laureate. For these readers of poetry, its future is fat, fly, brown, and online.

Notes

1 "Chingona" translates to "badass" or "kickass" when used as an appreciative descriptor, but derives from a common Mexican Spanish expletive.

2 The student quotations used in this chapter come from written assignments in the form of online discussion posts, specifically focused on Salgado's poetry and critiques of Instapoetry. Students are not named, so as to protect their privacy, but they are quoted verbatim. My thanks to all of these students for their willingness to lend their voices to this chapter.

3 All data on publishing and diversity is pre-pandemic. Before that crisis, the industry's resistance to diversification had become news fodder in the scandal over *American Dirt*, a novel about Mexican immigration written by a white US woman and scoring a seven-figure publication deal.

4 VIDA surveys both small and large publications yearly, though again, the latest information is pre-pandemic.

5 For example, twenty-first-century poets laureate Natasha Tretheway, Tracy K. Smith, and Juan Felipe Herrera boast 3,346, 1,141, and 193 followers on Instagram. The latter enjoys a greater audience on Twitter, where he is followed by 6,500 people. The range for these esteemed poets is considerable: current poet laureate Joy Harjo has approximately 15,000 Twitter followers, whereas Nobel Laureate Glück has just under 1,500 and an older figure like Rita Dove only 604. My point is not to chastise more established poets for their comparable lack of social media prowess (although Harjo's following, undoubtedly the result of her relentless outreach efforts while serving as laureate, is nothing to dismiss). Rather, comparing numbers such as these with Salgado's and with those of better-known instapoets like Rupi Kaur and R. M. Drake, both of whom have Instagram followers numbering in the millions, reveals how these poets have relied on different institutions to make their names, and continue to do so. All figures gathered on May 26, 2021.

6 UNCG's MSI status is based upon its population of African American students, who composed "34.7%… of the undergraduate enrollment for Fall 2019," the latest non-pandemic semester for which information exists. Its Title III status is based upon "the significant enrollment of students that are eligible for need-based federal grants (e.g., Pell Grant eligible) is 51.8%…" The university also has a Latino population of 11 percent, and its student body overall is 68 percent female. See UNCG Office of Sponsored Programs.

7 For Fall 2019, UNCG's undergraduate enrollment was 31 percent first generation, and 25 percent of that population qualified as low income. That year, the university was recognized by *U.S. News and World Reports* as "the top university in North Carolina for social mobility." See *UNCG News*.

8 Greensboro garnered praise from the Human Rights Campaign for its achievements, though the organization noted that it and all other North Carolina cities are hampered by legislation enacted at the state level prohibiting the passage of local anti-discrimination ordinances. See WUNC.

9 The specifics of what students studied are as follows: selections of poems from Salgado's first two books, *Corazón* and *Tesoro*; video readings of several poems available on YouTube from Mitú, Button Poetry, All Def Poetry, and Not a Cult Media; an episode of Kat Lazo's Mitú series "Kat Call" focusing on fat phobia; Salgado's TEDx talk; and her Instagram page. Students also read an interview with Salgado from the *Los Angeles Times*, and a small but provocative body of Instapoetry critique: essays in *PN Review* and the *Spectator* by Rebecca Watts and Thomas Hodgkinson, and a personal appeal for "better poetry" by Talah Bakdash writing for *the Tempest*.

References

Aguirre, Angela. 2021. "About." *Millennial Mija*. https://www.millennialmija.com/bio. Accessed June 21, 2021.

Bakdash, Talah. 2017. "Those Instagram Poets Are Ruining Everything Good in the World – This Is Why I'm against Them." *The Tempest*, August 20, 2017.

Barajas, Julia. 2021. "5 Poets Address Complications of Calling L.A. Home. How Will a Reopening City Treat Them?" *Los Angeles Times*, April 11, 2021.

Castaneda, Vera. 2019. "Poet Yesika Salgado Blew Up on Instagram. Now Her Books Are Breaking Literary Boundaries." *Los Angeles Times*, April 9, 2019.

Hodgkinson, Thomas. 2019. "Instapoetry May Be Popular, but Most of It Is Terrible." *The Spectator*, November 23, 2019.

Maher, John. 2020. "New Lee and Low Survey Shows No Progress on Diversity in Publishing." *Publishers Weekly*, January 29, 2020. https://www.publishersweekly.com/pw/by-topic/industry-news/publisher-news/article/82284-new-lee-and-low-survey-shows-no-progress-on-diversity-in-publishing.html. Accessed June 21, 2021.

Not A Cult Media. 2020. "So Your Friend Just Published a Book?" *Instagram Story*, November 27, 2020. https://www.instagram.com/p/CIG3EK-FwqL/. Accessed June 21, 2021.

Rothblum, Esther and Sondra Solovay, eds. 2010. *The Fat Studies Reader*. New York: NYU Press.

Salgado, Yesika. 2017a. "After Another Bad Date." In *Corazón*. Los Angeles: Not a Cult Press.

Salgado, Yesika. 2017b. "Ansiedad." In *Corazón*. Los Angeles: Not a Cult Press.

Salgado, Yesika. 2017c. "Blind Date." In *Corazón*. Los Angeles: Not a Cult Press.

Salgado, Yesika. 2017d. "Good Love." In *Corazón*. Los Angeles: Not a Cult Press.

Salgado, Yesika. 2017e. "Gorda." In *Corazón*. Los Angeles: Not a Cult Press.

Salgado, Yesika. 2017f. "Molcajete." In *Corazón*. Los Angeles: Not a Cult Press.

Salgado, Yesika. 2017g. "My Depression Has Questions." In *Corazón*. Los Angeles: Not a Cult Press.

Salgado, Yesika. 2018a. "1995." In *Tesoro*. Los Angeles: Not a Cult Press.

Salgado, Yesika. 2018b. "First Kiss." In *Tesoro*. Los Angeles: Not a Cult Press.

Schlemmer, Liz. 2018. "Greensboro Ranked Most LGBTQ-Inclusive City in NC." *WUNC.org*, October 17, 2018. https://www.wunc.org/news/2018-10-17/greensboro-ranked-most-lgbtq-inclusive-city-in-nc. Accessed June 21, 2021.

UNC Greensboro, Office of Sponsored Programs. 2017. https://sponsoredprograms.uncg.edu/wp-content/uploads/2017/07/MSI-FAQ-2015v6-final.pdf. Accessed June 21, 2021.

UNC Greensboro, Office of Sponsored Programs. 2020. *UNCG News*, March 4, 2020. https://news.uncg.edu/uncg-honored-first-gen-student-success/. Accessed June 21, 2021.

VIDA: Women in Literary Arts. 2020. https://www.vidaweb.org. Accessed June 21, 2021.

Watts, Rebecca. 2018. "The Cult of the Noble Amateur." *PN Review*. January–February 2018.

9

"Healing Is Everyday Work": Instapoetry, Intimate Publics, and the Language of Self-Help

Millicent Lovelock
University of Manchester

Using Lauren Berlant's (2008) work on "intimate publics" and Eva Illouz's (2007) writing on emotional capitalism, I argue that Rupi Kaur's frequent use of simple and unambiguous written and visual language on the subject of trauma and healing can be understood not as the product of limited poetic skill, but as a reproduction of a pervasive neoliberalism which centers the self as a site of labor and elides the specific societal conditions that might produce trauma. Through a close reading of Kaur's poetry and an examination of her social media celebrity, I will argue that the pleasure of reading Kaur's work for her readers does not simply lie in the poetic strength of its writing, but instead in the potential for self-transformation it appears to offer. Kaur's readers share a certain experience of womanhood that may be marked by trauma or failure to meet normative standards. Kaur's poetry is preoccupied with such experiences, and by consuming this poetry, her readers hope to achieve a sense of belonging or to be reassured that there is a way through any obstacles they may face. My reading will show that the promise of transformation in Kaur's poetry, however, does not go beyond self-transformation and consequently reproduces a neoliberal logic that centers the self as a site of labor.

Kaur is known for her short, emotive, and prose-like poems posted on Instagram. In 2015, she received widespread recognition when photographs she had taken depicting menstruation went viral after being removed from Instagram (Saul 2015; Tamarkin 2015; Tsjeng 2015). In 2014 Kaur self-published her debut collection, *milk and honey*, and shortly thereafter signed with Andrews McMeel Publishing, who reprinted the collection. An interview with *The Huffington Post* in 2015 described Kaur as "The Poet Every Woman Needs to Read," with interviewer Erin Spencer declaring that "the beautifully honest poems read like the everyday, collective experiences of today's modern woman" (2015). Later that same year, the removal of the "Period" photographs received a significant amount of media attention, with the story picked up by websites such as *Dazed Digital* (Tsjeng 2015) and *Buzzfeed* (Tamarkin 2015). The "Period" incident, wrote Mallika Rao at the time, "dovetailed with the celeb-backed backlash against the site's [Instagram] censoring of breastfeeding photographs, making Kaur an accidental icon of a feminist movement" (Rao 2015). Like those campaigning against the censoring of breastfeeding photographs, Kaur's series again aligned her with something women are seen to "experience collectively" (*The Huffington Post* 2015). By 2016, Kaur had sold over half a million copies of *milk and honey*, surpassing even the expectations of her publisher (Flood 2016). To date, per her publisher, Kaur has sold around five million copies of *milk and honey* (Andrews McMeel Publishing 2021).

Much has been made of Kaur's contribution to diversity in publishing and of her willingness to speak openly on often taboo, private, and difficult subjects (Kassam 2016; Khaira-Hanks 2017; Kruger 2017; Miller 2019). Often, the attention paid to her politically transformative potential neglects to engage with exactly what kind of transformation is promised and championed in Kaur's work. I will begin here by elaborating on the terms of the intimate public that I argue has formed around Kaur and her work before turning to the ways in which her work promises transformation. Kaur evokes a sense of collective womanly experience (and a concurrent feeling of intimacy) across both written and visual media. Crucially, through both forms of media, Kaur asserts that women share a particular kind of embodied experience and, as a result of this, are privy and subject to particular kinds of pain and, beyond this, trauma. This version of femininity is integral to the intimate public that exists in relation to Kaur's work and to the tantalizing transformative potential this work appears to offer. Kaur's conflation of womanhood, pain, and trauma lends her work a political edge that hints at social transformation while perpetually reiterating—to maintain intimacy with her readers—that pain and trauma are inextricable from the experience of being a woman. Further, Kaur's mobilization of the language of "emotional capitalism" (Illouz 2007) promises relief from the weight of the pain and trauma of being a woman. This relief, however, can only be found by engaging in emotional work that promises to transform from within the personal, emotional, and social conditions under which one lives.

Berlant's writing on intimate publics is part of their project on national sentimentality and the construction of gendered national identity in the United

States. Crucially, however, they explore the notion that all women have shared experiences that can be elaborated upon through a commodified "women's culture," which shapes a particular mode of belonging to and engaging with the world socially and politically (Berlant 2008: 7). For Berlant, an intimate public is "distinguished by a view that the people marked by femininity already have something in common and are in need of a conversation that feels intimate, revelatory, and a relief even when it is mediated by commodities" (2008: ix). Kaur's poetry acts as a means of instigating a particular conversation on womanhood that offers intimacy, revelation, and relief as it is shared between herself and her followers on her Instagram and through her published collections, which are purchased as commodity items. Commodity culture as the social adhesive that binds intimate publics in this context, however, must also be examined in relation to social media and, in particular, to Kaur as a social media celebrity who is as much a commodity item to her readers and followers as her books and other merchandising. In this respect, Kaur's poetry and her "Period" photo series must be analyzed in tandem in order to fully understand the kind of womanhood, sharing, intimacy, and transformation Kaur's poetry and Kaur herself offer.

In *milk and honey*, pain and trauma are established as foundational to the experience of womanhood, particularly in relation to sex. The collection is divided into four sections: "the hurting," "the loving," "the breaking," and "the healing." Sexual violence is established as the root cause of "the hurting" when in the second poem, Kaur describes sexual assault at the hands of another child at five years old. In the third poem Kaur writes within a line drawing with breasts and spread legs: "you / have been / taught your legs / are a pit stop for men / that need a place to rest / a vacant body empty enough / for guests" (Kaur 2014: 13). The drawing establishes that womanhood entails a particular kind of body. The allusion to a physicality that is specific to women is then further reinforced by the assertion that this body is a "pit stop for men." Here Kaur plays on heteronormative assumptions about sexual relations—that these relations always occur between women (with certain bodies) and men—and emphasizes the notion that these relations are inherently exploitative, unequal, painful, and/or traumatic. Further, Kaur's use of "you" seems to address the reader directly, encouraging the reader to identify themselves in what the poem depicts. At the same time, the simple, declarative language here suggests a level of knowingness on the part of Kaur, and beyond that, a level of shared knowledge: Kaur as poet can presume to know what her readers have been taught because it is what she has been taught too.

As Berlant explains, the narratives of an intimate public are "deemed expressive" of a shared history between its participants, they express the "sensational, embodied experience of living as a certain kind of being in the world" (2008: viii). Kaur's poems refer unrelentingly to the body and to the physical, and most often she does so through the lens of sex. In "the hurting" section of *milk and honey*, sex and rape are referred to directly and indirectly eleven times, while there are seven poems specifically dedicated to the body. Of course, there are near infinite ways one might experience having a body, though a presumed shared experience of violence and exploitation allows Kaur to circumvent the potentially fracturing nature of infinite bodily experience. Even when not writing explicitly on the subject of sexual assault, Kaur figures sex as a violent act of consumption at the hands of a male partner. "he guts her" she writes, "with his fingers like he's scraping / the inside of a / cantaloupe clean" (Kaur 2014: 31). And again, "you must have known / you were wrong / when your fingers / were dipped inside me / searching for honey that would not come for you" (Kaur 2014: 101).

The oscillation in her poems between "you," "her," and "me" works to build connections between herself and her readers. The first poem cited here refers obliquely to "her" but the potency of the image and the violent intimacy of it suggest a personal acquaintance with the physical act it describes. In the second poem, Kaur addresses a nameless and faceless (presumed) male figure, who stands in as a kind of universal sexual aggressor, before linking the experience to the narrator of the poem (who we are tempted to think of as Kaur herself). Kaur refers back to sexual violence as a painful, traumatizing event that is knowable to anyone who has lived as a woman. This pain or trauma is not just her own but is part of the package of womanhood; it is what connects Kaur to her readers and her readers to each other, allowing them to participate in an intimate public.

Berlant's work on intimate publics can be read fruitfully alongside Eva Illouz's writing on emotional capitalism. Illouz employs this phrase to describe what arises when emotional and economic discourses collide and we begin to understand our emotions and emotional processes through an economic or transactional lens, which suggests that our general well-being, happiness, and social successes are directly contingent upon the amount of emotional "work" we are willing to put into ourselves. Kaur's readers not only consume and share her work, they also engage with a narrative which suggests investment in the self as a way of overcoming whatever trouble one might be having personally, emotionally, socially, or culturally, potentially at the expense of broader collective political action or structural change.

According to Illouz, the idea of our emotional lives requiring work is so compelling because, since Freud's lectures in America, the Second World War, and the subsequent advent of advice and self-help literature, we have grown accustomed to seeing, reading, and hearing about our emotional lives through various iterations of "advice," "admonition," and "how-to-recipes," which are themselves by-products of a psychotherapeutic language that has entered the mainstream and shaped the way we think about ourselves and our emotional lives (Illouz 2007: 10). It is this language and this cultural material that instructs one on how to "alleviate" one's misery. Kaur's poetry is infused with the language of popularized psychoanalysis. Her work is not only preoccupied with the family, the body, and sexuality, subjects often associated with psychoanalysis, but her collection *milk and honey* and her work in general often trace the process of experiencing and then endeavoring to recover from a traumatic event. Kaur describes the necessary steps to recovery with a great deal of clarity, relying on direct, often literal language. For instance, in one poem she writes: "do not look for healing / at the feet of those / who broke you" (Kaur 2014: 155), and in another she simply writes: "accept yourself / as you were designed" (Kaur 2014: 172). There is little that is complex or challenging in these poems: they are short, direct and instructive. Their clarity is the product of a pervasive therapeutic language which, as Illouz writes, "dictates that we purge everyday language of unclear and ambivalent statements" (2007: 35).

In "the healing" section of *milk and honey*, Kaur's poems take an instructional tone, occasionally bordering on admonition before reverting to affirmation and reassurance. In a poem near the beginning of the section Kaur writes: "it is part of the / human experience to feel pain / do not be afraid / open yourself to it" (152). The poems that follow begin to offer strategies to cope with this inherent pain and even to transcend it. "do not look for healing / at the feet of those who broke you" (155), she writes, and, "how you love yourself / is how you teach others / to love you" (156). Further, her instructional platitudes suggest the kind of transcendence promised by an intimate public, as they flow on from the outpouring of grief and pain that occurs in the previous sections of the collection. These poems seem to manifest, in the aftermath of intense emotion, the requisite "agency" to overcome the obstacles inherent to living as a woman (Berlant 2008: 2). "if you were born with / the weakness to fall / you were born with / the strength to rise" (Kaur 2014: 156), she writes, and, "the world / gives you so much pain / and here you are making gold out of it" (185). These poems suggest not only that individuals can find total control of their social and emotional circumstances within themselves, but that the level of hardship one might experience is directly correlated to the amount of success or joy or comfort one might experience as the result of putting in enough emotional "work." The poems are short and clear. There is no space in the poems for ambiguity or for emotional complexity. They point to pain as a shared experience among women, suggest ways to alleviate or cope with said pain, and then suggest that you might even gain something from it if you put in enough effort.

There is a marked and significant shift in tone in "the healing." In the preceding sections of *milk and honey*, Kaur writes of pain as it is inflicted upon women by external actors, whether directly or indirectly. She writes about sexual violence, the weight of beauty expectations, and internalized misogyny, experiences which Kaur suggests are part and parcel of womanhood, but which are nonetheless dependent upon some external influence or interference. "The healing" then represents a shift in the way Kaur approaches the question of pain and trauma: rather than poems that recount these kinds of experiences, the poems in "the healing" attempt to provide instruction on how to cope with or transcend those experiences, but this requires an inward turn. Such an inward turn obfuscates the fact that these experiences are shaped by external, societal factors beyond the individual and beyond a presumed biological marker that renders women inherently predisposed to pain and persecution.

In the poem that opens "the healing" Kaur begins in the first person. "Perhaps / i don't deserve / nice things" she writes, "because i am paying for sins i don't remember" (147). Here, Kaur appeals to the experience she shares with her readers, alluding to original sin and to the idea that women carry with them the very reason for their persecution, that there is something innate, even bodily, that provokes scenarios in which they may be hurt. The poem, however, plays on the idea of sin and persecution in a number of ways. First, "sin" is indeterminate here as the speaker does not remember, suggesting that the "I" may not have actively, knowingly, or meaningfully done anything that should deprive them of "nice things." This indeterminacy provokes a degree of empathy in the reader; there is a sense that the idea of not deserving nice things is potentially unwarranted. Second, the poem evokes the idea of punishment in economic terms, the speaker is "paying" for these sins. On the one hand, paying in this context suggests a degree of responsibility or culpability that belongs to the speaker; they may not know exactly what it is they have done but this does not mean they don't have to take responsibility in some way, either passively or actively through the loss of "nice things." On the other hand, "paying" in the context of emotional capitalism, and in the context of the poems that follow in "the healing," gives the sense that the speaker is paying in the wrong way, that this paying could and should be redirected, that the speaker should pay instead into ensuring that in future they do deserve nice things, that they are not bound to misery by sins of the past.

Furthermore, this poem is significant for the way Kaur's narrator maneuvers in and out of the driver's seat. The section begins in the first person while the large part of the rest of the poems takes an instructional tone, addressing an unnamed "you." The first poem emphasizes that Kaur's narrator both knows pain intimately and that she has been approaching dealing with it all wrong. The poems that follow suggest that there is a right way to deal with pain, and it can be communicated clearly and simply. However, it is not only the practical, instructional promise that transcendence is possible that makes Kaur's poetry compelling. The pleasure of the work is, in part, extratextual: Kaur's poetry is inextricable from Kaur herself. Kaur, and what she represents as a celebrity figure, contributes significantly to the reading experience, and to both the appeal and popularity of her work. Graham Huggan writes that, in her poetry, Kaur "is both reaching out and reeling in, skillfully fashioning a community of like-minded (female) readers whose appreciation and approval stoke her own celebrity image" (2020: 821). Kaur's use of first person and direct address in "the healing" suggests that she is included in the experiences about which she writes, that both pain and recovery are things she understands intimately. Her celebrity, however, which cannot be separated from the reading of her work, suggests that she is also in some way exemplary. It is the interplay between her exemplary nature and her sameness that "reels in" her readers, but it is her celebrity that most potently promises transformation.

Similar to her poetry, the visual language of Kaur's "Period" photo series speaks simply, unambiguously, and even declaratively on a particular version of womanhood, presuming that what the images depict is universally understood among women. The "Period" series deploys easily recognizable signifiers of womanhood or femininity and plays upon the bodily functions presumed to be both associated with and inextricable from the experience of womanhood. In the photographs, Kaur is shown in muted colors, wearing blood-stained sweatpants and bleeding variously on sheets, in the shower, and in the toilet. The color scheme is soft grays and pinks, punctuated by bright red menstrual blood against fabric and white porcelain. Pink motifs run throughout the images; in one Kaur is pictured lying with a pink hot water bottle across her stomach and crotch. The powerful feminine associations of the color pink blend with the positioning of the water bottle so that femininity, menstruation, and ultimately vaginas are associatively merged; these photographs are for and about a particular kind of woman. Further, Kaur herself is the subject of the photographs and although her face is turned away from the camera or cropped out of the pictures, her presence brings her directly into the narrative, binding her explicitly to the embodied experience depicted in the series.

Beyond this recognition of a shared bodily experience, Kaur's response to Instagram removing her photographs also works to establish a link between womanhood and pain, trauma, violence, and exploitation. In an impassioned Instagram caption and Facebook post[1] Kaur critiques Instagram for the kinds of images they are willing to leave up on their platform at the same time as removing hers and explains that they have proven the point she was trying to make with the pictures in the first place. She writes that she aimed to "demystify the period and make something that is innate 'normal' again cause rape categories in porn are okay. Objectification and sexualization is [*sic*] okay" (*The Huffington Post* 2015). She continues: "abuse is okay but this [the "Period" photographs] makes them uncomfortable. that's what this work is supposed to do. make you as uncomfortable as you should feel when you watch others get abused and objectified" (*The Huffington Post* 2015). Kaur's point here, though a little fuzzily expressed, seems to be that people should interrogate why an image of blood-stained sweatpants makes them uncomfortable while porn does not. The sparsely punctuated, run-on style sentences in her response, however, serve more to suggest that both periods and abuse are normal, and align menstruation with other instances of violence against women.

The associative links between womanhood and pain in this instance are significant because, in the "Period" series, Kaur begins to draw herself and her work into a broader feminist political context. She asserts in her response to Instagram that, by association, her series was much more than just a statement on menstruation, it was a statement on unacknowledged and unaddressed instances of violence against women perpetrated and tacitly allowed by the platform every day. As Rao wrote for *The Huffington Post* at the time, these photographs made Kaur an accidental feminist icon, aligning her specifically with a burgeoning celebrity feminist moment (2015). This alignment, I suggest, has been critical to Kaur's popularity. Not only is she seen to represent women and their experiences, but she is also seen as someone who champions women and challenges the inequalities and obstacles they face. Significantly, Kaur is viewed as someone with exceptional transformative power. Part of the pleasure, then, of reading

Kaur's work lies specifically in the fact that it is her work and her image, and her perceived transformative potential (be it realized or otherwise) is integral to the reading experience and to readers' participation in the intimate public that has formed around Kaur's work.

Celebrity in this context works in tandem with a particular kind of personal-political currency. Hearn and Schoenhoff write that "the celebrity embodies exemplary forms of selfhood, models how those forms of selfhood might be achieved and lived, and functions as a catalyst in and through which desire and power are seen to coalesce" (2015: 195). The "Period" series makes clear the dynamic of Kaur's celebrity. First, her selfhood is exemplary in that she has confidently made public what might be considered private, taboo, or vulnerable. Second, this act of exposure, of public vulnerability is, counterintuitively, what establishes her power. In her response to the removal of her "Period" series, Kaur points to the pain and abuse women suffer, and consequently received screeds of abuse directed at herself for having posted the images and her written response in the first place (in a 2017 interview with *Rolling Stone* Kaur revealed she had "never experienced 'so many people saying so many mean things and telling me they were going to kill me'"). Further, after her photographs and her response to Instagram went viral, Kaur went from having around 35,000 followers on Instagram to 185,000 within days (*The Huffington Post* 2015). Within a year of the viral photographs, she had sold half a million copies of *milk and honey*, and since then she has sold copies in the millions (*The Guardian* 2016). At the time of writing, she has over four million followers on Instagram. All of these things endow her with immense cultural capital both as a poet and as a social media celebrity. Alyson Miller asserts, however, in spite of her industry and commercial success, "Kaur as Instapoet is framed as an activist who resists and rejects authority, turning from the status quo to highlight the structural inequalities that have traditionally sought to keep the 'other' on the outside" (2019). Her power is a recapitulation of vulnerability, marginality, and disempowerment; she represents simultaneously this vulnerability and the capacity to overcome it.

Miller continues, explaining that Kaur is a cult-personality "whose rhetoric of difference reveals only an astute act of commodification" (2019). The commodification of difference and political discourse in Kaur's work is made possible by her elevation as icon or celebrity. As a celebrity figure, Kaur is seen to embody diversity and inclusion at the same time as she serves to represent various inequalities and injustices, both in publishing and in broader society. She is seen as exemplary in a number of ways: she has made public on a massive scale intimate and painful experiences; she has been immensely commercially successful as a poet, and specifically as a poet from typically underrepresented communities; and, she has herself faced no small amount of criticism and resistance from the very industry in which she has found success (Watts 2018). At once, Kaur must be transformative and resisted or excluded by mainstream cultural tastemakers, as Miller notes, as this paradox produces a dynamic in which buying into Kaur, buying her work, sharing her work, and/or investing in her as a celebrity figure is itself constitutive of a political or transformative act. But exactly what kind of transformation does Kaur offer? Just as her celebrity status and therefore her cultural capital depends upon the tension between radical change and social exclusion, the transformational promise held in her work must be continually rerouted through trauma and pain. The commodification of difference and of politics in Kaur's work then functions only with Kaur as an ever-present celebrity figure whose singular transformational potential renders Kaur herself a commodity item.

For Huggan, Kaur's celebrity is "an open invitation to others, not just to share her personal experiences but, potentially at least, to intrude into her personal life" (2020: 817–18). The relationship Huggan highlights here between Kaur and her fans might be considered fairly typical, with a celebrity often operating on the illusion of access and insight while maintaining boundaries and control via tactical inaccessibility and careful publicity and marketing strategies. Kaur does not follow anyone on Instagram, though the vulnerability she displays in her poetry allows her followers to feel as though she is sharing something profoundly intimate with them, that they are in some way being allowed into her personal world, as Huggan describes. I suggest, however, that the "open invitation" of Kaur's celebrity is more precisely calibrated to sell her readers and/or followers on the idea that she is allowing them into her world in the hope that it will encourage them to change their own lives as she has changed hers. Put simply, Kaur's readers invest in Kaur herself, buying her books and merchandising and increasing her social media reach, all the while believing that this investment in Kaur is in some way a transformative investment in themselves. The result here is a double investment in an individual. First, the narrative of Kaur's work—the ways in which she establishes a shared, embodied experience and mobilizes a therapeutic self-help language—suggests investment in the self as a viable means of social and political transformation. Second, Kaur as a celebrity figure and as the motivating commodity in which readers invest in order to participate in the intimate public that has formed around her work suggests that political and social transformation can be achieved by investment in one extraordinary individual.

I would like to turn now to two poems published on Instagram around the time Kaur's most recent collection, *home body* (2020), was released. The poems are titled "you have all of you on your side" and "home." Between them, they illustrate how, in Kaur's work social transformation is trapped and limited by the body. The transformation offered by Kaur's work is confined to bodily experience and to the individual—be it Kaur or the reader—who is compelled to find the strength to change their circumstance from within. In this respect, Kaur's poems do not simply center the self as a site of labor through their use of therapeutic, self-help language, but they do so by representing the body as an infinite resource from within which any individual can locate both the terms of their oppression and the means to overcome it.

"i dive into the well of my body," writes Kaur in "home," "and end up in another world / everything i need / already exists in me / there's no need to look anywhere else" (2020). We can of course trace an emotionally capitalist discourse through this poem, the persona looks within and finds that they are able to change the world from within themselves, thus reproducing a neoliberal logic that centers the self as the site of all transformation. This logic, however, is expressed in the poem in explicitly bodily terms. Diving into the "well" of the body calls to mind wells of experience, as well as the image of drawing water from a well. The opening line here gives the sense that the persona is immersed in bodily experience, experience that they are able to draw from in order to "end up in another world." Her body is a deep and bountiful resource that provides simultaneously everything that she requires and offers the potential for change. There is a sense here too, if we return to the idea of drawing water from a well, that an altered internal world may also lead to altered circumstances externally, that the transformation of our personal circumstances can be broadly socially and/or politically transformative as we literally draw change from the inside to the outside. The poem does not simply suggest that the narrator is able to transform her world to another through reserves of psychic strength and willpower, but that she is able to do so for reasons that are intimately connected to her bodily experience. "There's no need to look anywhere else," she writes, because the body intrinsically holds gendered experiences of pain and trauma, and, as is illustrated by poems from "the healing" and in Kaur's work more broadly, pain and trauma are seen to be transformational if they are attended to properly. Kaur's language here collapses notions of broader societal change and draws them into the body and, crucially, into the individual. The poem suggests that another world is possible, but it locates that world within the individual, tacitly suggesting that even transformation at scale begins and ends with the self.

In "you have all of you on your side" Kaur builds an image of community through the narrow lens of an individual body and its vital and constituent parts. "you are not alone" she writes, "alone would be if / your heart no longer beat / and your lungs no longer pulled / and your breath no longer pushed / how are you alone if / an entire community lives in you" (2020). In this poem, Kaur describes multiple organs working in tandem to sustain life. The organs are endowed with a certain intentionality and a communal spirit that renders a person less alone and asserts again that they contain everything they might need inside. Of course, you might also consider that every living person has, in some combination and to some extent, organs working together to keep them alive. In this respect, the poem suggests again that it is through our bodies that we are connected to other people. However, there is an isolating quality to this poem. The vital organs listed are confined within the human body, they do not act as points of contact with other people in any meaningful way, and the poem emphasizes that their function is to keep "you" alive. The "community" of organs serves one person: you. Community in this poem is subsumed by the individual, and, crucially, by the individual body.

What is significant in both these poems is the way in which they merge the body with an individualist discourse that (often) draws from the language of emotional capitalism. They take what acts as the binding for a collective shared intimacy (the body and its experience of the world) and reconfigure it as a capacious and transformative yet highly individual means of negotiating the world. As Huggan writes, "Kaur's is clearly a literature that *inhabits* the world, but it tends to organize its worldly sensibilities around the incorporation of others into an all embracing self" (2020: 821). The community might be inside you, but it is composed of endless reiterations of yourself; you might find another world, but you will find it only within yourself. Transformative potential in Kaur's writing is subsumed by the self at every turn. She alludes to and occasionally even confronts directly the specific inequalities and acts of violence women are subjected to in the world through the lens of the body. She then directs her readers to turn inward. This instruction to turn inward, however, relies upon Kaur's readers investing in Kaur, who represents a certain way of being and a certain way of dealing with life's obstacles. Through her poetry and her celebrity

Kaur appears to be both exemplary and the same as her readers. There is a sense then, that investing in Kaur constitutes also an investment in oneself. As a result, the intimacy shared between Kaur and her readers structures a public of individuals who feel like a collective and who feel "ethical" (Berlant 2008: 6), but who transform only themselves.

There is little doubt that Kaur and her poetry have begun to alter how we might think about poetry in an increasingly networked world. And, perhaps more significantly, how we think about what form transformation might take in such a world. Kaur and her readers are bound by a shared understanding and acknowledgment (often implicit and sometimes explicit) that the world presents various obstacles and inequalities, and that these obstacles and inequalities must be challenged and ultimately transformed. However, what is shared must be perpetually reiterated in order for the intimacy of this public to be maintained, and what is shared is traumatic. Thus, the transformation that Kaur and her poetry promise cannot ever be fulfilled, as true transformation would disestablish the terms of the intimate public. Kaur's work, then, is only able to offer relief, something consolatory that hints at change while the source of pain persists. The political thrust of Kaur's work is subsumed by the self, though it offers a tantalizing view of a world in which transcendence from within is not only desirable but entirely possible.

Note

1 The Facebook post is available in Mallika Rao's 2015 interview with Kaur for *The Huffington Post* and a link to her Instagram post can be found in the references for this chapter.

References

Andrews McMeel Publishing. 2021. *Milk and Honey by Rupi Kaur*. Available at: https://publishing.andrewsmcmeel.com/book/milk-and-honey/.

Berlant, Lauren. 2008. *The Female Complaint: The Unfinished Business of Sentimentality in American Culture*. Durham, NC: Duke University Press.

Carlin, Shannon. 2017. "Meet Rupi Kaur, Queen of the 'Instapoets.'" *Rolling Stone*, December 21, 2017. https://www.rollingstone.com/culture/culture-features/meet-rupi-kaur-queen-of-the-instapoets-129262/.

Ferguson, Donna. 2019. "Keats Is Dead … : How Young Women Are Changing the Rules of Poetry." *The Guardian*, January 26, 2019. https://www.theguardian.com/books/2019/jan/26/new-generation-young-women-poets.

Flood, Alison. 2016. "Poet Rupi Kaur's Milk and Honey Sells More than Half a Million Copies." *The Guardian*, September 13, 2016. https://www.theguardian.com/books/2016/sep/13/poet-rupi-kaurs-milk-and-honey-sells-more-than-half-a-million-copies.

Hearn, Alison and Stephanie Schoenhoff. 2015. "From Celebrity to Influencer: Tracing the Diffusion of Celebrity Value across the Data Stream." In *A Companion to Celebrity*, edited by P. David Marshall and Sean Redmond , 194–212. Chichester: John Wiley & Sons.

Huggan, Graham. 2020. "Re-evaluating the Postcolonial Exotic." *Interventions*, 22 (7): 808–24. DOI:10.1080/1369801x.2020.1753552.

Illouz, Eva. 2007. *Cold Intimacies: The Making of Emotional Capitalism*. Cambridge: Polity Press.

Kassam, Ashifa. 2016. "Rupi Kaur: 'There Was No Market for Poetry about Trauma, Abuse, and healing." *The Guardian*, August 26, 2016. https://www.theguardian.com/books/2016/aug/26/rupi-kaur-poetry-canada-instagram-banned-photo.

Kaur, Rupi. 2014. *Milk and Honey.* Kansas City: Andrews McMeel Publishing.

Kaur, Rupi [@rupikaur_]. 2020. "Home." *Instagram photo*, November 17, 2020. https://www.instagram.com/p/CHtJHKZhtm8/.

Kaur, Rupi [@rupikaur_]. 2020. "You Have All of You on Your Side." *Instagram photo*, November 22, 2020. https://www.instagram.com/p/CH4CSl0BcGm/.

Khaira-Hanks, Priya. 2017. "Rupi Kaur: The Inevitable Backlash against Instagram's Favourite Poet." *The Guardian*, October 4, 2017. https://www.theguardian.com/books/booksblog/2017/oct/04/rupi-kaur-instapoets-the-sun-and-her-flowers.

Kruger, Sasha. 2017. "The Technop(o)litic of Rupi Kaur: (De)colonial Aesthetics and Spatial Narrations in the Digifemme Age." *Ada: A Journal of Gender, New Media, and Technology*, 11. DOI: 10.7264/N38G8J0x.

Miller, Alyson. 2019. "'Poetry's Beyoncé' on Rupi Kaur and the Commodifying Effects of Instapoetics." *Axon Journal*, 9 (1). https://www.axonjournal.com.au/issue-vol-9-no-1-may-2019/%E2%80%98poetry%E2%80%99s-beyonc%C3%A9%E2%80%99.

Rao, Mallika. 2015. "About That Period Photo That Broke the Internet." *The Huffington Post*, June 5, 2015. https://www.huffingtonpost.co.uk/entry/rupi-kaur-instagram-period-photo-series_n_7213662?ri18n=true.

Saul, Heather. 2015. "Menstruation-themed Photo Series Artist 'Censored by Instagram' Says Images Are to Demystify Taboos around Periods." *Independent*, March 31, 2015. https://www.independent.co.uk/arts-entertainment/art/menstruation-themed-photo-series-artist-censored-instagram-says-images-are-demystify-taboos-around-periods-10144331.html.

Spencer, Erin. 2015. "Rupi Kaur: The Poet Every Woman Needs to Read." *The Huffington Post*, January 22, 2015. https://www.huffpost.com/entry/the-poet-every-woman-needs-to-read_b_6193740.

Tamarkin, Sally. 2015. "This Instagram Was Deleted Because It Showed a Woman's Menstrual Blood." *Buzzfeed*, March 27, 2015. https://www.buzzfeed.com/sallytamarkin/the-patriarchy-is-leaking.

Tsjeng, Zing. 2015. "Why Instagram Censored This Image of an Artist on Her Period." *Dazed Digital*, March 27, 2015. https://www.dazeddigital.com/artsandculture/article/24258/1/why-instagram-censored-this-image-of-an-artist-on-her-period

Watts, Rebecca. 2018. "The Cult of the Noble Amateur." *PN Review*, 44 (3): 13–17. https://www.pnreview.co.uk/cgi-bin/scribe?item_id=10090.

10

Poetry-by-Numbers: Machine-Generating Instapoetry

Ryan Prewitt
Saint Louis University

Max Accardi
Independent Scholar

In a memorable section of Mark Twain's *Huckleberry Finn*, Huck inhabits a room that once belonged to Emmeline Grangerford, a prolific teenaged poet who loved to "write about anything you could choose to give her to write about, just so it was sadful." Most of Emmeline's poems are "tributes" to recently deceased people. In one tribute, she describes the death of a boy named Stephen Dowling Bots: "Then list with tearful eye, Whilst I his fate do tell. His soul did from this cold world fly, By falling down a well." Huck is sincerely impressed with Emmeline's poetry, and in one of the funniest, unintentionally backhanded compliments in literature, marvels that Emmeline "could rattle off poetry like nothing. She didn't ever have to stop to think" (Twain 1884: 142–3).

There are parallels between Emmeline's tributes and a typical Instapoem. Both are short,[1] both center on a single theme, and neither is especially subtle about communicating that theme. Both mostly eschew figurative language, and the metaphors they do use are quite straightforward. Both strive to induce an "authentic" affective response (in the author as well as the reader).[2] Most importantly for our purposes, both Emmeline and many Instapoets seem to "rattle off" poems without stopping to think, as if by mechanical function rather than poetic prowess.[3]

Instapoetry is thus an ideal genre to use in exploring the relationship between writing, thinking, and meaning. And because Instapoetry is digitally accessible and exhibits consistent syntactical features, it is also well-suited to Natural Language Processing ("NLP") techniques. This chapter combines those threads, documenting our attempt to answer two questions: Is it possible for an algorithm to write passable Instapoetry? If so (or if not), what does that mean for the genre and for poetic production generally?

This chapter proceeds in four sections. The "Instapoetry" section identifies qualities of Instapoetry which we believe make it well-suited to machine generation. The "Technology" section discusses the technical details of our project. The "Results" section presents our results, highlighting some of the noteworthy machine-generated Instapoetry we produced and other statistical information we derived. Finally, the "Theoretical Implications" section discusses the theoretical ramifications of the results.

Instapoetry

Compare Huck's account of Emmeline to a few lines by popular Instapoet r.h. Sin:

Selection 1:
never let a confused man
waste your time, love or energy

Selection 2:
the women with the highest
walls, have the deepest love

Selection 3:
you can't find safety in the arms of a man who
is the reason for your heartache.

These are among the first several posts the authors found when visiting r.h. Sin's Instagram page in early 2023 (Sin 2023).

These poems showcase what we believe are the signature characteristics of Instapoetry. Formally, Sin's poems are short and simple—they seldom exceed a few lines. The poems feature amorphous subjects: they either refer to an unnamed singular third person pronoun (most often "she/her/hers"), or directly address the reader ("you"). Sin's poetry fixates on a single theme: living up to women's expectations in the context of romantic relationships. Although his poems are addressed to both men and women, virtually all of them could be replaced with "RESPECT WOMEN" and lose nothing of their thematic content. The "message" of each poem is usually a fortune-cookie truism. "you can't find safety in the arms of a man who / is the reason for your heartache" means that people should treat their romantic partners with kindness if they want kindness in return; "never let a confused man / waste your time, love or energy" means that you can't always get what you want out of a (male) romantic partner.

Like most Instapoets, Sin tends to forego figurative language, and when he does try his hand at metaphor, it often doesn't work. Take this example:

you gave an angel hell
and she became a phoenix

The poem clearly uses a mixed metaphor—she is an angel *and* a phoenix—and while the poem registers the character of change that a phoenix connotes, the transition takes place not in the phoenix's rebirth, but in the transition to a phoenix from some entire other thing. In sum, Sin's poems are simple, generic, direct, and centered on a single theme. Like Emmeline, Sin seems to be able to "rattle off poetry like nothing" without "ever hav[ing] to stop to think," provided the subject of the poem is respecting female romantic partners.[4]

Sin's poetry is largely representative of the genre; however, other poets operate in slightly better faith, in that their work appears to be a sincere effort to represent their own experiences in an honest and relatable way. Rupi Kaur, the genre's foremost representative, writes about her struggles against patriarchal impositions rather than, in the case of Sin, preying upon an affect of empowerment in young women. Indeed, scholars have praised Kaur's ability to give voice to trauma and have found efficacy in her accounts of the constraints placed on gender. Sasha Kruger, for example, notes that Kaur's poetry "creates the space for women to speak, and therefore, allows for communal and self-healing" (Kruger 2017).

Others, while acknowledging Kaur's legitimacy and aesthetic appeal, still note the simple or even rudimentary character of her poems. J. M. Rue observes that Kaur marshals her signature confessional tone effectively, but critiques Instapoetry as a "remediated form of (poetry)" (Rue 2019: 1). Others are more critical: Alyson Miller describes Kaur as a "cult-personality," whose "rhetoric of difference reveals only an astute act of commodification" (Miller 2019). Miller comments on the genre more broadly: "Derided as 'fidget-spinner poetry,' it is a form excoriated as a consequence of a contemporary environment in which technological advancement has supposedly reduced an audience's capacity for effort and complexity" (Miller 2019).

Instapoetry, at least according to its critics, is a genre where most of the poems expound on similar themes in simple, direct language, targeted toward a market of consumers eager to validate their current emotional states. Instapoetry, in other words, seems to require relatively little creative "thought." This project tests that characterization empirically by creating an algorithm that takes a sample of real Instapoetry, and then authors poems of its own. In the remaining sections of this chapter, we discuss the technology underlying our algorithm, the results of the algorithm, and the theoretical implications of the project according to two contrasting theories of communication.

Technology

This project required two basic steps: first, collecting a large and representative sample of poems posted on Instagram and converting them to machine-readable text; second, using NLP techniques to gain insight from the sample. All of the scripts we wrote in the course of completing this project are available on our GitHub page.[5]

Sample Selection and Extraction

There is a staggering quantity of poetry disseminated on Instagram; the hashtag "#instapoetry" alone appears on more than four million posts. Along with popular and successful Instapoets like Sin, Atticus, and Tyler Knott Gregson, there are many Instapoetry accounts with few followers and little clout. To achieve a genuine cross-section of the genre, we wanted our sample to include both prominent and obscure Instapoets, and both high- and low-quality content. To accomplish this, we selected several prominent Instapoets (e.g., Sin, Atticus, Kaur), along with several hashtags commonly used in the Instapoetry community (e.g., #instapoetry, #instapoem, #instapoet). We then used an Instagram scraping tool to download a large number of Instagram posts (approximately 2,000 in total).[6]

The next challenge was to extract machine-readable text from the Instagram posts comprising our sample. The process of extracting text from images is known as optical character recognition, or OCR. Before attempting to perform OCR on our sample, we first pre-processed the images by converting them to grayscale, increasing their contrast, and orienting the text horizontally; we found through experimentation that these steps improved our OCR.

We performed the OCR itself with Python-tesseract, a Python interface for Google's OCR engine. After an initial round of OCR, we found that many of the results were unsuited for our project; some poems were unreadable, not written in English, or appeared to lack any textual content. We post-processed our sample by breaking each poem into a list of words, eliminating non-alphabetic characters, and checking the spelling of the remaining words. Where a poem appeared to be in a foreign language or did not appear to have many recognizable words, we discarded it. We then performed a second cleaning to sift out unnecessary words that related to the identity of the author rather than the content of the poem—like the author's name and Twitter handle.

Text Generation

To generate our poems, we used the concept of a Markov chain, a mathematical model that predicts the next "state" of a system based on its current state (Soni 2018).[7] We surveyed every word in each of the poems in our corpus and aggregated all the words directly following that word within the corpus. Thus, if one poem contained the two-word phrase "and then," and another contained the two-word phrase "and she," we counted both "she" and "then" as words that may follow "and."

The result was a "dictionary" that paired each word in our sample with a list of all of the words that followed that word. After assembling the dictionary, the algorithm began writing a poem by selecting a starting word at random from the dictionary, and then randomly selecting the subsequent word from among the words that followed the starting word anywhere in the corpus. The algorithm repeated this process until it achieved a poem of appropriate length based on the averages from across our sample.

Results[8]

The Poems

Our text generation algorithm produces a wide range of results. Because the Markov chain considers only the current state (in our case, the last word selected), it only sometimes achieves correct syntax and grammar. As a result, some of the poems we generated are incoherent, scrambled words in seemingly arbitrary order. But we also got some poems that achieve successful syntax. Although the Markov chain is random, it only pairs words that have, at some point in the corpus, appeared together.[9] This means that it is unlikely that something like a subject pronoun would be paired with a mis-conjugated verb (e.g., "they is"). This is to say that, although the Markov chain seems on the surface to be simply random, linguistic patterns still emerge in the generated material, and we sometimes achieve syntactically successful poems as a result. Like a human poet, our algorithm writes some poems that are better than others.

Here we will present a sample of some of the material our algorithm has produced. Because the algorithm can generate as many poems as we want it to, in order to present our results, we necessarily had to make decisions on which poems to represent in this chapter. We've tried to select poems that fairly represent the results we typically achieve.

Sometimes, our algorithm produces semantically and syntactically sound material. See the following example of the material that we have been posting to our Instagram account:[10]

> she was the dust
> settled deep inside

Note that in this case (as well as many others), our algorithm's poetry is comparable to most Instapoetry in its basic formal attributes: the poem is short, direct, and uses the third person feminine pronoun as its focus. Interestingly, however, it is possible to view this poem as having a greater degree of poetic sensibility than some real Instapoems—the metaphor is uniform, concise, and relatively effective.

Indeed, the algorithm occasionally writes poems that are not just passable, but almost *profound*. One such poem reads:

> can I soak up enough to feel nothing?[11]

This poem is interesting because it not only features figurative language but seems to communicate an abstract insight about human nature: the fact that people "soak up" or consume things to avoid reckoning with their emotions.[12]

Equally interesting are the instances in which a generated poem is syntactically poor but semantically rich. See the following example:

> knew she was she sleeps a castle in
> your life be in their behavior
> make you were pulled together to
> find someone after every direction

If you squint, it looks like a normal Instapoem. Again, we find a high frequency of the second person as well as the third person singular feminine pronoun. Although the syntax is incorrect, the algorithm has strung together linguistically associated words like "she," "sleeps," and "castle" (which calls to mind a fairy-tale princess asleep in a castle) or "every" and "direction." The poem doesn't deliver a meaningful metaphor using these signs, but it at least calls to mind a fragmented image. Take another example, with parts that function and parts that do not:

> memories giving more than a muscle lifting mask
> I've learnt from a high me

In this case, we have a mixed phrase, where "muscle" is clearly associated with "lifting," and "lifting" is clearly associated with "mask," but the three together create a symbol amalgam. This could be a type of decontextualizing language that many poets are praised for.

And of course, some poems are simply gibberish and resist any kind of coherent interpretation, like these lines:

> production leads to
> make you still not
> and diet james
> ce eat aid at he canst choose to import now and[13]

In short, the poems our algorithm writes are a mixed bag—some are incomprehensible, most are varying degrees of bad, and a few are quite good. (That ratio is, in our opinion, not far off from human-authored Instapoetry.) The following we present unadorned with any commentary:

- play on the more often we loved you / cuz darling some men lie
- those posters in the only ones / who prefers / to and you loved / because the storm one story about myself / fully but the earnestness / and nights when you said / you let it doesnt want to
- to live a burning with the / fears and hope / you have always used / in a bewildering / phenomenon in time i / wish you brought meter favorite drink beer / es tk a er i deep clear without thinking

Topic Modeling

In addition to procedurally generating our own Instapoetry, we also used Latent Dirichlet Allocation ("LDA") to ascertain some of the common topics in our corpus (Ganegedara 2018). LDA assumes that any document involves one or more "topics" (meaning concepts, themes, motifs, etc.), and that each "topic" comprises a group of related words. LDA thus considers each word in a corpus and measures its proximity to other words; when it finds that certain words often occur near one another, like "cat," "whisker," and "meow," it treats those words as a "topic." Here are the top five topics we identified in the corpus:

1. Love, yourself, something, beautiful, tell, someone, smile, heart, life, still
2. Phase, years, things, four, away, would, beauty, feel, heart, love
3. Love, phase, feel, soul, people, know, could, even, everything, still
4. Know, want, words, love, nothing, keep, year, anything, last, heart
5. Time, heart, words, life, need, everything, eyes, still, look, before

These results prompt several observations. The word "love" appears in four of the five topics, but each topic appears to reflect a different type of "love." In Topic 1, the second most frequent word is "yourself," and the third is "beautiful." One way to interpret this data is that Instapoets often use "love" to discuss *self-love*, urging their readers to rejoice in themselves and feel beautiful without needing external validation. In Topic 3, "love" appears with "soul," "people," and "everything," suggesting a more general "love" for the world or humankind. And in Topics 2 and 4, "love" appears in connection with words suggesting duration ("phase," "year" or "years," "keep," "last") and words suggesting romance ("beauty," "feel," "heart"), which may indicate a focus on the fleeting nature of romantic love.

The fifth topic is the most distinct from the other topics, and the most puzzling: it consists largely of words suggesting duration ("time," "life," "still," "before"), but unlike Topics 2 and 4, features fewer "romance" words. This could indicate that some Instapoems are reminiscent of the *ubi sunt* genre of analogue poetry (the most famous of which begins with "where are the snows of yesteryear?"), which tends to focus on nostalgia and impermanence. But while the first four topics comport with our qualitative impressions of Instapoetry—as a genre focused on romance, self-worth, and emotional authenticity—the "*ubi sunt*" topic does not. We have no strong opinions on why this could be the case, but it may bear further study.

Theoretical Implications

Based on the above results, we believe that we have created a moderately successful algorithm for writing Instapoetry; although its poems are a mixed bag, real Instapoems are also a mixed bag. Importantly, what our algorithm does not do is *think*, at least in a traditional sense—it randomly pairs words that have appeared together in our large corpus. And yet, at least some of its poems (1) resemble some human-generated Instapoetry such that it is difficult to tell the difference, and (2) contain seemingly insightful (or at least coherent) metaphors and messages.

Like Anakin Skywalker, we're left wondering "what have I done?" (Lucas 2005). More specifically, what does the fact that an algorithm can generate passable Instapoetry mean for the genre, and more generally, for communication in the digital age? In this section, we present two contrasting interpretations of our algorithmic poetry based on different theoretical perspectives on communication, and then attempt to synthesize those interpretations to raise questions about Instapoetry as a genre.

Distributed Cognition and Posthumanism

Now that we have established a baseline of what the algorithm is and does, let us return briefly to Huck Finn's contemplation on Emmeline's poetry. Our algorithm follows a similar process to Emmeline—we tell it to run and within milliseconds it churns out twenty poems that frequently operate within the affective mode that is specific to Instapoetry. In this technical sense, our algorithm does not "(stop) to think," in part because the thinking has already taken place by the poets who generated the material that forms its corpus.

The process by which our algorithm generates poetry gives literal application to posthumanism's theory of distributed cognition. In the introduction to their treatise *A Thousand Plateaus*, Deleuze and Guattari complicate traditional ideas of thinking. They argue that cognition is distributed across different "assemblages." These assemblages "connect the human to outside elements without recourse to a privileged interior subjectivity" (Broglio 2008: 22). In other words, being and cognition depend on receptive registers outside of one's interior subjectivity, such as the mind, the body, the material and technological environment. Katherine Hayles describes this process in the context of reading digital media:

> [S]ound, vision, haptic responses, kinaesthesia and proprioception work together to create complex sensory/cognitive experiences. Moreover, these experiences occur through the mediation of intelligent machines, resulting in the further in-mixing of human and non-human cognitions. (Hayles 2008: 16)

The practitioners of Instapoetry embody this process—the cognitive functions that underlie their poetic practices are already distributed across several cognitions.

If we consider this in the context of Instapoetry, we can recognize some assemblages of cognition immediately, such as the onus to generate engagement, and to that end the visual rhetoric, the tonal qualities, and the consistent symbolic content. We can consider the assemblage of commodification, which closely follows the highest levels of success in the genre. Deleuze and Guattari argue, however, that these assemblages are neither unique nor isolated, and form only parts of the root system that bear relation to a continuous whole:

> An assemblage, in its multiplicity, necessarily acts on semiotic flows, material flows, and social flows simultaneously ... There is no longer a tripartite division between a field of reality (the world) and a field of representation (the book) and a field of subjectivity (the author). (Deleuze and Guattari 1987: 22–3)

Although Deleuze and Guattari wrote in a pre-digital era, their language of "flows" aptly describes the Instapoetry landscape. Language is the core of its mission, hence semiotic flows; commodification (via publication and other peculiar product associations) operates at the goal line, hence material flows; Instagram is a social media network hence social flows. Of course, to Deleuze and Guattari, these are fluid and non-complete; but it may still give us distinct insight into the situationality of production of our particular content of interest.

Further, and more importantly for the purposes of this chapter, it resonates with our project and methods in important ways. Here is where our algorithm diverges from the mechanistic description Huck attributes to Emmeline. Deleuze and Guattari give us the language and means to consider the ways in which cognition is already distributed when a poet writes; thus, it isn't that there is no thinking taking place, but rather that the thinking takes place in different ways and across different registers. This is a useful analogue to our algorithm. In drawing from over 1,000 Instapoems and nearly as many individual Instapoets, we have effectively given a literal application to the deconstruction of the poet-subject that we can draw from Deleuze and Guattari's conditions of distributed cognition.

Under this theoretical framing, the relative success of our algorithm suggests that the production of poetry does not, as we typically assume, require "thinking" in the traditional sense; there is no central, autonomous subject producing the material, but rather a networked system of cognition and language. The algorithm empirically replicates Deleuze and Guattari's concept of the assemblage, in which the boundaries between reader and writer blur; each becomes a participant within a nonbinary, interconnected system of language and meaning.

This theory of communication prompts us to reconsider our hermeneutics of suspicion with regard to Instapoetry—what matters more than the innate or autonomous quality of the poems, as this line of thinking suggests, is the *life and effects* of the poems in the context of their ever-proliferating web of communication. The staggering levels of engagement the genre achieves suggest that its life is vibrant and meaningful to its many participants. Following these logics, our Instapoetry algorithm instantiates theories of posthuman poetry and communication that signal how communication and meaning occur in emergent digital landscapes.

Deconstruction and Hyperreality

> Everyone just lives in their own cell, and the system tames them by giving them each their own personal serenity ... Everyone is alone. Everyone is empty. People no longer have need of others. You can always find a spare for any talent. Any relationship can be replaced.
>
> — Makishima Shogo, *Psycho-Pass*, episode 22

Posthumanism is an optimistic take on Instapoetry—optimistic in that it views digital literature as the "next stage" of human interconnectivity, which surpasses previous modes of expression by incorporating multiple registers beyond the text. A less optimistic interpretation is that Instapoetry is the next stage of the disintegration of meaning in late-stage capitalism; under this interpretation, the fact that passable Instapoetry can be generated by an unthinking algorithm confirms the emptiness of the genre.

Deconstruction asserts that "texts ... do not have definable meanings and determinable missions, that they are always more than any mission would impose, that they exceed the boundaries they currently occupy" (Caputo 1997: 31). In other words, any linguistic description fails to encompass the incomparable meaning of the referent: words can only imitate an underlying reality.

Jean Baudrillard adds sociological insight to deconstruction's analysis of communication. Baudrillard argues that as societies become more advanced and scientific and artistic discourse progresses, people begin to delude themselves into thinking a complete understanding of reality is possible. Consequently, they start to create increasingly sophisticated representations of reality, which will never pindown their fundamentally ineffable referent. Representation begins as a faithful effort to imitate reality (stage 1 simulacra); then, some representations begin to mask the underlying reality (stage 2 simulacra); then, because there is no longer an identifiable "original," the imitations come to mask the *absence* of the original (stage 3 simulacra); then, at last, representations begin to refer only to other representations, without any connection to a referent (stage 4 simulacra). The dream of rendering reality as a coherent, representable whole leads to a chain of imitations with increasing verisimilitude, until no "real" is left (Baudrillard 1988: 6).

Baudrillard's theory is at its most cogent as applied to expressive acts in late-stage capitalism. Baudrillard argued convincingly that in late-stage capitalism, both language and physical objects constitute an exchange of signs: language is "a structure of exchange contemporaneous with meaning itself, and on which is articulated the individual intention of speech" (Baurdillard 1981: 58), while tangible products fall into "categories of objects which … undertake the policing of social meanings" (Baurdillard 1968: 20). By consuming a Lexus, or a Big Mac, or a book (or a poem on a website that pays content creators for traffic?), the consumer indelibly marks herself. Consumption, whether of language or of objects, is simply the "systematic act of the manipulation of signs" (Baudrillard 1968: 25).

Due to the ever-increasing consumption of products and language, late-stage capitalism produces more and more "culture," but at the expense of "art." As Baudrillard writes, "The logic of the disappearance of art is, precisely, inversely proportional to that of the production of culture … [T]his disappearance is not negative or depressing—no more than merchandise is" (Baudrillard 1987: 173, 179). In a society driven by the logic of consumption, what once was art is now merchandise—born from the same cycle of production and consumption as any other widget.

What better embodiment of this state than Instapoetry, the authors of which directly peddle their words, superimposed on artsy backgrounds, on a website that functions as a marketplace for creators to advertise their content? On popular Instapoetry pages, the authors intermingle their poems with advertisements for books, journals, clothing, and greeting cards, all of which form an essential part of their "brand." As Clare Bucknell put it in a piercing review of Instapoetry as a genre, Instagram "[p]osts present poems in the same way adverts place products" (Bucknell 2020).[14] There is no essential difference between the poems and the products: both function as what Bucknell calls "markers of a lifestyle" (Bucknell 2020).

The next question is what type of meaning this merchandise is capable of holding. Obviously Instapoems have subjective meaning to their readers, as evinced by the startling number of fans who choose to tattoo Instapoet Atticus's poem "love her, but leave her wild" on their flesh (Edwards 2017). But the poems themselves are often either unrelated to any concrete thought, a concrete reference to another consumable product, or both. Consider two poems by Kaur: "love is giving all we can / even if it's just the bigger slice of cake" (if this means anything at all, it's that sometimes when you love someone, you do nice things for them) and "mint chocolate chip ice cream will fix just about everything" (the sole meaning of which is to invite the beleaguered reader to consume mint chocolate chip ice cream). Note that the metaphor of both poems is the consumption of something pleasurable—cake or ice cream (or perhaps the poem itself). As Bucknell writes, "The sheer inoffensive sweetness of the writing—and its brevity—means it works anywhere."

Language that can mean anything to anyone, ironically means nothing in and of itself. This is distinct from poetic ambiguity, which invites multiple interpretations that emerge from some feature of the text itself. After all, researchers tried and failed to use a better algorithm than ours to generate *analogue* poetry, and the results were readily distinguishable from the original; a Maya Angelou algorithm came up with "I will speak, because my voice shall be heard," which instantly betrays its robotic authorship (Tang 2020). But our algorithm as well as many of Instapoetry's prominent practitioners suggests that Instapoetry is an assembly line product, no different from a Lexus, the meaning of which is the subjective emotion experienced by its consumer in the act of consumption. The only connection between author and reader is a commercial transaction; each lives in her own cell, writing or interpreting poems—consuming language—to achieve personal serenity. The notion of shared meaning becomes obsolete. Is Instapoetry the last stage of the "chain reaction of simulacra [that] put an end to art?"

If this analysis is correct, Instapoetry is a third-order simulacrum. Its existence masks the absence of a real meeting of the minds between author and reader—it disguises itself as something more than the production and consumption of the indicia of a desirable lifestyle. Our algorithmic poet is the logical next step; it is a fourth-order simulacrum, which takes the words other Instapoets have written and arranges them within the formal features of an Instapoem, but without the intermediary of conscious thought. In other words, it is the automated reproduction of representations.

Synthesis and Conclusion

In this chapter we have sought to represent the results of our Instapoetry algorithm and explain their possible significance. The results invite opposing interpretations of Instapoetry as a genre; is it the natural development of poetic communication, or an embodiment of the hollow expressive acts that characterize late-stage capitalism? The interpretations share many of the same factual precepts—that authors do not operate in a vacuum, but instead draw their vocabulary from the culture that they themselves consume. Our algorithmic poet makes this process literal; its vocabulary (the words and word-pairs it employs) are drawn directly and exclusively from a corpus of poems other people have written.

Yet this paints a troubling picture of Instapoetry as a genre. Whether we accept the posthumanist assertion that cognition is a distributed process and that Instapoets draw their vocabulary from Instapoetry writ large, or the deconstructionist notion that much of writing is simply copying, while the referent slips ever further away, Instapoetry is the product of the platform that hosts it. And Instagram is, fundamentally, a marketplace, not just for products but for the indicia of a lifestyle. Baudrillard's metaphor for a hyper-commodified, late-capitalist environment was a mirror: a shiny chrome surface, perfectly reflecting other shiny chrome surfaces in an endless loop (Baudrillard 1988: 166–88). But Instapoetry seems to suggest that, in the digital age, the marketplace simulation presents quite differently—not as perfect industrial products, but reproductions of imperfection, displaced onto the level of affect. Instapoetry's principal commodity and point of appeal is its honesty and authenticity—yet the genre minimizes the distance between composition and commodification.

Baudrillard, above all, believed that commodification accelerates the collapse of meaning. Thus, the process by which cognition results from a poet's exposure to and interactions on Instagram, which is fundamentally a platform for commodification, results in poetry that is essentially a product. Whether that divests the poems of meaning is a question we simply hope to provoke.

Notes

1 Emmeline's Ode to *Stephen Dowling Bots, Dec'd* is six lines; the average Instapoem from our sample is 3.5 lines.

2 Fans of Instapoetry often praise the genre as a vehicle for authentic, unmediated emotional expression (Matthews 2019: 395).

3 Instapoet Atticus acknowledged this in an interview, writing that the genre is replete with "[p]eople throwing up poems that they didn't spend a lot of time on" (Lederman 2017). We don't have any data on how much time it takes most Instapoets to write a poem, but it can't have taken Atticus too long to come up with: "Swimming pools were invented to kiss girls in the rain / and if they weren't, they should have been."

4 Sin is a successful Instapoet by any metric. He has over 2 million followers on Instagram (Sin 2023). In 2017, two of his print books were among the top five best-selling poetry books through Barnes & Noble (Sin 2017). Instapoetry, in other words, is big business.

5 https://github.com/Nadogan/Instagram_Poetry_Processing. The readme and requirements.txt files provide additional technical information for readers who want to use some of these techniques for their own projects. Our code bears the Unlicense License and may be used freely for any application.

6 The tool we used is "instagram-scraper," which is available here: https://github.com/arc298/instagram-scraper. Unfortunately, while we were completing this project, Instagram changed its algorithm to resist automated traffic. As a result, instagram-scraper no longer appears to work—and in fact, the Instagram account of one of the authors was banned due to his use of instagram-scraper.

7 Markov chains are a relatively crude method for generating texts, but that's the point of our project: we wanted to see whether randomly pairing words from the vocabulary of many Instapoets could generate passable poetry. Projects using more sophisticated techniques to generate poetry have produced dismal results; for instance, the advanced GPT-2 algorithm, tasked with writing a sonnet based on samples of Shakespeare's work, came up with the closing lines: "And the sky is not bright to behold yet: Thou hast not a thousand days to tell me thou art beautiful" (Tang 2020). Nevertheless, AI communications technologies continue to advance and to impress, and by now ChatGPT, an AI chat bot built on the highly advanced GPT-3 algorithm has caused significant shocks to the higher education system (D'Agostino 2023).

8 We have made the sample we used available at: https://drive.google.com/drive/folders/1oGATLmX6-W6vRwkt8tpqqmvNzU5BzDCv?usp=sharing

9 The only exception is where an indecipherable word has been omitted—"pairing" the words before and after it, even though they did not appear next to one another in the original text.

10 https://www.instagram.com/vesper.rose.poems/. We are not the first to come up with the idea of posing as an Instapoet; for an amusing account of a person who gained a considerable following posting the most generic sentiments he could think of ("That's the thing about feelings, you have to FEEL them"), see Lloyd (2019).

11 Our algorithm does not account for punctuation. We found experimentally that our OCR process would often interpret random marks as punctuation, yielding low-quality results. Additionally, accounting for punctuation could disrupt the Markov chain, because words do not share any semantic connection with the punctuation adjoining them. Accordingly, where our algorithm generated a poem that seems to demand a punctuation mark, we have inserted one.

12 Almost all of the "good" poems our algorithm produces are very short. This makes sense given how Markov chains work: the longer the poem, the greater the likelihood of randomly linking a word that doesn't fit with the previous words.

13 Poems like this can occur for a variety of reasons: imperfections in our sample (due to non-English poems slipping through the cracks), imperfections in our technology (due to our OCR script failing to accurately read the words in the poem, or interpreting nontextual elements of an image as letters), or both.

14 This piece by Bucknell sparked a backlash among fans of the genre. Katie Ailes, for instance, lambasted Bucknell's "sneering tone" and alleged reliance on "racist, sexist, classist, and prejudiced stereotypes" (Ailes 2020). Unlike Bucknell, we have no wish to assess Instapoetry's normative value; instead, we attempt to characterize what goes on when people produce and consume Instapoetry. And we believe Bucknell offers insight on that topic.

References

Ailes, Katie. 2020. "'Instapoetry' in the LRB: Toward a Better Criticism of Popular Poetics." *KatieAiles.com*, May 21. Available online: https://katieailes.com/2020/05/21/instapoetry-in-the-lrb-towards-a-better-criticism-of-popular-poetics/. Accessed January 23, 2023.

Baudrillard, Jean. 1968. "The System of Objects." In *Jean Baudrillard: Selected Writings*, edited by Mark Poster, and trans. Jacques Mourrain, 12–28. Stanford: Stanford University Press.

Baudrillard, Jean. 1981. *For a Critique of the Political Economy of the Sign*, trans. Charles Levin. London: Verso Books.

Baudrillard, Jean. 1987. "Beyond the Vanishing Point of Art." In *Post-Pop Art*, edited by Paul Taylor, and trans. Paul Foss, 171–89. Cambridge, MA: The M.I.T. Press.

Baudrillard, Jean. 1988. *Simulation and Simulacra*, trans. S. Glaser. Ann Arbor: University of Michigan Press.

Broglio, Ron. 2008. *Technologies of the Picturesque: British Art, Poetry, and Instruments, 1750-1830*. Lewisburg: Bucknell University Press.

Bucknell, Claire. 2020. "Instapoetry." *London Review of Books*, 42 (10). Available online: https://www.lrb.co.uk/the-paper/v42/n10/clare-bucknell/instapoetry. Accessed January 23, 2023.

Caputo, John D. 1997. *Deconstruction in a Nutshell: A Conversation with Jacques Derrida*, 3rd edn. New York: Fordham University Press.

D'Agostino, Susan. 2023. "Designing Assignments in the ChatGPT Era." *Inside Higher Ed*, January 31. Available online: https://www.insidehighered.com/news/2023/01/31/chatgpt-sparks-debate-how-design-student-assignments-now. Accessed February 1, 2023.

Deleuze, Gilles and Felix Guattari. 1987. *A Thousand Plateaus : Capitalism and Schizophrenia*, trans. Brian Massumi. Minneapolis: University of Minnesota Press.

Edwards, Samantha. 2017. "How Instapoetry Is Changing the Way We Read Look at Poems." *Fashion Magazine*, December 18. Available online: https://fashionmagazine.com/culture/instapoetry/. Accessed January 23, 2023.

Ganegedara, Thushan. 2018. "Intuitive Guide to Latent Dirichlet Allocation." *Towards Data Science*, August 23. Available online: https://towardsdatascience.com/light-on-math-machine-learning-intuitive-guide-to-latent-dirichlet-allocation-437c81220158/. Accessed January 23, 2023.

Gibson, William. 1989. *Neuromancer*. New York: Berkley Publishing Group.

Hayles, N. Katherine. 2008. "Distributed Cognition at/in Work: Strickland, Lawson Jaramillo, and Ryan's *seippingglimpse*." *Frame*, 21 (1): 15–29.

Kruger, Sasha. 2017. "The Technopo(e)Litics of Rupi Kaur: (De)Colonial AestheTics and Spatial Narrations in the DigiFemme Age." *Ada: A Journal of Gender, New Media, and Technology*, 11. Available online: https://scholarsbank.uoregon.edu/xmlui/handle/1794/26772. Accessed January 23, 2023.

Lederman, Marsha. 2017. "Meet Atticus, the Most Famous Canadian Poet You've Never Heard Of." *The Globe and Mail*, July 19. Available online: https://www.theglobeandmail.com/arts/books-and-media/meet-atticus-the-most-famous-canadian-poet-youve-never-heard-of/article35730003/. Accessed January 23, 2023.

Lloyd, Andrew. 2019. "I Faked My Way as an Instagram Poet, and It Went Bizarrely Well." *Vice News*, September 12. Available online: https://www.vice.com/en/article/zmjmj3/instagram-poetry-become-successful-scam. Accessed January 23, 2023.

Lucas, George (Dir). 2005. *Star Wars: Episode III—Revenge of the Sith*. USA: Lucasfilm Ltd.

Matthews, Kristin L. 2019. "'Woke' and Reading: Social Media, Reception, and Contemporary Black Feminism." *Participations Journal of Audience & Reception Studies*, 16 (1): 390–411.

Miller, Alyson. 2019. "'Poetry's Beyoncé': On Rupi Kaur and the Commodifying Effects of Instapoetics." *Axon: Creative Explorations*, 9 (1): 1–2.

Poetzsch, Markus. 2008. "Ron Broglio, Technologies of the Picturesque: British Art, Poetry, and Instruments 1750–1830." *Wordsworth Circle*, 39 (4): 178.

Rue, James M. 2019. "The Future of Poetry in the Digital Era-Instapoetry and Remediation," MA thesis, Utrecht University.

Sin, r.h. 2017. "Top 5 Best Selling #poetry Books via @barnesandnoble." *Facebook*, February 19. Available online: https://www.facebook.com/RHSinWrites/photos/top-5-best-selling-poetry-books-via-barnesandnoble-the-big-3-tomorrow-is-the-las/1210468429061325/. Accessed January 23, 2023.

Sin, r.h. 2023. [@r.h.Sin]. 2023. [Instagram profile]. *Instagram*. Available online: https://www.instagram.com/r.h.sin/?hl=en. Accessed March 9, 2021.

Soni, Devin. 2018. "Introduction to Markov Chains." *towards data science*, March 5. Available online: https://towardsdatascience.com/introduction-to-markov-chains-50da3645a50d. Accessed January 23, 2023.

Tang, Dennis. 2020. "The Machines Are Coming, and They Write Really Bad Poetry." *Lithub*, January 27. Available online: https://lithub.com/the-machines-are-coming-and-they-write-really-bad-poetry/. Accessed January 23, 2023.

Twain, Mark. 1884. *The Adventures of Huckleberry Finn*. New York: Harper and Brothers.

Urobuchi, Gen. 2011. *Psycho-Pass* [TV program].

11

How to Be a Successful #instapoet: Defying Jean Baudrillard's Hyperreal with Marketing Strategies Based on Hollie McNish

Melissa Sarikaya
Friedrich-Alexander-Universität Erlangen-Nürnberg

Introduction

Academic research on Instapoetry predominantly focuses on the evolution of Instapoets and finding key characteristics to define the genre. The discussion of whether Instapoetry is a serious art form or an internet phenomenon to gain followers has also been a substantial field of academic attention along with the accusatory discussion of the capitalist side of publishing Instapoetry. Instapoets face harsh criticism for their online presence and are called out because of their self-marketing strategies. The inherent judgment of contemptible (self-)marketing, however, clashes with the assertion of the economic belief that marketing is necessary, even beneficial as an exchange between two partners (the customer and the marketing agent) who share the joint value of enriching the customer's life. Satisfying the customer needs is key (Drummond and Ensor 2005: 2; Kotler and Keller 2016: 25; Armstrong et al. 2017: 5–6)—and not a red flag for a deficient product. Good marketing is as vital as a good product.

The purpose of this chapter is to analyze marketing strategies commonly employed by Instapoets to produce their authenticity on a supposedly shallow platform like Instagram. My post-structuralist approach is a hybrid of Jean Baudrillard's theory of the hyperreal and an economic turn to marketing strategies on Instagram. I will apply those ideas to Hollie McNish, a writer with 83,200 followers as of 2021, who is winning her online and offline readers with her reputation as an accessible and honest poet. Instapoets' success in maintaining a genuine image can be explained by bursting Instagram's hyperreal bubble.

Instapoetry has often been defined as a brief and simplistic form of poetry, derogatively as an artless form, with its key features being repetitions and iterations as well as a plagiarized and cliché language (Watts 2018; Berens 2019; Edmond 2019: 2; Chasar 2020: 190–1).[1] Rebecca Watts's infamous *PN Review* denying Instapoets any artistic or cultural value, demonizing them for their honesty and accessibility and Soraya Roberts's denunciation of Instapoetry as poor with the premise of quality over quantity are just some instances of gatekeepers eagerly erasing Instapoets from their elite world of letters (Roberts 2018; Watts 2018). Yet, instead of evaluating the quality of Instapoetry, with a case study on Hollie McNish this chapter investigates the strategies Instapoets employ to resonate with their audience.

My argument is that Instapoets employ the (marketing) strategy of bursting the hyperreal Insta-bubble by deliberately referring to the offline persona to constitute their authenticity online while forging the online personality to match the poets' desired offline image. I do not scorn Instapoets for claiming online authenticity using marketing strategies but I want to emphasize how Instagram is a platform that plays along similar rules as economic-based enterprises in the "real" world.

Hollie McNish's Label as an Authentic Instapoet

Hollie McNish is an award-winning poet with five published books, which are also advertised on her Instagram profile's bio. She was granted the prestigious Ted Hughes Award for her book *Nobody Told Me* (2016). Although this chapter focuses on McNish's Instagram platform, she resists the label of "Instapoet," since she is a spoken word artist and performance poet, and also shares visual poetry recordings on YouTube. With *Nobody Told Me* (2016) and *Slug and Other Things I've been Told to Hate* (2021), McNish expands into the realm of prose writing. Her work *Cherry Pie* (2015) especially stresses her multidimensional facets as a writer-artist and is probably the most performative of her poetry books.[2]

Hollie McNish is generally perceived as a candid poet with humorous and personal works. McNish is a fan of Instagram because it is a democratic way of sharing poetry and a valuable platform to make poetry more accessible (Brown 2014; O'Keeffe 2017; Evans 2020). The core principle of inclusivity is evident in McNish's addition of image descriptions to her Instagram posts. Her poetry is accessible both physically through online distribution and mentally through a relatively simple language. She transgresses taboos, for instance, by writing about the female body, female sexual pleasure, misogyny, racism, and homophobia, but keeps the poetry relatable and witty. McNish's niche is to verbalize the hushed-up and therefore constructs her reputation as an authentic artist—in other words: she is "real." Yet, how does that connect to a reality that is more and more taking place online?

Jean Baudrillard's Hyperreal and Instagram

Jean Baudrillard, the "high priest of postmodernism" (Gane, Mike "Introduction," in: Baudrillard 1993: X), associated today's world with a tech-fetishism as early as 1968 in *Le Système des Objets*, and it is a phenomenon that Baudrillard kept studying throughout his works (Baudrillard 2003: 43; 2005). According to Baudrillard, each period is governed by a specific schema—*simulacrum*—which expresses the time's law of value. Baudrillard initially identifies three levels, the *Order of Simulacra*. From the Renaissance onwards, primarily, the natural law of value was *counterfeit*, hence the guiding principle was *mimesis*, an exact replication of the real item or world. The Industrial Era modified the goal of exact replication into a mass production of the item. The market law of value in *production* weighs higher than the exact replication, leading to blurry lines between reality and its representation. The dominant schema in today's code-governed phase is *simulation* (Baudrillard 1993: 50). Each law of value is subsumed in following the order. In later works, Baudrillard adds a fourth level to the Order of Simulacra, in which there is no relation to reality whatsoever. Therefore, the fourth state is equal to a loss of the real.

This loss is particularly immanent in today's obsession with online platforms. Along with Walter Benjamin, Marshall McLuhan was one of the first to acknowledge the immense force of technology as a medium, which is also the starting point for our code-driven generation today. Characteristic of today's simulacrum is its indeterminacy of genetic codes, digitality in every area and reliance on programs. The strife toward the "smallest indivisible element" with the credo of cellular entities is the ultimate goal (Baudrillard 1993: 56–9). We are ruled by a cybernetic system that relies on binary codes, particularly the principle of question/answer mimics the dual digital code of stimulus/response. This leads to a vanishing of actual interrogative questions resulting in pre-designed

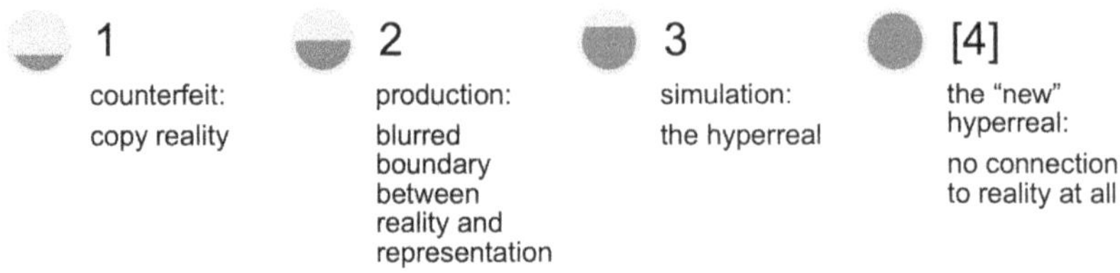

Figure 11.1 Schema of Baudrillard's Order of Simulacrum with the four levels of simulacra. Author's own image, 2023.

questions to fit the response mechanisms. Thus, meaning dissolves into a prescripted system that equals polling statistics (Baudrillard 1993: 62–3).[3]

The foundation of today's code-structured society is illusory tactile simulation. The necessities for a deceptively real simulation are thus contact, sensory mimicry, and tactile mysticism to create the illusion of an entire ecology (Baudrillard 1993: 71). Because all of these generate an operational simulation, Baudrillard calls this state the *hyperreal.* It is a reproduction equivalent to the real, but actually not real itself because "[i]t is the generation by models of a real without origin or reality" (Baudrillard 1983: 2). The signs of reality have become the substitutes for the real, in that signs are used to represent reality, but this representation is incomplete and reductive; ultimately with no relation to reality after all (Baudrillard 1983: 4, 11). To be precise, the reproduction is already governed by the hyperreal. Baudrillard argues that our entire reality is hyperrealist (Baudrillard 1993: 73), resulting in a reality, "whereby *the reversal becomes irrelevant*" (Lane 2009: 84). To "bring a new world into being is in itself to produce that world, and the real has only ever been a form of simulation" (Baudrillard 2003: 41). The simulation is a transcendence from the real into the imaginary. This hyperreal state of imaginary reality is homogenized, digitized, and operationalized, for instance in binary question/answer structures. This "perfect" but illusionary hyperreality is more "complete," for it is more structured, neater, and tidier than reality, and thus seemingly more real (Baudrillard 2003: 41–5).

Where can Instagram be located on Baudrillard's Order of Simulacra? If reality serves as the basis, hence a zero within Baudrillard's Order of Simulacra, then me trying to find an adequate representation of the world, for instance a globe-emoticon (cf. Figure 11.2), shows that I cannot even fit the world into this model. The globe-emoticon is already a second-order simulacrum. There is a blurry boundary between the emoticon and the world enhancing only certain features, for instance this representation focuses on America, neglecting other continents. But there are other stresses: the earth as a globe, blue and green color scheme, shadows, etc. This unsuccessful substitution of the world with a correspondent emoticon shows that a mimetic representation of the world's complexity is impossible.

Instagram supposedly represents actual people, but the internet is already an entire separate alternate world, to which not every human being has or wants access. Thus, Instagram, as a social media platform of the World Wide Web is a fourth-order simulacrum. Profiles on Instagram cannot represent the real "self." The self-portrayal is random, at times even fake (e.g., fake profiles, fake likes, or bought followers). Thus, I argue that scrolling through the Insta-feed equals an immersion into a pseudo-real hyperrealist platform. Still, Instagram is satisfying because humans crave simplicity (Baudrillard's term is "primitivity"). The hyperreal symbolizes a desire to return to a simplified reality. Humans like things to be simple, ordered, structured—which Instagram allegedly offers.

Figure 11.2 Emoticon of the globe showing insufficiency in mimetic representation. Author's own image, 2023.

What we can take from here is that Instagram is hyperreal. Instagram's appeal is to suggest simplicity and order. Users crave realness on Instagram to uphold the illusion of Instagram as a model of the real world. Therefore, Instagrammers cultivating the illusion of verisimilitude in their profile are more successful in omitting the accusation of shallowness. To claim credibility, Instapoets employ marketing strategies, which I will now take a closer look at.

Case Study: Strategies to Defy the Hyperreal

Social media platforms open up a new sphere for marketing. Today's internet is called Web 2.0 and indicates a shift in the online world, particularly on social media, toward more interactive user-centricity instead of publisher-centricity. Interactive marketing enables a bilateral communication between customers and companies (e.g., feedback) (Wilcox, Cameron, and Reber 2015: 360–3; Kingsnorth 2016: 31–2; Quesenberry 2019: 8–15). With the rise of more lifestyle Insta-influencers, the pressure increases to establish a channel as an appealing visual brand to resonate with followers. Essential marketing strategies for both private users and the "big players" on Instagram are, for instance, a consistent color palette and upload schedule, which help with the aesthetics and follower numbers of profiles. Likewise, Instapoets are employing strategies of visual branding due to the rising awareness of an online presence. Rupi Kaur, Instagram's Poet Laureate, wisely applies visual branding (utilizing lower-case spelling, presenting delicate pictures of herself) on her Instagram channel, which probably contributes to her major success (Leszkiewicz 2019).

In the article "No Filter," Soraya Roberts criticizes Instapoets for their capitalist and commercial purposes and even calls out Rupi Kaur's writing as "poetry of capitalism." Roberts states that the feel-good atmosphere celebrated on Instagram intentionally encourages prodigal purchases. This hostility toward Instapoets, particularly regarding their high sales numbers, is often to be found in critics who intend to discuss the quality of Instapoetry. Lilli Pâquet, a scholar who identifies Instapoetry as a hybrid between poetry and self-help and studies Instapoetry's ekphrastic characteristics, states that "self-branding allows [Instapoets] to appear authentic by giving readers more immediate access to the authors, but at the same time it can appear commercially necessary for authors bypassing traditional gatekeepers" (Pâquet 2019: 301). Instapoetry's minimalism pleases the masses—so much that their writers perform incredibly well in book sales records. While critics may scorn these success stories, marketing experts delight in them. These writers manage to overcome the hyperrealist barrier and sell their work outside of Instagram in the real world. Their recipe is dissemination through marketing strategies.

In an Insta-world of followers and algorithms, it's hard out there for Instapoets to recruit their devotees. The content that generates more likes and followers tends to be pursued more vigorously. Hashtags are a common means to attract new followers and discover new profiles. Of course, Instagram's algorithms for promoting content relating to a certain hashtag are deliberately obscure. Instapoets usually promote their content with well-known but dull hashtags such as #poetry (over 57 million posts) and #poetsofinstagram (over 15 million posts) simply to generate more followers. Yet, that hashtags are a common way to navigate one's way through the endless waters of content (Quesenberry 2019: 148) is often ignored. However, Hollie McNish's eschewal of hashtags resists categorization and labeling, relying on the audience to figure out the content. Although McNish refrains from Instagram's game of hashtags, she promotes her account in a more "traditional" manner of marketing. In the following, I link McNish's Instagram to common marketing strategies meant to achieve accessibility and authenticity.

Audience as Follower-Consumers

Kevin Stein argues in *Poetry's Afterlife* (2010) that the way art is encountered shapes its significance. Today's greatest technological advancement is to overcome the need of physical proximity in order to enjoy art. The ability to access everything on affordable smart devices frees users from physical and local restraints. Art can now be experienced conveniently on the couch. Poetry lovers can listen to readings, watch performances, and with click-and-buy even purchase poetry (e-)books without leaving the house. These options create intimacy when absorbing art (Stein 2013: 89–90).

In consuming Instapoetry, intimacy is created by entangling followers wherever they want to be with their smartphones. This supposed intimacy between content producers and followers is constantly reestablished with posts, uploads, and particularly with the popular Snapchat-inspired feature of sharing stories that last up to twenty-four hours. Helicopter-poets can constantly buzz around followers' minds with limitless poetry consumption. Instagram as a concealed simulacrum is equivalent to an alternate reality. This new reality calls for a new role. Poets' audiences are no longer just consumers; their role instead shifts into a more active one. Therefore, I introduce the term "follower-consumer" because of the dual role of an Instapoet's audience. First, they are "following" the poet by subscribing to their content. Second, more implicitly and less intendedly, they automatically become "consumers" who are expected to leave more than just a like. And the follower-consumers happily oblige, e.g., by asking to sponsor McNish on platforms like Patreon or donate money to help advance her career.

Through daily updates—and in some cases hourly reminders of their solidarity through the story feature on Instagram—follower-consumers morph into becoming a part of an Instapoet's supporting base. Through easily digestible poetry resonating with the users' beliefs, the follower-consumers slide into increasing accordance with the Instapoet. However, studies on participatory culture have shown that by purchasing, people are more likely to identify as advocates of a cause, rather than receiving services for free (Mahoney and Tang 2017: 65). Active participation—either by purchasing, or by actively engaging with an Instapoet's site (e.g., by tagging, commenting, or liking)—is one of the main pillars of marketing strategy. If a brand becomes so popular among its consumers that they advertise the brand among their peers, those satisfied consumers become deliberate brand ambassadors. Hence, the brand can refrain from self-advertisement because word-of-mouth advertisement from peers is generally perceived as more credible than a brand's self-advertising. Thus, the consumers' active participation in promoting the brand is one of the most effective strategies to gain new consumers. In Hollie McNish's case, she can deliberately rely on her follower-consumers to spread the lyric word. While McNish mostly passively relies on her followers to tag and share her posts, at times she also actively encourages her followers to do so. Many comments even offer to spread the words by reposting or tagging other people.

On a Baudrillardian note, this means that in the midst of living in an alternate universe detached from reality (fourth-order simulacrum), Instagram users acquire a new identity congruent with their profile. This leads to a new social role of the follower-consumer, who actively engages with sites that the self advocates for. The aim is to encourage hyperreal follower-consumers to participate on Instagram and to eventually slide them off Instagram into real-life profitable consumers. Thus, an Instapoet's key concept is to take consumers off Instagram into the real world. Therefore, self-promotion is linked to real-life items, such as books, shows, tours, and readings (products that McNish also advertises on her

Instagram channel). Instapoets' followers involuntarily become consumers. To enhance the consumerist aspect or side-effect of Instapoetry, I will use the term "follower-consumer" to bring this double effect into mind.

Audience-Targeted Widespread Dissemination

Marketing works best if it is audience-targeted but still reaches a large crowd. Thanks to social media, these two dialectic approaches can be united: consumers identify with messages seemingly applying to them individually rather than being directed at a homogeneous group. Social media efficiently disseminates outwardly personal messages that are in fact spread into the vast world of potential follower-consumers (Mahoney and Tang 2017: 14). Therefore, the masquerade of seeming confidential while reaching a mass audience is a typical pattern on Instagram. What drives Instapoets to spill their supposedly private lives so bluntly? And why does their audience cherish this?

Macha Louis Rosenthal coined the term "confessional poetry," an expression for the shared feeling of aspiring poets that their writing is a product of their own "soul's therapy." Instead of a Romanticist course of hiding the personal behind a curtain of universal emotions, modern writers de-mask "the poet's actual face and psyche," resulting in a blunt and direct sharing of the poet's self (Rosenthal 1960: 226–8). This maskless confession is also apparent in contemporary poetry's self-presentation—particularly on social media platforms. The lens of social media is biased because of the strife to present oneself in the best light to survive in today's tech-society. On the one hand the "private face" is what people actually feel, whereas on the other the "public face" is how people present themselves to the outside world and this public self-presentation aims for perfection, for instance through endless editing (Valkenburg and Piotrowski 2017: 218).

The psychologists Duane Buhrmester and Karen Prager argue that the two guiding principles of communication in (pre-)adolescence are self-presentation and self-disclosure (Buhrmester and Prager 1995: 33–4), in which "[s]elf-presentation is the presenting of aspects of identity within the normative standards of a certain audience [and] [s]elf-disclosure is the sharing of intimate information, also according to the normative standards within a certain group" (Valkenburg and Piotrowski 2017: 221). Equivalently, users need to balance their self-presentation and self-disclosure of their public face on social media. Fans and followers have a constant craving for their idols' self-disclosure; the more intimate the details, the better. However, to maintain mental and physical health, Instagrammers and influencers try to establish a pattern of self-presentation. Yet, if the self-presentation remains too superficial, followers might lose interest, resulting in decreasing follower numbers. Kevin Stein diagnoses modern-day society with a "restless call for attention," and it is the media that satisfies this "human craving." This has a double effect: the individual's yearning for attention is satisfied while the audience's voyeuristic desire to pry is fulfilled. The first is a sign of today's "primary narcissism," which is "a core ingredient of one's mental health." The need for external validation is what drives humans into online exposure (Stein 2013: 92–8). Social media suggests the illusion of control with the aim of maintaining psychological privacy (the "possibility to control when, what, to whom and how" private information is shared) (Valkenburg and Piotrowski 2017: 222–3). Hollie McNish is very private with certain topics such as her daughter (who remains anonymous) and her home (which McNish avoids to exhibit). In opposition to her privateness her autobiographic poetry is highly confessional; it is about romantic and non-romantic relationships, self and body image, sexual intercourse, and masturbation. McNish balances self-disclosure and privacy in sharing her intimate poetry while strategically keeping other private topics off Instagram. Thus, her psychological privacy is not endangered. The captions under her Instagram posts often reveal how McNish juggles self-disclosure and privacy. For instance, one caption reads: "For the person asking for this poem from last week's gig. It was written a while ago for anyone else who wants to be a grandkid again." This is followed by self-marketing of her printed work: "It's not in any book but will be in Slug" (McNish 2020). The poem accompanying this caption deals with the loss of grandparents. McNish manages to stay in the sphere of individualized personal connection while widely sharing the experience of grief with her followers. It also sends the message that she sees and acknowledges every single person/follower-consumer. McNish's messages/poems are soaked up by her follower-consumers, as they celebrate McNish's ability to touch their emotions while often directly addressing McNish and hoping for an individual response to their comment.

Certain aspects can be concealed on a hyperreal platform because a new agency and personality are created. Reality on the internet may be constructed according to the created hyperreal personality balancing privacy and (over-)sharing. The masquerade in the hyperreal sphere allows for a discrepancy between the private face and the public, confessional, self-disclosed online face.

Interaction and Transaction

According to Meghan L. Mahoney and Tang Tang, who investigate the role of social media and its influence on users in *Strategic Social Media* (2017), the three cardinal functions of social media are "diffusing information, providing a sense of community for audiences, and mobilizing users into action" (Mahoney and Tang 2017: 2). Through social media, audiences or consumers are rather active users who participate and engage in sculpting the social media platform. Crucial for the success of social media platforms is their interactive and transactional nature (Mahoney and Tang 2017: 9–15). The appeal of Instagram for poets lies in its community and interactivity, particularly regarding feedback on their work (Kovalik and Curwood 2019).

Instagram nurtures the idea(l) of community by offering interactive tools on Instagram (liking, commenting, reacting, tagging). Of course, the community on Instagram is just a simulacrum. From an economic perspective, the user-interaction is supposed to result in profitable transaction. By engaging with the follower-consumers on a pseudo-same level, the real agenda remains obscure. Instagram naturally aligns with today's expectations of a transactional mode of communication. One can immediately interact with an Instagram story or post, creating an illusion of intimacy. Hollie McNish, however, engages with her follower-consumers through her captions, while staying silent on her followers' comments. Nevertheless, her devotees share their personal stories and information. The narcissistic craving of sharing also applies to the follower-consumers. They are eager to be "seen" within the Instapoet's community. The Instapoet's platform is constructed as a safe space where confidentialities may be exchanged such as intimacies on various topics ranging from childbirth, to aging, to death. The illusion of psychological privacy encourages follower-consumers to also let others consume their privacy.

Social networking is very important in marketing, as humans trust people who are like themselves more (Strauss and Frost 2014: 225). Hence, a transactional goal is to engage follower-consumers in marketing their lauded Instapoet. When poetry-lovers tag other people (or rather: hyperreal profiles) below a comment, they are more likely to check out McNish's poetry, compared to Instapoets vigorously trying to advertise their poetry themselves. McNish connects with her follower-consumers through captions. Of course, the communication between Instapoet and follower-consumer is less bilateral than it seems. Instead, the internet obscures the simulacra of meaningful interactions. McNish skillfully detaches herself from the hyperreal Insta-world in referring back to the real world, for instance with her emotions: "Writing poems has always helped me sort out my thoughts. These were thoughts about grief I wrote a while back" (McNish 2020). At other times McNish refers to in-person gigs and even involves her audience, such as in asking for recommendations when hosting an event in Barcelona. McNish sometimes even interacts with people who were at the shows, and thus subverts the hyperreal with allusions to the real. To successfully blend the real and the hyperreal, it is essential to build a consistent narrative.

Transparency and Narrative

The Instapoet's projected personality is key to whether a profile will be successful or not. Nevertheless, the danger of an Instapoet's fugacity is real. In a time of multitasking as the new credo, people's ability to pay attention to a single thing over a longer period of time decreases. Thus, the poetry is only shortly pondered upon before the next post pops up. Users lose the capacity for perpetual focus. Does that make Insta-poetry rather superficial?

Kevin Stein, fathoming poetry's role in the digital age, addresses the new mode of attention in which distraction has become the primary aesthetic reception of art because the lines are constantly blurred. He calls this new state the "polyfocal-attention-dis-traction." Stein concludes in the end that a "surprising efficiency," thanks to users' ability to multitask, can often be detected (Stein 2013: 101–2). This means that follower-consumers' ability of efficient polyfocal attention due to high-frequent use of the internet will acknowledge a poem's value of comprising meaningful exchange in a few poetry lines. Instapoets are experts at grabbing their follower-consumers' short-lived and widely spread attention by weaving them into their personal narrative. It is essential to have a brand and to keep the values aligned through a consistent personality ultimately resulting in credibility (Kingsnorth 2016: 37).

Another feature of Instapoetry is the possibility to explain poems in the posts' captions, thus steering the reader's attention into a favorable direction. Sharing personal stories is in fact a key feature for transparency in order to create one's own (company) narrative (Mahoney and Tang 2017: 29–33), and Instagram as a social media platform is an excellent space to tell brand stories (Quesenberry 2019: 22). Successful marketing is to share personal narratives since audiences will then identify with the story, which enables authenticity and claiming a niche in the market (Mahoney and Tang 2017: 57). In the case of McNish, her open honesty about her situation, daily struggles, and work process let her follower-consumers relate to this otherwise remote hyperreal Insta-person. McNish weaves her narratives of credibility by deliberately pointing to artificiality (e.g., by calling her poetry "scribble" and giving contexts to the origins of the writing). During lockdown, McNish established some live Insta-readings to replace her gigs on tours. The readings were often advertised with photos of the aesthetically pleasing comfort of the improvised living room "stage" but hinting toward its fakeness (e.g., "All set up now" [McNish 2020]). The hypertidy-Marie-Kondo[4]-Insta aesthetic McNish used for the readings might not be unusual for Instagram, but it is for McNish, as she often stresses the struggle to balance all of her social roles as a "wife," "worker," "lover," and "mother" (Instagram post of McNish 2020). By pointing out fakeness, McNish proves her authenticity and reclaims credibility by undermining Instagram's hyperreality in reminding her follower-consumers that the neat picture that is often displayed online is "just a show."

Likewise, to claim reliability, McNish posts photos from her computer screen with typos, the visible mouse, and the ongoing formatting process. The oftentimes rather poorly shot images create a tempting atmosphere of authenticity. While these photos seem as if taken and posted in a hurry, undeniably though it is McNish's conscious choice what and when to upload on her Instagram channel. Posts like these reclaim mimetic first-order representation, which is of course an endeavor doomed to fail. Nevertheless, stressing fakeness and Instagram's un-reality, McNish enhances her own relatability by subverting Instagram's simulacrum with glimpses into real-world projects. Particularly with the recent publication of *Slug*, McNish mobilized her follower-consumers' forces into buying her book—a major success that ranked her on the *Sunday Times* Bestseller List. She understands the significance of referring to the real outside of the hyperreal Insta-platform.

Selling an Idea/Lifestyle

Consumers favor brands whose ideas are in line with their lifestyle. A consumer's lifestyle counts into psychographic variables of audience-targeted marketing strategies (Drummond and Ensor 2005: 75; Strauss and Frost 2014: 224–5; Kingsnorth 2016: 25; Armstrong et al. 2017: 241; Quesenberry 2019: 61). Ever since the emergence of social marketing in the 1970s, marketing experts figured that consumers react positively toward a product if it is in line with their lifestyle, reinforcing existing beliefs, opinions, and patterns (Wilcox, Cameron, and Reber 2015: 270; Mahoney and Tang 2017: 14). Thus, it is vital to sell an idea or a lifestyle choice surviving once taken home, rather than a purposeless product. And what better way to exhibit modern feminist, liberal choices by showcasing one's bookshelves and gig tickets, or a casual poetry book lying on the coffee table? These signs of conspicuous consumption are markers of a self-fashioning habitus. Thus, McNish's marketing strategy is very successful: Through self-focused messages she refrains from forcefully pushing herself upon potential follower-consumers. The follower-consumers then identify with Hollie McNish on an imaginary personal level (although of course, real personal proximity is impossible through a hyperreal mass medium like Instagram). McNish confidingly advertises her ideas to her follower-consumers. This imagined personal link may be brought home—by buying affordable poetry books showcased as physical representations of lifestyle choices. Through Insta-engagement, the illusion of solidarity toward Hollie McNish and her poetry topics is created. The constructed online persona influences the real offline person. In solidarizing with McNish, the follower-consumer becomes an assimilated open-minded, feminist, liberal, and confident person. Daily Instagram updates and poetry books showcased at home remind the follower- and real-life-consumers of these principles. The advertised poetry books are purchasable reminders that the proclaimed lifestyle and ideas are "real" and that she is not a hyperreal, non-realistic simulacrum.

Positive Reinforcement

One goal of marketing is to ensure that the product is positively reinforced continuously and in different places (online, in retail stores, and at home) (Wilcox, Cameron, and Reber 2015; Mahoney and Tang 2017: 14). Positive reinforcement ensues every time McNish posts content agreeing with the follower-consumers' lifestyle choices as well as their ideas (Drummond and Ensor 2005: 73; Kotler and Keller 2016: 340–1; Armstrong et al. 2017: 211–2).[5] McNish's retail store is Instagram, and her follower-consumers enter it multiple times a day to check for updates. Just in case the follower-consumers forgot, the poems originate from her books—of course available for purchase to guarantee positive reinforcement in the bookshelf. Mike Chasar, author of *Poetry Unbound* (2020), the latest book on the phenomenon of poetry emerging from the bookish sphere into a globalized transmedial world by studying different examples, argues that one of the new liberties gained by Instapoets is their "leveraging digital interfaces to become best sellers." Implicitly, publishing poetry has an economic purpose. Instapoets nourish "the desire to recapture an authentic originality and to locate and curate source texts that are unencumbered by traditional authorship" (Chasar 2020: 76, 184, 190). The hyperreal can only be escaped by real-world engagement, such as going to poetry gigs, buying poetry books, or sharing poetry with real-life friends (though Instagram's tagging options once more conceal the hyperreal simulacrum of friendship interaction).

Conclusion: Further Strategies to #stayreal

Apart from these marketing strategies, McNish also employs other strategies to escape the hyperreal. Posting fragments from her writing process in the form of little notes, or adding snippets of the pages of her text-editing systems, allows McNish to include her follower-consumers into the evolution of a poem. The spelling mistakes and typos that can be found in her captions and poems contribute to her effortless social media appearance. McNish also engages in public and global topics, an element which was particularly dominant in her pieces about coping with the lockdown due to the COVID-19 pandemic, as well as the movement Black Lives Matter and #justiceforgeorgefloyd. McNish's self-affiliation by having a mixed-race daughter is usually a topic she prefers to leave sealed, however, she felt the need to speak out in light of emerging racism. The mix of poetry and poetry-non-related content results in seemingly genuine content, which strategically builds on the follower-consumers' trust.

In fact, all the items just listed are strategies to escape a detachment from reality. However, in a Baudrillardian approach, these are just symptoms for an already lost realm of the real. Instagram as a web-based app is inevitably a simulacrum. Although Instagram's filter-culture and face-tuning apps are highly popular, there is a craving for "realness" on Instagram (e.g., #nofilter with over 284 million posts). The desire for tearing up the hyperreal state is evident in the trend toward defying digitality in cherishing digital anonymity. Hollie McNish avoids Instagram's fourth-order virtual common playground by not obeying the generic rules of lifestyle influencers (e.g., avoiding hashtags, focus on poetry and words instead of selfies and images). By reclaiming authenticity and producing intimacy on a hyperreal platform like Instagram, she uses her own marketing strategies to establish herself as a "real" person outside of Instagram.

This subversion of a hyperreal simulacrum is only successful if the interaction between poet and audience transcends the hyperreal medium into actual engagement in the "real" world. However, more likely, the follower-consumer will not transgress the hyperreal state remaining in the simulacrum of (online) intimacy.

Notes

1 Therefore, Instapoetry is also prone to parody (Pâquet 2019: 301), cf. Andrew Lloyd's social experiment in how quickly followers can be gained by faking an Instapoetry account (Lloyd 2018).
2 Besides rhythmic poetry, *Cherry Pie* consists of recipes, illustrations, and intertextual references to pop music culture. Throughout the book, its title is deconstructed into ambiguous symbols that need to be deciphered.
3 Here is an example: When I contacted the flight companies to receive a refund for my canceled flights due to the COVID-pandemic, their websites had scripted responses, thus, only specific questions could be asked. A website's FAQs are also a perfect example: since the answers are already given, the dynamics of language dissolve in pre-formatted questions.
4 Marie Kondo is famous for her minimalist interior design. Her fans love her decluttering tips and her catch phrase: "Does it spark joy?"—if the item in question does not, one is supposed to get rid of it.
5 Positive reinforcement is a learned stimulus of consumer behavior (Armstrong et al. 2017: 211–12).

References

Armstrong, Gary, Philip Kotler, Valerie Trifts, Lilly Anne Buchwitz, and David Gaudet. 2017. *Marketing: An Introduction*. 6th ed. Toronto: Pearson.

Baudrillard, Jean. 1983. *Simulations*, trans. Paul Foss Paul Patton and Philip Beichtman. New York: Foreign Agents Series, Semiotext(e).

Baudrillard, Jean. 1993. *Symbolic Exchange and Death*, trans. Iain Hamilton Grant. London: SAGE Publications.

Baudrillard, Jean. 2003. *Passwords*, trans. Chris Turner. London and New York: Verso.

Baudrillard, Jean. 2005. *The System of Objects*, trans. James Benedict. London and New York: Verso.

Berens, Kathi Inman. 2019. "E-Lit's #1 Hit: Is Instagram Poetry E-literature?" PDXScholar. electronicbookreview.com/essay/e-lits-1-hit-is-instagram-poetry-e-literature/. Accessed May 14, 2021.
Brown, Rivkah. 2014. "Interview: Hollie McNish." *Varsity*, Last Modified March 12, 2014. https://www.varsity.co.uk/culture/7041. Accessed May 20, 2021.
Buhrmester, Duane, and Karen Prager. 1995. "Patterns and Functions of Self-disclosure during Childhood and Adolescence." In *Disclosure Processes in Children and Adolescents*, edited by Ken J. Rotenberg, 10–56. Cambridge: Cambridge University Press.
Chasar, Mike. 2020. *Poetry Unbound. Poems and New Media from the Magic Lantern to Instagram*. New York: Columbia University Press.
Drummond, Graeme, and John Ensor. 2005. *Introduction to Marketing Concepts*. Amsterdam: Elsevier.
Edmond, Jacob. 2019. *Make It the Same. Poetry in the Age of Global Media*. New York: Columbia University Press.
Evans, Louise. 2020. "The Candid Works of Instapoet Hollie McNish." *Brizo*, Last Modified October 19, 2020. https://brizomagazine.com/2020/10/19/the-candid-works-of-instapoet-hollie-mcnish/. Accessed May 14, 2021.
Kingsnorth, Simon. 2016. *Digital Marketing Strategy: An Integrated Approach to Online Marketing*. London: Kogan Page.
Kotler, Philip, and Kevin Lane Keller. 2016. *Marketing Management*. Boston: Pearson.
Kovalik, Kate, and Jen Scott Curwood. 2019. "#poetryisnotdead: Understanding Instagram Poetry within a Transliteracies Framework." *Literacy*, 53 (4): 185–95.
Lane, Richard J. 2009. *Jean Baudrillard*. 2nd ed. New York: Routledge.
Leszkiewicz, Anna. 2019. "Why Are We so Worried about 'Instapoetry'?" *New Statesman*, Last Modified March 6, 2019. https://www.newstatesman.com/culture/books/2019/03/instapoetry-rupi-kaur-genre-rm-drake-rh-sin-atticus-hollie-mcnish. Accessed May 17, 2021.
Lloyd, Andrew. 2018. "I Faked My Way as an Instagram Poet, and It Went Bizarrely Well." Last Modified September 12, 2018. https://www.vice.com/en/article/zmjmj3/instagram-poetry-become-successful-scam. Accessed December 20, 2020.
Mahoney, L. Meghan, and Tang Tang. 2017. *Strategic Social Media. From Marketing to Social Change*. West Sussex: Wiley Blackwell.
McNish, Hollie [@holliepoetry]. 2020. "Photo of McNish's Poem 'Grandchild'". *Instagram*, November 5, 2020. https://www.instagram.com/p/CHOamWQhsKA/?utm_source=ig_web_copy_link.
McNish, Hollie [@holliepoetry]. 2020. "Photo of McNish's Poem 'Holy Trinity'". *Instagram*, April 10, 2020. https://www.instagram.com/p/B-0FjwoBwVc/?utm_source=ig_web_copy_link.

McNish, Hollie [@holliepoetry]. 2020. "Photo of McNish's Reading Chair". *Instagram*, May 28, 2020. https://www.instagram.com/p/CAvcsJ1BsT4/?utm_source=ig_web_copy_link

McNish, Hollie [@holliepoetry]. 2020. "Raindrop". *Instagram*, May 14, 2020. https://www.instagram.com/p/CAKZ8QvhFjD/?utm_source=ig_web_copy_link.

O'Keeffe, Alice. 2017. "Interview with Hollie McNish: The Politics and Poetry of Boyfriends, Babies and Breastfeeding." *The Guardian*, Last Modified June 17, 2017. https://www.theguardian.com/books/2017/jun/16/hollie-mcnish-politics-of-poetry-ted-hughes-prize-winner. Accessed May 20, 2021.

Pâquet, Lili. 2019. "Selfie-Help: The Multimodal Appeal of Instagram Poetry." *The Journal of Popular Culture*, 52 (2): 296–314.

Quesenberry, Keith A. 2019. *Social Media Marketing: Marketing, Advertising, and Public Relations in the Consumer Revolution*. 2nd ed. Lanham et al.: Rowman & Littlefield.

Roberts, Soraya. 2018. "No Filter." *The Baffler*, Last Modified January 24, 2018. https://thebaffler.com/latest/instapoetry-roberts. Accessed May 14, 2021.

Rosenthal, Macha Louis. 1960. *The Modern Poets. A Critical Introduction*. Oxford: Oxford University Press.

Stein, Kevin. 2013. *Poetry's Afterlife. Verse in the Digital Age*. 4th ed. San Francisco, CA: University of Michigan Press and University of Michigan Library.

Strauss, Judy, and Raymond Frost. 2014. *E-Marketing*. Boston: Pearson.

Valkenburg, Patti M., and Jessica Taylor Piotrowski. 2017. *Plugged In: How Media Attract and Affect Youth*. New Haven and London: Yale University Press.

Watts, Rebecca. 2018. "The Cult of the Noble Amateur." *PN Review*, 44 (3): 13–17.

Wilcox, Dennis L., Glen T. Cameron, and Bryan H. Reber. 2015. *Public Relations: Strategies and Tactics*. 11th ed. Boston et al.: Pearson.

12

Platform Poetics: Instapoetry in the Age of Platformization

Zak Bronson
University of Western Ontario
Warren Steele
University of Western Ontario

On June 29, 2021, Instapoet Nikita Gill posted a series of messages to her Twitter account that criticized the Instagram platform that helped launched her career. Upset at the ways the platform had profited from her poems, partly by generating an unhealthy obsession with likes and recognition, Gill explained that "[i]t's impossible to keep up with an algorithm that turns art into daily content generation."[1] In response, Gill urged her readers (and fellow Instapoets) to ignore the attention and recognition that accrue through the social media platform and to "[t]ake the time to work on the art that no one has seen and enjoy the process."[2] Several weeks later, fellow Instapoet r.h. Sin posted something similar to his Instagram page. Noting that his poems and posts were not being seen by all of his followers, Sin wrote, "What's the point in posting here when the messages don't reach all the people who followed this account. It's wild how people can press the follow button and still not be able to follow along with the things they want to see."[3]

Gill and Sin's comments are a stark contrast with the abundance of praise attributed to Instapoets' use of Instagram, and to claims that the platform enables writers to build successful literary careers outside of the print-based publishing industry. Rupi Kaur, often seen as the figurehead of Instapoetry, has been at the forefront of these discussions with detailed accounts of her rapid rise to fame. Kaur's career began when she shared her poems on Tumblr, but her success skyrocketed after switching to Instagram, at which point she gained a large number of followers attracted to her expressive poems and distinctive hand-drawn images. After releasing her self-published collection *milk and honey* in 2014, Kaur built enough of an online reputation—due, in part, to a viral photo posted to her Instagram account—that she was offered a deal by Andrews McMeel Publishing. The company promptly republished *milk and honey* in 2016, which as of writing has sold over three million copies and remained on the *New York Times* bestsellers list for 165 weeks. Since that time, Kaur's fame has only expanded, resulting in appearances on late night talk shows, countless interviews, and press for her live reading events.[4] Kaur is only one of many popular Instapoets, but unlike Atticus, r.h. Sin, Cleo Wade, and R. M. Drake, she is by far the most successful and well-known.

In contrast to Kaur, Gill's and Sin's comments demonstrate the complexities of Instapoets' reliance on a highly commercialized, digital platform over which they have little power or control. Despite the fact that Instapoets depend on the Instagram platform for their livelihood and careers, they have very little understanding of how the platform's algorithms work or why some posts are seen by some and not others. This asymmetrical understanding of the platform's algorithms is a counternarrative to the praise conferred on the platform by literary critics, and speaks to the ways that poetry's transformation into digital content produces an unequal power dynamic between the platform and the Instapoet, as creators need the platform to share their work, but are left in the dark about how it works to leverage, engage, and prioritize their content. Ultimately, Gill's and Sin's comments demonstrate the need to pay more attention to how platforms, algorithms, and the "platformization" of poetry change the shape, content, and distribution of Instapoems. Indeed, because platforms remain central to both Instapoetry and contemporary media industries, critical discussions of Instapoetry need to account for the new social industries responsible for this powerful amalgamation of digital technologies, neoliberal economics, and postindustrial consumption habits that occur on platforms like Instagram.

In this chapter, we seek to explore these ideas by examining Instapoetry within the wider context of the platform economy and the commodification and quantification of social media. As a creature of the Instagram platform, and a product of the social industry to which Instagram belongs, Instapoetry is firmly integrated with the practices of the platform economy as typified by TikTok, YouTube, and others. Normally named "platform capitalism,"[5] "surveillance capitalism,"[6] "social media entertainment,"[7] or "the social industry,"[8] the platform economy is typified by its combination of uniform interfaces, participatory audiences, unpaid labor, user-generated content, and personalized algorithms. While critics have been quick to highlight the economic aspects of this industry, much less attention has been paid to the realm of cultural production. Here, we attempt to fill this gap by analyzing Instapoetry and the ways in which Instagram's integration with cultural production and mobile app systems shape the production, distribution, and consumption of Instapoems by arguably co-creating the poems themselves through the offer of market incentives—i.e., the embrace or rejection of that which makes one's poetry *visible* or *invisible* on the site. As such, this discussion aims to dispel more optimistic claims about Instagram and its value as a site of cultural expression and political resistance by women and people of color, since the aim is to demonstrate how these platforms stifle originality and disincentivize the creation of a unique voice by compelling young and aspiring poets to privilege algorithmic visibility over the development of personal artistry.

The Platformization of Poetry

Since its emergence, scholars have attempted to define Instapoetry by examining it in relation to social media. In his recent book *Poetry Unbound*, Mike Chasar argues that Instapoets can be read as part of a long tradition of poets interested in utilizing new media technologies—including the magic lantern, radio, television, film, and now social media—to break down barriers between poet and reader, and as a means to foster new levels of connection not afforded by print-based publishing industries. For Chasar, Instapoets such as Kaur and Tyler Knott Gregson have utilized social media to foster a level of authenticity built from social media's appearance of intimacy and connection.[9] Similarly, Seth Perlow's recent discussion of the presence of handwriting in the work of older poets like Emily Dickinson and Instapoets like Kaur underlines how Instapoets built on the tradition of handwritten poetry in ways that "heighten its lyrical intensities" and present it as "an intimate, affectively rich expression of the poet's thoughts and feelings."[10] For both of these writers, therefore, Instapoetry needs to be considered in relation to the technological affordances of Instagram itself, since interrogating poetry in any era requires engagement with the affordances of the medium for which it was written. For if "poems are shaped by the media of their transmission," critics and scholars must attend to these media so as to discern how they shape the production and reception of poetry at a given time.[11]

Still, in the context of Instapoetry, what constitutes the medium? What *is* the "technology" of social media? Is it the social media platform that writers and audiences use to interface with the poem, as well as design applications like Canva that determine how it looks? Or is it social media's combination of digital platforms, algorithms, protocols, metrics, and user-based interfaces, which creators utilize to generate and share work? If poems are shaped by their mode of transmission, which aspects of social media should researchers attend to in order to understand the variety of expressions and emotions produced through the Instagram site?

To answer these questions, we can turn to the growing discussions around digital platforms and the subsequent "platformization" of the creative industries, especially literary publishing. That is, to the process by which poetry is transformed into digital content distributed through the Instagram platform, and combined with data mining in order to direct content to users by matching them to their "preferred" posts.

Since Instagram launched in 2010, the platform has undergone a series of technological, economic, and cultural transformations that have brought significant changes in how it can be used, and currently is being used, by "content creators," and how that content is monetized by them and by the platform. While Instagram was originally a relatively straightforward photo-sharing app intimately tied to the smartphone camera, and structured according to the logics of social media sharing, it has now expanded to include a host of socio-technological functions, encompassing video creation, personal messaging, stories, advertisements, and algorithmically targeted content. Instagram's transformation is thus indicative of what Anne Helmond (2015: 1) terms *platformization*; that is, "the extension of social media platforms into the rest of the web and their drive to make external data platform ready."[12] As Helmond details, platformization can be understood as a process by which social media applications progressively integrate commercialized networks into their programs in order to monetize and capitalize on social networks. It is through this process that companies like Facebook (which purchased Instagram in 2012) have expanded their power and control over the internet and the digital creative industries as a whole. Instagram, for example, is no longer just a social media site; it is a fully developed social industry composed of over 1 billion active accounts, composed of millions of businesses, and countless numbers of content creators, including celebrities, "micro-celebrities," beauty vloggers, lifestyle gurus, and social media influencers. All of whom depend on the platform to carve out successful online careers.[13] Understanding Instapoetry, therefore, requires sustained engagement with the variety of technological and cultural affordances produced by the process of platformization and its role in shaping digital media and culture as a whole.

However, platformization entails more than just an expansion of the Instagram platform; it also entails a transformation in how content is produced and distributed on the platform. Platforms operate through what Jean Burgess refers a "platform paradigm," a term she uses to refer to the ways that "platforms like YouTube or Facebook have a lot of power within the information sector and creative content industries," and how "their *logics* … are more deeply reshaping our society and culture."[14] Although each platform is different, these logics—as defined by how they operate and their systems of value—ensure Instagram functions by extracting personalized information about each user, in order to then utilize it strategically to make more profitable decisions about which content to prioritize in users' scrolls. Gill's and Sin's comments, especially their concerns around "reach" and "attention," capture the ways that Instagram operates by algorithmically personalizing content to each user. To do so, the platform extracts hundreds of data points about their users, including demographic information (age, gender, location, race), and contextual information ("likes," interests, tastes, interactions), which it then utilizes to profile user behavior and "push" content to them.[15] Although the precise elements of these measurements are concealed, the Instagram platform is allegedly designed to give users the content you "care about the most based on your interests, relationships, and timeliness of the *posts*."[16] Through this, the platform determines the type and variety of content received and the method by which users can see it on the site.

Given these various forces, platforms are not neutral conduits for, nor neutral arbiters of, the content they exist to circulate, but are powerful gatekeepers that influence and shape online cultural production, choosing who wins and who does not on the basis of engagement—that is, which posts users scroll to the most. As Burgess details, platform logics contain a set of technological and cultural affordances that define the very conditions of what counts as *value* on the platform (via measurements such as interactions, attention, engagement), as well as how that value is measured through "likes," clicks, and saves.[17] Based on these types of factors, platforms determine exactly which type of content is made visible or invisible. In this respect, platforms normalize a set of rules and conditions around which types of content are allowed, encouraged, and amplified on the site. In order to be visible on the Instagram, therefore, creators have to learn to comprehend the metrics, code, and means of algorithmic visibility necessary to become visible to the most number of users. Kelley Cotter's discussion of

Instagram influencers, for example, examines how content creators have to play the "the visibility game" by attempting to interpret the platform's concealed or hidden measurements, and interpret the rules of the platform by deliberately "gaming" it—posting at different times, in different styles, or by adapting their online behavior in order to be seen.[18] Since visibility mediates the possibilities of success, platforms establish the "participatory norms" that determine the type of content produced and promoted on the platform, and in this way establish an internalized and largely unspoken set of instructions that incentivize both what and when to post.[19] Bucher calls this internalized state the "algorithmic imaginary."

Given these implications, platforms like Instagram not only determine how creators share or produce their content, but how that material is made visible to audiences. Although creators are certainly free to ignore these concerns around visibility, the platform's various protocols, logics, and algorithms encode technological constraints that determine the conditions under which their content appears. As we discuss in the next section, the platformization of poetry has impacted the ways that artists now produce their work with maximum visibility in mind. To explore these ideas in more depth, we will now turn back to Instapoets, Gill and Sin, to investigate their comments more closely and explore just how platform logics shape the production of Instapoetry.

Being Seen and Heard

Although it is difficult to assess the degree to which Instagram's platform logic influences the styles of individual Instapoets, it is clear that platformization fundamentally changes how Instapoets produce and distribute their work. While print-based poets typically achieve success by publishing their poems in prestigious literary journals and collections, or by accruing enough cultural capital that they are recognized for their craft, Instapoets produce content for the platform's combination of audience-based metrics and platform logics. This means they must continually struggle to capture algorithmic visibility, and that they not only utilize the platform to share their work, but remain attentive to the success of various styles, aesthetics, themes, or poetic approaches to algorithmically boost their work for the sake of gaining followers, attracting new readers, and garnering the attention of the legacy media by going sufficiently "viral." Since being "visible" on the platform is necessary for success or attention, users must continually battle against the "threat of invisibility"—the fear that their content won't be seen by enough audiences, or that it won't be "relatable" enough to attract new followers.[20] In an attention economy, capturing recognition and visibility operates as technological limitations that shape the conditions under which artists produce work. As Bucher puts it, "The problem [of social media] is not the possibility of constantly being observed, but the possibility of constantly disappearing, of not being considered important enough. In order to appear, to become visible, *one needs to follow a certain platform logic.*"[21]

The implications of platformization can be read in many of the criticisms directed by various writers and poets who have mocked Instapoets' concerns with capturing attention and recognition online. In her now well-known essay on Instapoetry, Rebecca Watts argued that writers such as Rupi Kaur and Hollie McNish were not poets, but *personalities* who utilized their social media accounts to brand themselves in lucrative ways, or, in the case of McNish, to craft attention-grabbing poems more focused on capturing momentary interest instead of artistic integrity.[22] Watts's criticisms have been elaborated by numerous poets and journalists who have mocked the ways that Instagram has elevated poorly crafted poems lacking artistic merit. For example, in 2017, poet Thom Young created a fake Instagram account for "Tyler" (@tyypoet), a young, brooding male poet purposely crafted to replicate the styles and aesthetic of Atticus. Writing purposely short, banal poems such as "love made her wild" and "wait," "Tyler" gained unexpected recognition when a poem featuring a sole, typewritten "her" on an off-white background went viral. Similarly, in 2019, a writer for *Vice* magazine published "I Faked My Way as an Instagram Poet, and It Went Bizarrely Well," where he detailed his creation of RavenStares (@ RavenStares), a young poet that purposely replicated the lowercase fonts and moody images common to the genre, and gained 646 followers in only four weeks, as well as the recognition of Atticus who publicly praised his poems.[23]

Although these criticisms are certainly elitist in their disdain for Instapoetry—and ignore how difficult it can be to attract attention on an online platform utilized by over 1 billion users—they each speak to the ways that the platformization reworks the lines between artistic integrity and platform visibility. Because Instagram is an attention economy, success depends on knowing and interpreting one's audience to make one's work more marketable. Indeed, one must be *seen* and *heard* to capture attention and gain recognition, and Instapoets must continually battle with internal pressures that privilege their own artistic integrity as well as external pressures exerted by Instagram's algorithm and user-base. As an artist, should one abandon the former for the promise of commercial gain? Or sacrifice appealing to the latter to maintain and develop one's voice? In many ways this is nothing new; this has been the story of art since it was first imbricated with commerce. However, the novelty of the present moment cannot be ignored. Not when social media metrics, rather than nebulous market concerns, grasped only partially and never in real time, determine the contours of that struggle, and, we argue, its outcomes.

Instapoets' work is mediated through the Instagram platform on which they depend. To aid creators, the Instagram platform provides users with instantaneous measurements such as "likes," views, comments, shares, and interactions. Additionally, Instagram provides Creator accounts to users with over 10,000 followers, giving them the opportunity to receive detailed information on potential reach, audience demographics, daily numbers of followers and unfollowers, and instantaneous feedback about which content receives the most likes, comments, and interactions. Based on this, Instapoets have the ability to gain unique insights about their readers' tastes and interests, and can modify their work to target specific interests, or to evolve their poems to better capture audience recognition much more quickly than print-based publishers striving to cater to popular tastes. As book critic John Self (2019) puts it, "the poet knows which poems have the most likes and comments, and can tailor future writing to amplify the effect."[24] In doing so, Instapoets can not only target specific audiences, but learn to target certain emotions or audience concerns more effectively over time.

We can see how this works with r.h. Sin, a writer who has gained a significant following online (over 2 million followers), and has produced an enormous amount of work (at least 23 poetry books), including many books jointly written with his wife Samantha King Holmes and fellow Instapoet R. M. Drake. Sin's success is dependent on his use of the Instagram platform. Like many of his fellow Instapoets, Sin has received very little recognition in the mainstream press, and has never been reviewed by major journals or the cultural press. Yet, as a former social media marketer, Sin is well-placed to utilize the platform to gain attention and recognition. In a rare profile published in *The New Yorker*, Sin is quite overt about his utilization of metrics and data as a means to capture platform visibility. To capture the algorithm's "attention," Sin engages in a series of practices, like crafting "pithy bits of fourth-wave feminism," turning trending topics into epigrams, and writing 7,200 words a day. Describing his ability to gain new followers, Sin states:

> I came into 2016 with 251,018 followers … I entered 2017 with 515,164. I am a workhorse. I think a lot of people in my industry are content with the "struggling artist" ideology. I'm not. On any given day, my account brings in 600,000 to one million "likes." The object is to be seen or heard, and I make a lot of noise.[25]

Sin's references to word counts, "likes," and "trending topics" are all illustrative of the ways that his poetry is fused with the logics of platformization, resulting in a near obsession with algorithmic recognizability and follower counts. He proudly employs a host of techniques designed *not* to improve his work, but to capture and maintain visibility and attention by posting up to fifteen times a day. In addition to his poems, Sin shares blog posts, articles, self-improvement tips, inspirational messages, and photographs—all of which are intended to expand on the thematic concerns of his poems for the sake of maintaining audience engagement.

Sin's engagement with metrics and measurements has also resulted in significant criticism from fans and critics who suggest that he is gaming the system by exploiting audience interests. Most notably, fellow Instapoet Bianca Sparacino (@rainbowsalt) lumped Sin in the category of Instapoetry's numerous "bad boy" poets, including Atticus and R. M. Drake, who each utilized social media to exploit women readers, and, in the words of Sparacino, to "become wealthy off of the female experience."[26] For Sparacino, Sin not only utilized social media to share poetry, but wrote poems to specifically target a marketable and lucrative female audience. Indeed, since 2016, Sin has almost exclusively written short, aspirational poems that overtly cater to a female demographic, often through detailed explorations of female empowerment, self-help messages, or short, snappy messages about toxic male relationships. Although his earliest works of poetry, like his *Whiskey Words & a Shovel* trilogy, are more varied in their styles and themes, his later work has almost exclusively focused on these gendered concerns. As such, some readers have praised his poems for their raw, emotional accounts of female heartbreak, while others have routinely complained about his attempts to "mansplain" the female experience, leading one disappointed Goodreads reader to protest, "I am so done with trash male poets who write solely to police female body politics, sexuality, and emotions under the guise of 'teaching' or 'empowering' them because frankly, who asked you."[27]

Sin's most recent book, *One More Before Goodbye* (2020), which was written and published during the midst of the COVID-19 pandemic, builds on these themes. Addressing how the pandemic engendered feelings of isolation and depression, Sin writes in his introduction that "these words are my offering to you who has often found themselves endlessly scrolling through a phone … I am writing this to encourage you to set yourself free because I, for one, believe that there is something that is currently keeping you from being all that you can be."[28] Sin's book expands on this with poems that resemble inspirational stories or pithy one-liners more than poetic verse. In fact, the book's first untitled poem begins "No one is perfect but when you are dating someone, pay attention to how often they disregard your peace of mind and emotional well-being."[29] Sin's simulated stream of consciousness style demonstrates his particular means of capturing success on a platform where readability and clarity are central to attracting attention, and the cultivation of directness and spontaneity is crucial to appearing authentic. Yet the numerous criticisms lobbed at his work also illustrate the limitations of writing poetry on a digital platform that rewards visibility and relatability above all else, since universal praise is impossible, no matter how much he adapts his work to achieve maximum visibility and maximum appeal.

Sin's emphasis on self-help and inspiration is certainly not unique. Many of Instapoetry's most popular writers, including Atticus, Cleo Wade, Humble the Poet, Morgan Harper Nichols, and Alexandra Elle, all firmly fit within these conventions, posting poems that blur the lines between poetry and prose. This style is no doubt shaped by the limitations of the Instagram platform which makes it easier to read short, expressive messages over long complex verse. But it is also linked to the nature of the Instagram network, which remains largely dominated by a variety of self-help influencers, and which indirectly encourages Instapoets to produce content that resembles this material. As Brooke Erin Duffy notes, content creators often utilize expressions of self-help and personalized inspiration as a means to capture digital visibility since it tends to attract followers through feelings of interconnection and para-social intimacy.[30] Such practices are clearly illustrated through many of these writers whose popularity and success can be linked to the logics of platform amplification. Because Instagram's algorithms align users to "relevant" content, they simultaneously privilege posts that resemble the styles or approaches of the wider social network. Writers whose work taps into tropes of self-help and personal aspiration are likely to receive additional "boosts" that can attract new followers, while those seeking platform success are incentivized to adapt their content to more closely align with what is already popular on the network.

After all, for many Instapoets, gaining and maintaining platform visibility can be a lucrative process. While traditional print-based literary poets derive economic value from the publication and republication of poems in collections or journals, Instapoets earn no income for sharing their works on the Instagram platform. Unlike YouTube, Instagram does not offer artists any advertising revenue for sharing their content online. As a result, Instapoets must attempt to generate an income by securing book contracts and advertisements which they can then integrate into their posts, or by producing poetry-themed commodities, such as clothing, outfits, and jewelry. For Instapoets, the creation of short, inspirational expressions and self-branded images that can be turned into poetry-themed commodities provide opportune ways to earn additional income. Atticus, for example, has turned his simple, but memorable poems (including his most popular poem "love her but leave her wild") into a host of poetry-inspired merchandise and accessories: hats, sweatpants, jewelry, wine tumblers, scrunchies, stickers, and even Atticus-branded wine. Likewise, Sin's short, straight-forward messages (e.g., "woman, the original poem," "be good to her, she's rare") perfectly lend themselves to stylized products: hats, sweatshirts, and COVID-19 masks.

While this commercialization of poetry is by no means new—the poems of Walt Whitman and Rumi have long been turned into branded commodities utilized to sell products—Instapoetry is unique in the ways that the platforms have artists engage in these acts of personalized branding and self-promotion, further eroding the boundaries between artist and economics. Whitman never sold Levi's, for example, in the pages of his books, but Sin and others are happy to do so on their Instagram pages for the right price. Instapoets such as Sin and Kaur are *poet-entrepreneurs* who utilize distinctive modes of self-branding, entrepreneurialism, and professionalization in addition to their poetry as a means to capture platform visibility. Kaur, for example, was once described by *The Atlantic* as the "ultimate poet-entrepreneur," and has said that she approaches her poetry as though she were "running a business."[31] This includes the act of writing and touring, as well as "time spent in the office with her [media] team to oversee operations and manage projects," including curating and developing her personal brand across her social media platform, her poems, published books, interviews, and live performances. The combination of poetry and entrepreneurialism is thus a unique phenomenon borne from the platformization of poetry and Instagram's reliance on the creative labor of users and content creators. While much of these practices were previously done by book publishers, in the platform economy, writers and artists must combine their artistry with personalized branding in ways that distinguish them as a brand in order to earn an income. On a digital platform where recognition remains essential to attracting attention, the combination of personalized styles, thematic concerns, and even coordinated color patterns can be a way of maintaining a sense of consistency that gains instant recognition.

The Perils of Platformization

But if Instagram can give, it can also take away. In contrast to Kaur, lesser known figures such as Nayyirah Waheed, Amanda Lovelace, Makenzie Campbell, and Zack Grey have achieved only a fraction of Kaur's success, and many others have developed a fraught relationship with the platform. In 2019, journalist Jonathan Ford published an article in the *Financial Times* that profiled a number of Instapoets, including Gill, Lovelace, and South African Instapoet Iain Thomas, who were upset at the ways that Instagram had monetized their creative labor, stifled their success, and deprioritized their poems on the platform. According to Ford, much of this originated in 2016 when Instagram switched from a chronologically arranged newsfeed (that displayed the most recent posts at the top of a users' scroll) to an algorithmically organized feed that was said to prioritize the posts that users engage with the most. For many Instapoets, this meant that many of their posts were unseen and invisible to their followers. According to Gill, this switch meant that she lost the majority of her audience: while her pre-algorithm posts were seen by 70 percent of her over 600,000 followers, her post-algorithm posts reached only 25 to 50 percent of them.[32] Faced with this decreasing audience, Gill lamented, "Instagram is making the platform more and more inaccessible for artists and small businesses unless we pay it money to boost our posts."[33]

Criticisms like these demonstrate how the platformization of poetry leads to a precarious form of artistic and financial success, as writers are continually subject to the nature and power of platform changes—some of which are subtle, some of which are not. Gill's criticisms of Instagram's algorithmic changes demonstrate how Instapoets live, as it were, in a state of "platform precarity," as their posts are often deprioritized, and their income affected, due to Instagram's consistent tweaking of the platform's algorithmic measurements.[34] In recent years, numerous reports have detailed how platforms like TikTok, YouTube, and of course Instagram have deprioritized, or "shadowbanned," content, particularly in the case of LGBTQ2S+ creators whose posts were concealed due to hidden metrics. Although it is not always possible to fully understand all of the behind-the-scenes measurements going on beneath platform's protocols, all creators are subject to the "popularity game," meaning that those posts that do not appeal to mass audiences are disadvantaged on the platform.[35] As a result, Instapoets can be left "playing the game" by modifying their content to stay successful, or risk toiling away in obscurity.

Given these issues, it is not surprising that many of the more successful Instapoets are those who overtly engage with non-confrontational messages or simplistic expressions meant for easy readability online, while writers such as Nikita Gill, whose style and themes differ from many of her more successful peers, have repeatedly struggled to achieve platform visibility. Despite being one of the early success stories of Instapoetry and having her name frequently mentioned as one of the leading Instapoets, Gill's online following has stagnated over time (as of writing, she has 628,000 followers). Although much of her early Instapoetry success was attributed to her engagement with complex themes around feminine trauma, mental health, and depression, which "attracted audiences from black, Asian or minority ethnic backgrounds," Instagram's algorithmic switch rather abruptly undermined her audience.[36] As she recounted to Ford, "I had been getting about 20,000 likes but then I noticed they were just staying the same even though my follower numbers rose by almost 60 per cent last year."[37] As a result of this difficulty, Gill has almost completely abandoned Instagram by posting only about once a week, and has gained more recognition in recent years through traditional media outlets, including becoming a regular fixture on the BBC and a frequent guest at poetry festivals—something few Instapoets have achieved.[38]

In contrast to writers such as Sin, Gill often explores mental health issues in more complex and challenging ways. Instead of simply adopting straightforward empowerment messages, Gill frequently points to the legacies of gendered trauma, to lingering emotional pain, and the importance of communal connections over individual self-fulfillment. Her first published work, *Your Soul is a River* (2016), for instance, commonly replicates the self-help themes popular on social media, yet her works adds linguistic complexities that avoid the simplicity and repetitiveness typified by other Instapoets. Her most recent books *The Girl and the Goddess* (2020) and *Where Hope Comes From* (2021), for example, have been praised for their historical explorations and revisions of Greek mythology and Hindu history, issues not readily comprehensible on social media platforms. In this respect, it is not surprising that Gill has backtracked some of her initial praise for Instagram, explaining in the same Twitter post mentioned above: "For artists, it's important to have the time to think about what we create and spend time working on our passions away in the silence of things."[39] Gill's comments—as well as her recent attempts to escape the "Instapoet" label—reflect her desires to free herself from the constraints of platformization. Yet, her simultaneous dependence upon these platforms to share poems, gain followers, and market books illustrates the extreme difficulties of trying to develop a career outside of the platform responsible for aiding it. For in a time when it has become harder and harder to gain entrance into literary poetry, platforms are a blessing that provide access to potentially millions of readers, and a curse that can instantly lose them.

Although there is more to be said and unpacked about the ways that platformization shapes Instapoetry, these two case studies demonstrate the appeals and limitations of platform-based publishing. Because while Instagram is certainly a venue in which artists can share their work, it is simultaneously one that shapes and determines the production, distribution, and creation of that content. Indeed, despite optimistic claims that platforms democratize literary publishing, the realities of platformization illustrate how obscure measurements and algorithmic protocols lurk behind-the-scenes determining which content is visible and invisible on the site. As the contrasting portraits of Sin and Gill attest, while some are rewarded for their efforts, many others aren't, and many more will tinker away attempting to gain visibility on a platform indifferent to their efforts.

Notes

1 Gill (2021).
2 Ibid.
3 Sin (2021).
4 For a discussion of Kaur's rise to fame, see Hill and Yuan (2018).
5 Srnicek (2017).
6 Zuboff (2019).
7 Cunningham and Craig (2019).
8 Seymour (2020).
9 Chasar (2020: 187–90).
10 Perlow (2021).
11 Chasar (2020: 11).

12 Helmond (2015: 1).
13 Cunningham and Craig (2019).
14 Burgess (2021: 22).
15 Kant (2020; Burgess 2021: 22).
16 Instagram (2016).
17 Burgess (2021: 23).
18 Cotter (2019: 899).
19 Bucher (2018: 89).
20 Ibid., 17.
21 Ibid., 84. Emphasis added.
22 Watts (2018: 13–17).
23 Thom Young has also detailed some of these criticisms in his novel *Instapoet*, co-written with Matt Blythe.
24 Self (2019).
25 Marikar (2017).
26 Sparacino (2017).
27 Leona (2017).
28 Sin (2020: 4–5).
29 Ibid., 7.
30 Duffy (2017).
31 Hill and Yuan (2018).
32 Ford (2019).
33 Ibid.
34 Cunningham and Craig (2019: 94).
35 Bucher (2018: 96).
36 Ford, "How Instagram Could Stifle a New Generation of Poets."
37 Ibid.
38 Interestingly, many Instapoets are almost excluded from traditional media outlets, including Rupi Kaur, who though gaining some recognition through talk shows, has received very scant attention from the press. Her most recent book of poems *Home Body* (2020), for instance, was not reviewed by any major newspapers, despite becoming a *New York Times* bestseller.
39 Gill (2021).

References

Bucher, Taina. 2018. *If… Then: Algorithmic Power and Politics*. Oxford: Oxford University Press.

Burgess, Jean. 2021. "Platform Studies." In *Creator Culture: An Introduction to Global Social Media Entertainment*, edited by Stuart Cunningham and David Craig, 21–38. New York: New York University Press.

Chasar, Mike. 2020. *Poetry Unbound: Poems and New Media from the Magic Lantern to Instagram*. New York: Columbia University Press.

Cotter, Kelley. 2019. "Playing the Visibility Game: How Digital Influencers and Algorithms Negotiate Influence on Instagram." *New Media & Society*, 21 (4): 895–913.

Cunningham, Stuart, and David Craig. 2019. *Social Media Entertainment: The New Intersection of Hollywood and Silicon Valley*. New York: New York University.

Duffy, Brooke Erin. 2017. *(Not) Getting Paid to Do What You Love: Gender, Social Media, and Aspirational Work*. New Haven: Yale University Press.

Flock, Elizabeth. 2017. "Why This Poet Is Posting Meaningless Verse on Instagram." *PBS*. Published June 12, 2017. https://www.pbs.org/newshour/arts/poetry/poet-trolling-everyone-instagram-show-social-media-glorifies-pop-poetry.

Ford, Jonathan. 2019. "Instagram Threatens to Stifle a New Generation of Poets." *Financial Times*. Published May 24, 2019. https://www.ft.com/content/7a84b216-6849-11e9-9adc-98bf1d35a056.

Gill, Nikita [@nktgill]. 2021. "It's Impossible to Keep up with an Algorithm That Turns Art into Daily Content Generation. Take the Time to Work on the Art That No One Has Seen and Enjoy the Process. You Deserve Rest and Self Care and Time away from Volatile Digital Spaces." *Twitter*, June 29, 2021. https://twitter.com/nktgill/status/1409902798905483265.

Helmond, Anne. 2015. "The Platformization of the Web: Making Web Data Platform Ready." *Social Media + Society*, 1 (2): 1.

Hill, Faith, and Karen Yuan. 2018. "How Instagram Saved Poetry." *The Atlantic*. Published October 15, 2018. https://www.theatlantic.com/technology/archive/2018/10/rupi-kaur-instagram-poet-entrepreneur/572746/.

Instagram. 2016. "See the Moments You Care About First." *Instagram*. Published March 15, 2016. https://about.instagram.com/blog/announcements/see-posts-you-care-about-first-in-your-feed.

I.T. 2017. "Rupi Kaur Reinvents Poetry for the Social-Media Generation." *The Economist*. Published November 1, 2017. https://www.economist.com/prospero/2017/11/01/rupi-kaur-reinvents-poetry-for-the-social-media-generation.

Kant, Tanya. 2020. *Making It Personal: Algorithmic Personalization, Identity and Everyday Life*. Oxford: Oxford, University Press.

Leona. 2017. Review of *Whiskey, Words, and a Shovel*, by r.h. Sin. *Goodreads*. Published June 27, 2017. https:// www.goodreads.com/review/show/2041766423?book_show_action=true&from_review_page=1.

Leszkiewicz, Anna. 2019. "Why Are We So Worried about 'Instapoetry'?" *New Statesman*. Published March 6, 2019. https://www.newstatesman.com/culture/books/2019/03/instapoetry-rupi-kaur-genre-rm-drake-rh-sin-atticus-hollie-mcnish.

Marikar, Sheila Yasmin. 2017. "The Life of an Instagram Poet." *The New Yorker*. Published March 8, 2017. https://www.newyorker.com/culture/culture-desk/the-life-of-an-instagram-poet.

Perlow, Seth. 2019. "The Handwritten Styles of Instapoetry." *Post45*. Published September 17, 2019. https://post45.org/2019/09/the-handwritten-styles-of-instagram-poetry/.

Self, John. 2019. "Was Emily Dickinson the First Instapoet?" *Penguin*. Published September 13, 2019. Available at: https://www.penguin.co.uk/articles/2019/sep/was-emily-dickinson-the-first-instapoet.html.

Seymour, Richard. 2020. *The Twittering Machine*. London: Verso.

Sin, r.h. 2020. *One More Before Goodbye*. Self-published, r.h. Sin.

Sin, r.h. [@rhsin]. 2021. "What's the Point in Posting Here When the Messages Don't Reach All the People Who Followed This Account. It's Wild How People Can Press the Follow Button and Still Not Be Able to Follow along With the Things They Want to See." *Instagram*, July 22, 2021. Post no longer available.

Sparacino, Bianca. 2017. "Where Have All the Good Male Poets Gone?" *Salon*, December 17, 2017. https://www.salon.com/2017/12/17/where-have-all-the-good-male-poets-gone_partner/.

Srnicek, Nick. 2017. *Platform Capitalism*. Cambridge: Polity.

Watts, Rebecca. 2018. "The Cult of the Noble Amateur." *PN Review*, 44 (3): 13–17.

Young, Thom, and Matt Blythe. 2018. *Instapoet*. New York: Bone Machine.

Zuboff, Shoshana. 2019. *The Age of Surveillance Capitalism: The Fight for the Future at the New Frontier of Power*. London: Profile Books.

13

What's the Carbon Footprint of an (Insta)Poem?: Reading #poetsofinstagram in the Anthropocene

James Mackay
European University Cyprus

Polina Mackay
University of Nicosia

Reading M-texts

Instapoems exist primarily to be read on mobile phones. They are not the only poems to be so encountered: Brian Bilston calls himself the "Poet Laureate of Twitter" and is only one of the voices to have emerged from that platform; Amazon's Kindle platform has long been mobile integrated; creators of avant-garde electronic literature have embraced the possibilities for dissemination offered by Google Play and the Apple Store (Duerden 2021). But there is a qualitatively different feel to the way Instapoems are written for the mobile screen. Rather than being adapted for it, squashed into it, or created in such a way as to escape the bounds of the screen, Instapoems entirely embrace both the brevity required to remain legible within the endless scroll of Instagram and the simplicity of message needed to stand out in the feed. Line lengths are ruthlessly trimmed to ensure blank space in the post, and (in contrast to almost every other branch of poetry) Instapoems often prioritize good graphic design over thematic heft, including visual elements such as colored backgrounds, photographs, grainy paper, or calligraphy.[1] In this chapter, we will ask what other affective elements emerge from this encounter between the lyric and new technology. Rather than treating Instapoems as escapees, "proper" poems that have accidentally found themselves in a feed and should be rescued and analyzed using all the New Critical scalpels at our disposal, we propose a reading that begins with the physical mobile phone screen on which they are created and via which they are overwhelmingly consumed. We also take account of the other context in which these poems have emerged: what we might call the last stage of the Great Denial, that period encompassing the late twentieth and early twenty-first centuries when it was still just about possible to pretend that anthropogenic climate change was not an immediate threat to human social cohesion. Such warming is a result of carbon dioxide and methane emissions necessary to maintain the lifestyles of, in particular, highly privileged Westerners, but also the lifestyles of middle classes around the globe. This is the grouping that also produces by far the bulk of the millions of Instagram poetry posts, and it will be our contention that we can trace some of the anxieties attendant on living an unsustainably high-carbon lifestyle in the poems themselves.

In her much-cited 2008 article "Hypertext Fiction Reading: Haptics and Immersion," Anne Mangen remarks that "[u]nlike print texts, digital texts are ontologically intangible and detached from the physical and mechanical dimension of their material support, namely, the computer or e-book (or other devices, such as the PDA [...], the iPod or the mobile phone)" (405). She goes on to argue that the phenomenological experience of reading a physical book, requiring sustained engagement with a single material object, creates a greater engagement with the words on the page, which, using the terminology of philosopher Don Ihde, she terms a *hermeneutic* relation. The haptics of engagement with an e-text (mouse clicks, keyboard engagement, continuously scrolling with one's forefinger) place one at a distance from the text and thus semi-permanently in an *alterity* relation. Studies of reader recall support this contention, showing that readers retain significantly more information from reading printed pages, not to mention interacting with the text in various ways, including highlighting, marginalia, or the simple act of marking one's place by folding the page (see, e.g., Owens et al. 2023). However, Mangen's essentially negative take on digital textuality is not the only possible interpretation. Reading on the mobile phone ("m-reading"), as Kuzmičová, Schilhab and Burke (2020) discuss, also allows readers to remain in constant contact with the text—dipping in and out of it while stuck in traffic, in line at the bank, etc.—to a greater degree than paper books allow. With their focus mainly on fiction, these researchers also note the utopian potential for m-readers to immediately look up unfamiliar words and concepts, or to pleasurably match their reading to their immediate environs. Perhaps betraying a certain unconscious class bias, the example they give is of accessing "collections of the Latin classics" during "a trip to Rome" (339). Kuzmičová, Schilhab and Burke further argue that Mangen fails to take into account both the alienating effects of a paper book and the possibility of gradual acclimatization to m-texts via immersion. Clearly, with so many different potential factors at play, it is hard to make a definitive statement about whether e-reading is in any particular sense "better" or "worse" than reading from a printed page.

What is clear in both the skeptical and affirmative strains of this discussion, however, is that the act of reading on a mobile phone can be differentiated in cognitive terms from the act of reading a text on paper. The television writer Charlie Brooker captures something of the *unheimlich* nature of the experience in the title of his anthology series *Black Mirror*. Like a mirror, the outer alkali aluminosilicate covering of the typical mobile phone screen reflects our image back to us during use, though the LCD display behind it absorbs much of the light, darkening our reflection.[2] The effect is palimpsestic: our image is narcissistically overlaid on the material we read. The invisible sensor grid of the capacitive touch screen between the glass and the light display responds to physical touch, which, given the small amount of text that can fit onto the typical phone screen, is needed frequently in the form of swipes for new content. The OLED or LED lighting display attracts the eye with its brightness (artificial lighting having been a marker of modernity since human relationships with the temporal were reset by street lighting), pulling at the reader's attention. This is especially true in the context of social media, which is designed to maximize active engagement, by generating what Shoshana Zuboff has christened "behavioral surplus": that is to say, information on consumer habits that can be mined for data to be sold on "behavioral futures markets" (2019: 93–7). M-reading, in other words, is not monolithic. Just as the Paperwhite technology of the Kindle screen produces a different reading experience to paper, so the social media environment of Instapoetry creates a wholly different experience from the Kindle app, even though both occur via mobile interface. Instapoetry, needing to fully participate in the attention economy, frames itself simultaneously as a respite from such an economy (poetry is an escape from the world) while working via hashtag links and engagement-inviting comments to manipulate the reader's future interactions (click the heart icon and subscribe for future posts).

This palimpsestic context lies behind one of the odder features of Instapoetry, namely, the confusion around what actually constitutes a poem. Scroll down any of the feeds generated from the most popular Instapoetry hashtags—for instance #poetsofinstagram, #poetry, or #instapoetry—and alongside the classic Instapoem (3–6 lines of vaguely haiku-like vers libre superimposed on an image) you will also find posts that are photographs with no discernable poetic content in either the image or the accompanying text. One might argue that the accompanying hashtags constitute a poem, but that level of sophistication does not seem to be justified by an examination of the accounts behind these posts. Rather, these posts elide the concept of the "poem" as literary object with a more insubstantial concept of "the poetic," an affectual descriptor that somehow conjoins somewhat diffuse ideas of beauty, calmness, experience, passion, innocence, and spirituality. This elision arises from the social media and m-reading experience: in the infinite scroll, poems are not valued as discrete units so much as they are experienced as parts of a seamless experience.

Reading at the Scale of the Anthropocene

What we have offered in the above is an analysis rooted in the immediate experience of the mobile phone user. After all, this approach mirrors how Instapoems are consumed and echoes the typical critical methods we apply to the examination of cultural artifacts, which are usually analyzed in relation to their cultural context. However, the act of reading on a mobile phone also insistently makes us conscious of another context, far removed from (and yet always present within) the immediate act of reading: the context of the Anthropocene. In this period, the graphs of the Great Acceleration show multiple indicators of planetary distress—surface temperatures, sea levels, ocean acidity, greenhouse gases, terrestrial biosphere degradation—shooting upward in an exponential curve (Steffen et al. 2015). These are matched with the graphs of globalization, showing the strong correlation between these earth system trends and socioeconomic trends such as urban populations, international tourism, mechanized transportation, primary energy use, and many more. As Timothy Clark has argued, this constitutes an "'emergent' event [...] one whose novelty meets no available, matching or adequate discourse in representation, discussion or judgment" (2015: 47).

The emergent cognitive challenge is one of simultaneously understanding our actions on a personal, societal, and planetary scale. The first of these is inherent: it is impossible for us not to bring our subjectivity to bear on our perceptions and decisions. The second is learned through our education and growing up in society: we are taught about social and cultural norms, we learn about structuring laws and codes, and we also observe the effects of our actions on others. Thinking on a planetary scale, however, is disordering. When we buy a cup of coffee, that is a pleasant and satisfying experience. If we buy a cup of coffee for someone who cannot afford one, then it becomes a societal good. However, planetary thinking also requires us to take account of the clearance of old growth forests to provide space for monocultural sun-cultivated coffee plantations, the use of water in growing the crop, the leaching of pesticides and herbicides into local water tables, the carbon cost of shipping the coffee from the other side of the planet, the use of non-recyclable materials in the packing and shipping process, the CO_2 generated in lighting and heating the café, and so on. We must consider all elements, right up to the fact that the plastic "splash stick" used to prevent hot coffee from spilling out the lid will likely end up either in a landfill or become microplastics in the ocean.

This new context is one that is simultaneously disordering and omnipresent. "Disordering" because the number of factors that suddenly need to be considered becomes so large that to let them affect the immediate situation seems ludicrous ("You won't buy a coffee for a homeless man because of the tiny individual carbon cost?"), yet when factored up to a species level become urgent. Keeping the splash stick as a focus, the pressure group Clean Water Action (2021) has estimated that Starbucks, the company that originated the splash stick, sells as many as four billion coffees in disposable cups per annum. This figure can be scaled up many times to account for other coffee chains and independents globally. It is not possible to recycle splash sticks at the time of writing. Therefore, every one of these six to ten billion sticks will be in the environment for decades or centuries. We also call the situation "omnipresent," because both governments and corporations have heavily invested in campaigns designed to convince consumers that the responsibility for myriad planetary system destabilizations lies at the feet of the individual, in a deliberate effort to blunt the force of demands for real change. While the audience for Instapoetry is diverse and global, it is certainly true that Gen-Z and millennials predominate among users and creators: precisely the group most likely to have received environmental messaging through education and social media.[3]

One of Timothy Clark's most useful insights is that this same idea of overlapping scale frameworks can be brought to the analysis of literature. He demonstrates this, in chapter five of his monograph *Ecocriticism on the Edge*, via a reading of Raymond Carver's short story "Elephant." Read within the micro-scale of the personal and psychological, this text concerns a man's gradual acceptance of his lot as someone constantly being harassed by family members for money. Such an intimate and familiar reading practice is how Eurowestern readers traditionally experience texts, especially in the (generally individualistic) forms of the prose short story or novel. A second scale is also familiar within academic literary criticism, where the reading expands to take in the general chronotope within which the story is set. In the case of "Elephant," that scale would most likely be one of the four or five decades in America following the Second World War: this would allow for a reading of the blue collar speaker's situation as being produced by the end of the boom years of expansion and economic growth in the mid-twentieth century. However, our situation in the Anthropocene, as demonstrated by the splash stick example above, demands that we add a third, much larger, scale, in which the space within which the story is to be considered expands to take in the entire planet as an (almost) closed system, and the time period expands to take in not just the past 300 years but the next 300 as well. At this scale, the psychological concerns of the individual disappear and the planetary effects of their actions, particularly the petrol burned during the course of the story come more sharply into view. The ending of the story, in which the narrator and his workmate George head out at speed over the American landscape, is normally framed on scales one and two as a form of liberation. Viewed via the third scale, this ending actually becomes an example of primitive "petro-minimalist" magic realism (Clark 2015: 104). In this view, the narrator's working-class status recedes in importance once placed in global terms, and his car, a nonhuman agent considered in most readings only as abstract symbol, actually becomes for Clark a central actor in demonstrating "the oppressive, all-pervading and destructive effects of being born into a fossil-fuel-based infrastructure" (Clark 2015: 104).

Reading M-texts in the Anthropocene

Over the rest of this chapter, we want to think through some of the ways that this idea of scale reading, and particularly its insistence on macrocosmic materiality, can be applied to a single Instapoem. In choosing the specific poem, we made one key decision. Although most Instapoetry discussion thus far has focused on those writers who have been able to successfully build a following and monetize it in the form of publishing deals and merchandise sales (Lang Leav, Cleo Wade, Atticus, the inevitable Rupi Kaur), the #poetsofinstagram feed is not made up of such superstars, and this chapter is not interested in canon creation. We therefore chose an account which much better embodies the amateur aesthetic of Instapoetry. The pseudonymous ms.poetry.ms has, at the time of writing, published 2,168 posts at the rate of three per day—a standard number of posts as it allows the Instagrammer to control the overall visual look of their feed—and has accrued 284 followers. Beyond that, there are few overt clues as to her identity (or gender, for that matter, though for the sake of convenience we will make the assumption based on the "ms" in her username), beyond a scattering of Christian-themed poems and a few posts promoting the work of British singer-songwriter Kris James. The posted poems, usually 4–6 lines without rhyme or meter, are usually written in san serif or cursive fonts. They appear superimposed on photographs, usually of either natural or urban landscapes: the wide variety of photographic style and the varied natural features suggest that these photographs are not being taken by the poet but are rather repurposed from a copyright-free image library or similar repository. There are occasional misspellings and grammatical errors which, given the generally high level of the writer's linguistic skill, suggest that these poems are written and published in a hurry and likely represent a personal creative practice more than they do any attempt to get a commercial publishing deal.

The specific poem that we will concentrate on here, posted to Instagram on January 22, 2021, reads, in full, "No matter how much you miss that person / Don't forget that you share the same sky." Imposed on a picture of treetops, shot from below and silhouetted against a bright blue sky partially covered by drifting white clouds, the post is accompanied by the maximum thirty hashtags allowed by the platform. All of these are familiar from other Instapoems—"#poet #poets #poetry #poems #poetsofinstagram #poemsporn" and so on (Figure 13.1).

Considered in its immediate context, this poem is straightforward. As with those posts earlier mentioned that are tagged "#poem" without containing any words, the aim is a generalized "poetic" quality: the speaker is doing the work of poetry, reassuring the reader that feelings of loss and discomfort can be overcome with perspective. Appearing in the general #poetsofinstagram feed, it attracts the eye more via artistic photography than with its particular easily graspable, and widely shared, sentiment. Read on the poet's own feed, where it is just one of many poems with similar themes, it seems mechanistic, just part of a production line of poetry—something reflected in the author's choice to remain anonymous. As with much Instapoetry, it is hard to talk about in isolation, since the levels of verbal craft, figurative imagery, and philosophical insight are highly

Figure 13.1 A poem from Instagram account @ms_poetry_ms (2022). The poem reads: "No matter how much you miss that person / Don't forget that you share the same sky."

straightforward. The visual element of the tree suggests an instrumentalist view of nature: like the diffuse "poetic," the "natural" is here seen only as a rhetorical device used to augment the writer's otherwise plainly stated sentiment.

The second scale Clark offers, what he calls the "middle" scale, places the work in a wider cultural context. In his reading of Raymond Carver, he suggests that this should be just the postwar decades, but we would argue that broader historical readings which remain within Eurowestern and anthropocentric contexts are still on the middle scale. To perform such a reading is tricky given that we cannot be certain of the writer's immediate geographical context, but just as we have assumed that the writer is female from her username, so we think it justified to assume from her promotion of Kris James and her use of British spellings (e.g., "coloured" rather than "colored" in a post from February 4, 2021) that she is from the UK. A middle-scale reading here might begin with situating the poem in a tradition of love epigrams that goes back beyond Catullus 85 ("Ōdī et amō. Quārē id faciam fortasse requires / Nesciō, sed fierī sentiō et excrucior").[4] This would lead to discussing the ways that such quotations have circulated within the tradition of commonplace books, collections in which educated people would copy down enlightened sayings, and in which "epigrams in particular remained much the most popular form of extract" throughout the early modern period: such a discussion might in turn think about the way that social media functions as a similar space in which to curate and create thoughts and sayings (Allan 2010: 142). We might therefore move on to consider the graphic design of the poem, which clearly owes a debt to motivational posters such as the Successories series (produced since 1985 in the United States, and marketed in the United Kingdom since the 1990s). Such posters also utilize white fonts and pictures of natural scenery, but in an explicitly capitalistic context, adding messages such as "WALK THE TALK / Take the initiative and lead the way / you can make the difference" below a picture of emperor penguins walking on a beach ("Walk the Talk"). Such comparisons might in turn lead to a consideration of the poem's place within a wider context of Western capitalism, in which the idea of the copied inspirational quote moved away from the private practice of the individual to become a mass market product. This was a move that was already underway when Benjamin Franklin began publishing his *Poor Richard* almanacs, though the two practices existed alongside one another for centuries. We might also specifically talk about commonplaces as a form of female rebellion; as Catherine Kerrison among others has noted, the eighteenth- and nineteenth-century practice of encouraging women to maintain commonplaces inadvertently created opportunities for reflection that helped women "understand [...] the constructed nature of gender" (Kerrison 157). Further, we might discuss the ways that the algorithmic management of contemporary digital experiences, by encouraging particular content and patterns of hashtags, may either enable or distort the ability to use curated short original thoughts and extracts to meditate on gender, race, or disability.

As can be seen from the above paragraph, the second scale—what we might call the Western humanist scale—is highly generative, as might be expected. Indeed, these are the two normal scales for literary criticism, the same ones we teach our students when we work on courses about literary theory: the one affording us a chance at close reading of the text, the second putting it into context. The third scale, however, asks us to place the poem into a spatial framework of the entire planet, considered as a closed system, and in a time frame of not only the past approximately 12,000 years but a projected future of at least the next several hundred. Twelve thousand years is considerably longer than the period that Clark suggests, but it better situates the poem as the product of what Timothy Morton has termed "agrilogistics." A pattern of thinking which Morton argues has at its root the comparative stability and hospitability of the climate of the Holocene, agrilogistics is the pattern of reasoning that emerges from the movement away from hunter-gathering and toward domestication and grain-based farming. It depends, according to Morton, on the idea that "it fails to matter how miserable you are, since you are alive": more existence, and indeed mere existence, is the only goal (2013: 100). The product of such thinking is inevitably a polluted and warming planet that will shortly no longer sustain agrilogistical civilizations.

A sort of conceptual horror creeps in at the idea of assessing ms.poetry.ms's Instapoem at this scale, a rejection of the possibility of assessing something so slight against something so inhumanly gigantic, and a distinct feeling of breaking the proverbial butterfly on a wheel. Yet the knowledge of the effects of petrochemical civilization, as we argued above, not only means that thinking at such a scale is morally necessary: it also means that *not* thinking at such a scale is becoming less and less possible. In a report for American Psychological Association (APA), Whitmore-Williams et al. suggest that both solastalgia (mourning for the pre-warming past) and eco-anxiety (fear of the coming climate-changed future) are on the rise in people who would not think of themselves as directly yet affected by climate change, while people who have been directly impacted by wildfires, drought, hurricanes, or other "extreme" weather events suffer from acute traumatic stress (2017: 22–7). The mobile phone screen is exactly the space most likely to surface such feelings, not only via all the mechanisms we mentioned in the introduction (constantly implanting the reader's images within the text they are reading, constantly calling on the reader to engage with others, constantly forcing contact with the unnaturally smooth screen), but also via the use of mobile phone advertising to promote green causes, not to mention that the relative youth of Instagram's core user base means that they have in many cases been the subject of national and local environmentalist educational campaigns.

Poetic Carbon Footprints

With the context above in mind, we want our third-scale analysis to literally assess the Instapoem as a material object. As our title asks, what actually is the carbon footprint of ms.poetry.ms's poem? How does it compare to the carbon footprint of an equally brief poem in a paper book? Beginning with the printed poem, we will follow Wells et al.'s study "Carbon Footprint Assessment of a Paperback

Book" (2012). Clearly a little out of date by now, this nonetheless remains the most detailed assessment we have found of the carbon costs of printing, from the initial harvest of wood pulp through paper manufacture and printing, all the way to end-of-life landfill or recycling. The authors calculate, based on a 320-page average-sized book, an average footprint per book of 2.71 kg CO_2-eq. Assuming that the publisher follows standard practice and prints even a short poem on its own dedicated page, and using the rough calculation of 2,710/320, this gives us an estimate of ≈8.47g of CO_2-eq per poem.

To think about Instapoems as discrete objects with effects, we can conceptualize them as selfies. Many posts to #poemsofinstagram are indeed just photographs of handwritten poems taken on mobile phones, so the comparison will be broadly correct. Not being environmental scientists, we will rely on the report "The environmental costs of being *selfie*sh," which aims to quantify the carbon output of a selfie (Salis, Cinquegrani and Colace 2019). As the authors observe, "A picture might not seem that much, but if we put it online, it goes through several networks and data centers that require plenty of electricity to function," with concomitant CO_2 emissions (5). The authors are careful to state that there are multiple ways to calculate the emissions required to upload 1GB of data, especially given that energy efficiency and use of renewables vary widely over different nations, so the figure they come up with can only ever be an approximation. Nonetheless, by first dividing the estimated energy usage of 5.12 kilowatt hours (kWh) per gigabyte by the amount of data (2 MB) in an average selfie, then multiplying the result by the International Energy Agency's figure of 506.312 g CO_2-eq/kWh, the authors estimate that each selfie—and thus each Instapoem—is responsible for ≈5.06 g CO_2-eq: for context, they add, the average tree absorbs ≈60 g of atmospheric CO_2 per day.

The above comparison might suggest that an Instapoem is more environmentally friendly than the printed book. However, selfies cannot just be assessed as uploads of pure data, but, as we argued in the beginning, they also must be seen as interdependent with the smartphone environment for which they are created (ms.poetry.ms would have been unlikely to publish books of illustrated poems, after all). We therefore also need to take into account the life cycle of smartphones. While several studies have argued that the e-reader is more ecologically friendly than the printed book, those assessments depend on the long life of such devices. Smartphones, by contrast, have life cycles of only a few years, and it is likely that Instagram users, who prioritize camera quality and high-memory-usage image manipulation software, are more likely than most to replace their phones often. Excluding the network usage accounted for above, the total Global Warming Potential of a standard smartphone has been estimated at 57 kg CO_2-eq (Ercan et al. 128). The impact of smartphones is also not limited to their climate effects. We should also find a way of accounting for the environmental destruction caused by lithium mining in the Congo, the lakes of toxic tailing left behind by rare earth extraction in China, and the fumes created by smelting old circuit boards in the last stage of the phone's life in the Philippines: a way that, ideally, would also account for the human misery involved.

Again, that perceptual horror looms. Yet all this information does indeed change our understanding of ms.poetry.ms's poem. Now it is the bald assertion that we "share the same sky" that swims into view. By accounting for the damage wrought by the smartphone for which the poem is designed, this statement now becomes a manifestation of the denialism noted by the APA as one of the symptoms of eco-anxiety, an attempt to elide the vast global inequalities and disregard for the future on which Instapoetry as a poetic practice depends. The poem's dependence on the idea of an eternal, never-changing sky is also revealed as not the expression of eternal truth which the poet no doubt intended, but rather a form of magical thinking. The pictured sky—Larkin's "deep blue air, that shows / Nothing, and is nowhere, and is endless"—is very different to the polluted skies of the cities where smartphones are made (Larkin 1982).

Moreover, if we can take "sky" as metonymically associated with "weather," as it often is, then this poem also manifests the agrilogistic belief in an essentially unchanging world as identified by Morton. In such thought patterns, the sphere of the human is conceptually divorced from that of "nature," figured as eternal, beneficial, and bountiful, and it therefore makes sense to only prioritize one's immediate wants and feelings ("no matter how much you miss that person"). When the poem itself is acknowledged as contributing to the gases pumped out by a machine civilization into the empyrean, however, sky and weather become symbols of the changeability, impermanence, and outright hostility of the biosphere. Reading this poem at this planetary scale is vertiginous precisely because the work itself is so slight and disposable—measurably so, given that it had garnered just seven "likes" from other users in the four months between its posting and our picking it up. Instapoetry's essence, if it has one, is exactly *to be disposable*: most poems on the #poemsofinstagram feed, like those of ms.poetry.ms, gain a few likes, a comment or two, and then disappear. Reminding ourselves that the technological disposable is never quite as disposable as it seems is no bad thing.

Yet the real challenge is not only to read at the third scale, but to take the other scales into account as well. The emotion expressed in this poem, of a longing for connection and "the poetic," should not be dismissed. Indeed, we should note that the poem is also hashtagged #poetryisnotdead, suggesting that we might also read it as longing for the return of something felt to be lost. Here we can broaden out our reading to comprehend the totality of all the poems that carry the various hashtags used by ms.poetry.ms, noting just how often these poems are accompanied with pictures of clouds, rain, waterfalls, petals, nutshells, twigs, ocean waves, rainbows, and the like—invocations of an agrilogistic ideal of nature that is the opposite of the world invoked by the screen on which these poems are experienced. We are not arguing that Instapoetry has any kind of radical potential as an environmental movement. Indeed, the second-scale readings explain exactly why this is not the case: social media platforms, particularly Instagram, could have been designed to dampen revolutionary potential, whether for reassessments of gender roles beyond the personal or for new perspectives on ecology. Nonetheless, by connecting the observable emphasis on nonhuman biological and geological features in Instapoetry's iconography with its clear climate denialism, we might end up seeing something unexpected in these individually insignificant poems—a mourning for a world passing, a desire for a world in which poetry and beauty still exist, and an implicit fear of the world to come.

Finally, these poems seem to crave constancy in the idea of beauty humanity has long associated with nature. Given that, as we identified before, making users desire to be in constant contact with their device is a core aim of the mobile phone industry, the Instapoem also expresses this connection within its content, becoming the embodiment of the connection between the user and the screen. Such a reading inevitably brings us back to the first scale of the individual, and even to the physical experience of reading an Instapoem in an Instagram feed. Other things become relevant in this context, the primary one being the location of the reader and how constant their connection to the internet—and by extension to the poem—might be. These contexts and the role they might play in the experience of reading the Instapoem illustrate the idea that first- and second-scale readings are not just useful but also inescapable. But this inevitability of our situation begins to emerge fully only when third-scale readings come into play, just as we have demonstrated in this chapter. The lens of third-scale readings, in our case in projecting even a single Instapoem into the geological time of the Anthropocene, brings to the spotlight humanity's imminent progression toward the end of the earth as we know it.

Notes

1 One could argue that concrete poetry is also highly visual, but visuality is thematic in the works of poets like Iain Hamilton Finlay in a way that is rarely true in Instapoetry (see Hair 2014: 193–5).
2 At the time of writing, the majority of mobile phones manufactured worldwide use Corning's Gorilla Glass technology and capacitive touchscreen technology in the way described here (Castelluccio 2020). Though the technology will likely continue to evolve (with foldable, dual-screen, and stretchable glass technologies coming to market), these are unlikely to change the effects we describe here.
3 See, for example, Kovalik and Curwood's assertion, "Young people are composing multimodal creative works, including digital poetry, to share with an online audience, using platforms such as Instagram" (2019: 185).
4 Of the many translations of this verse offered by Niall Rudd, we prefer Gilbert Highet's: "I hate and love. You ask, perhaps, how that can be? / I know not, but I feel the agony" (qtd. in Rudd 2005: 187).

References

Allan, David. 2010. *Commonplace Books and Reading in Georgian England*. Cambridge: Cambridge University Press.

Castelluccio, Michael. 2020. "Dual Screens and Folding Phones." *Strategic Finance*, 101 (9): 61–2.

Clark, Timothy. 2015. *Ecocriticism on the Edge: The Anthropocene as a Threshold Concept*. London: Bloomsbury Academic.

Clean Water Action. 2021. "Starbucks and Our Plastic Pollution Problem." *Clean Water Action*. https://www.cleanwateraction.org/features/starbucks-and-our-plastic-pollution-problem.

Duerden, Nick. 2021. "'Poet Laureate of Twitter' Brian Bilston: 'I'm Still Pretty Shy and Mostly Unconfident.'" *Inews*. January 11, 2021. https://inews.co.uk/culture/books/brian-bilston-alexa-what-is-there-to-know-about-love-interview-825075.

Ercan, Mine, Jens Malmodin, Pernilla Bergmark, Emma Kimfalk, and Ellinor Nilsson. 2016. "Life Cycle Assessment of a Smartphone." In *Proceedings of ICT for Sustainability*, January, 2016. Dordrecht: Atlantis Press. DOI: 10.2991/ict4s-16.2016.15.

Hair, Ross. 2014. "Models of Order: Form and Cosmos in the Poetry of Ian Hamilton Finlay and Ronald Johnson." *Texas Studies in Literature and Language*, 56 (2): 181–225.

Kerrison, Catherine. 2006. *Claiming the Pen: Women and Intellectual Life in the Early American South*. Ithaca: Cornell University Press.

Kovalik, Kate and Jen Scott Curwood. 2019. "#poetryisnotdead: Understanding Instagram Poetry within a Transliteracies Framework." *Literacy*, 53 (4): 185–95.

Kuzmičová, Anežka, Theresa Schilhab, and Michael Burke. 2020. "M-Reading: Fiction Reading from Mobile Phones." *Convergence*, 26 (2): 333–49. DOI: 10.1177/1354856518770987.

Larkin, Philip. 1982. "High Windows." In *The Faber Book of Modern Verse*, edited by Michael Roberts, Revised by Peter Porter, 357. London: Faber.

Mangen, Anne. 2008. "Hypertext Fiction Reading: Haptics and Immersion." *Journal of Research in Reading*, 31 (4): 404–19. DOI: 10.1111/j.1467-9817.2008.00380.x.

Morton, Timothy. 2013. "She Stood in Tears amid the Alien Corn: Thinking through Agrilogistics." *Diacritics*, 41 (3): 90–113. DOI: 10.1353/dia.2013.0016.

Owens, Erin, Soo-yeon Hwang, Dianna Kim, Tyler Manolovitz, and Lisa Shen. 2023. "Do You Love Them Now? Use and Non-use of Academic Ebooks a Decade Later." *The Journal of Academic Librarianship*, 49 (3): online publication. DOI: 10.1016/j.acalib.2023.102703.

Rudd, Niall. 2005. *Lines of Enquiry: Studies in Latin Poetry*. Cambridge: Cambridge University Press.

Salis, Matteo, Francesco Cinquegrani, and Michele Colace. 2019. "The Environmental Costs of Being *Selfiesh*." *CoreEcon*. https://www.core-econ.org/wp-content/uploads/2019/07/Data-competition-selfie.pdf.

Steffen, Will, Wendy Broadgate, Lisa Deutsch, Owen Gaffney, and Cornelia Ludwig. 2015. "The Trajectory of the Anthropocene: The Great Acceleration." *The Anthropocene Review*, 2 (1): 81–98.

"Walk the Talk." 2021. *Successories*. https://www.successories.com/motivational-posters/3672-walk-the-talk-motivational-poster.

Wells, Jean-Robert, Jean-François Boucher, Achille-Benjamin Laurent, and Claude Villeneuve. 2012. "Carbon Footprint Assessment of a Paperback Book: Can Planned Integration of Deinked Market Pulp Be Detrimental to Climate?" *Journal of Industrial Ecology*, 16 (2): 212–22. DOI: 10.1111/j.1530-9290.2011.00414.x.

Whitmore-Williams, Susan Clayton, Christie Manning, Kirra Krygsman, and Meighen Speiser. 2017. *Mental Health and Our Changing Climate: Impacts, Implications, and Guidance*. Washington, DC: American Psychological Association and ecoAmerica.

Zuboff, Shoshana. 2019. *The Age of Surveillance Capitalism: The Fight for a Human Future at the New Frontier of Power*. London: Profile.

List of Contributors

Max Accardi is a practicing attorney and occasional author. He is a graduate of Washington University School of Law and has an undergraduate background in political science and chemistry. Max's research interests include theories of communication and representation, natural language processing, the intersection between aesthetics and politics, and sometimes the law. Other forthcoming publications include an analysis of hegemonic incorporation as applied to simulations of prominent dead celebrities.

Kathi Inman Berens is a US Fulbright Scholar of digital culture, former Annenberg Innovation Lab Fellow, prize-winning author, and Associate Professor of Book Publishing and Digital Humanities at Portland State University (USA). She is co-editor of the Electronic Literature Collection Volume 4 (2022). Her current project historicizes handmade literary interfaces in the context of automated writing.

Zak Bronson is a Ph.D. Candidate and Instructor at the University of Western Ontario, where he teaches courses on media fandom, algorithmic culture, and genre film. His research focuses on the cultural significance of popular genre cinema, including science fiction, horror, and action. His most recent publications include an essay on China Miéville's *Railsea*, and a book chapter on the desktop horror film *Unfriended*. He is currently completing his dissertation on the representation of environmental catastrophe within contemporary science fiction cinema.

Yara Gawrieh Ekmark is a scholar and writer with a passion for contemporary literature and digital media. She holds a Master of Arts degree in English from Stockholm University and has participated in exchange studies in Creative Writing at Bath Spa University, where her literary fiction manuscript was nominated for the Janklow and Nesbit Bath Spa Prize 2021. With an academic background in English literature and a focus on creative writing, she possesses a deep understanding of the craft and nuances of storytelling. Yara's research interests revolve around the intersection of technology and creative expression, particularly focusing on the transformative impact of social media platforms like Instagram on modern poetry and literary communities.

Laura Gallon is Research Associate at the University of Sussex, UK, and works in academic publishing. She is currently writing a book entitled *Migrant Women Writers and the Short Story* and contracted with Palgrave. She previously worked on a research project on migrant narratives for the British Library, and as editor-in-chief of *Excursions* journal. She has published articles about instapoetry and inclusivity in cultural magazines such as *Archivoz* and *Voice*, and presented her work on contemporary short form writing by migrant women at national and international conferences.

JuEunhae Knox is Teaching Associate with the Digital Humanities Institute at the University of Sheffield. She is currently examining AI-produced poems against Instapoetry practices, and the effect that an over-inundated digital metaverse has on new poetic forms, from corecore TikTok reels to Notes app Instapoems. She also examines how counterpublics by marginalised groups form in resistance to algorithmic constrictions, and the challenges of resisting platformization tactics. Her PhD thesis at the University of Glasgow was the first to study Instapoetry and poe(t/m)-tagging in light of the Creator Economy. She led the inaugural global conference Reading #Instapoetry with James Mackay, and as well as a co-edited special issue with the *European Journal of English Studies* on Instapoetry as a global movement. Other recent works include "United We 'Gram," published by *Poetics Today*, which scrutinizes the hypertextual effects of consumerist Instapoetry trends; a piece with SigWeb entitled "Hooked on Access: Examining the Voice of Accessibility in Instapoetry"; and a chapter on "Rhyme with Good Reason" in Palgrave's *Teaching the New English* series.

Millicent Lovelock is President's Doctoral Scholar at the University of Manchester. Her work investigates how the formal features of social media are engaged in literary and televisual texts on the subject of feminism and sexual violence. Lovelock completed a research MA at the University of Otago on intimacy, identity, and the boy band One Direction. Her research was reported in *Teen Vogue*, *Nylon Magazine*, and *ID*. As a musician, Lovelock has attended residencies in Germany and New Zealand. In 2020 she was awarded a Taite Music Prize for her album *Relief*. She currently co-organizes the Sexuality Summer School in Manchester.

James Mackay is Associate Professor of Digital Cultures and Literature at European University Cyprus. Previous publications include *The Salt Companion to Diane Glancy* (2010) and *Tribal Fantasies: Native Americans in the European Imaginary 1900–2010* (2014, with David Stirrup). He is a founder-editor of the journal *Transmotion*, an open-access journal of Indigenous literary and cultural studies. Recent projects include a co-edited issue of the *European Journal of English Studies* on Instapoetry as a transnational phenomenon.

Polina Mackay is Professor of English Literature and Head of Department of Languages and Literature at the University of Nicosia. She is also Vice President of the European Beat Studies Network. Her research interests focus on gender and sexuality in modern and contemporary literature. She is the author of *Beat Feminisms: Aesthetics, Literature, Gender, Activism* and the co-editor of several other books and special issues, including *Global Beats* (with Oliver Harris), *The Beat Generation and Europe* (with Chad Weidner), *The Cambridge Companion to H.D.* (with Nephie Christodoulides), *Kathy Acker and Transnationalism* (with Kathryn Nicol), and *Authorship in Context* (with Kyriaki Hadjiafxendi). Her essays have been included in, among others, *The Routledge Handbook of International Beat Literature, The Cambridge Companion to the Beats, Out of the Shadows: Beat Women and Naked Lunch @ 50: Anniversary Essays.* She is also the co-author (with James Mackay) of a number of articles on gender and sexuality published in such journals as *Porn Studies* and *Studies in American Indian Literatures.* Currently, she is working on a Horizon-funded project on the political novel and on a new book on gender in the narratives of breast cancer.

Ryan Prewitt is a Ph.D. candidate at Saint Louis University specializing in twentieth century and contemporary American literature. He researches the relationships between aesthetics, radical politics, and digital platforms. He has a background in computation and deploys it in digital and computational humanities projects.

Eleonora Natalia Ravizza is Assistant Professor at the Department of Political Studies, University of Catania, Italy, where she teaches English Language and Translation. She received her Ph.D. in Literary and Cultural Studies from the International Graduate Centre for the Study of Culture (Justus Liebig University, Giessen, Germany) and the University of Bergamo (Italy). She has published several essays focusing on the work of contemporary Caribbean, Canadian, and Black-British authors. Her research interests include social media studies, language and memory, philosophy of language, stylistics, and contemporary poetry.

María Carla Sánchez is Associate Professor of English and of Women's, Gender and Sexuality Studies at the University of North Carolina, Greensboro. She specializes in US women's literatures, Latino/a/x and African American literatures, and the long nineteenth century. Her publications include *Reforming the World: Social Activism and the Problem of Fiction in Nineteenth-Century America* (University of Iowa Press, 2009); *Passing: Identity and Interpretation in Sexuality, Race, and Religion* (NYU Press, 2001); her current work-in-progress, *Imagining el Otro Lado: Protest and Print Across a Shifting Border*; and essays on literature, pedagogy, and US culture. She also serves as President of SSAWW, the Society for the Study of American Women Writers.

Melissa Sarikaya has been a lecturer at Friedrich-Alexander-University Erlangen/Nuremberg since 2019 and is currently writing her dissertation thesis on marginalized women poets of the late-Victorian/Modernist era. Her research interests are poetry, gender and queer studies, intersectionality, pop culture, and media studies. Her latest projects are a co-edited volume on social inequality. Melissa Sarikaya is speaker of the early career researchers' section of the Interdisciplinary Centre for Gender, Difference, and Diversity (IZGDD). Melissa Sarikaya and Dr. James Dowthwaite (University of Jena) founded MADS, a network on Modernism, Aestheticism, and Decadence Studies.

Camilla H. Soelseth is Assistant Professor in the Department of Archivistics, Library and Information Science at Oslo Metropolitan University, Norway. Her dissertation is situated in the fields of digital humanities and digital culture. It concerns the phenomenon of instapoetry from a media ecological perspective, focusing on the impact of platformization on the storing, transmission, and interpretation of poetry. Her research interests are everything at the intersection of culture and literary studies, social media, and the post-digital. She sees access to cultural resources, like poetry, as necessary for civic imagination.

Warren Steele is Assistant Professor in the Faculty of Information and Media Studies at the University of Western Ontario where he teaches the History of Communication, among other things.

Laura Tansley is a writer and tutor. Her academic and creative writing has been published in a variety of places in the UK and internationally, including in the visual prose collection, *Notes to Self* (2021). She co-writes fiction and non-fiction with Micaela Maftei and their collection of co-authored short stories, "The Reach of a Root," was published in 2019. Together they also co-edited "Writing Creative Non-Fiction: Determining the Form" in 2015. Tansley lives and works in Glasgow, UK.

Index

www.ingramcontent.com/pod-product-compliance
Ingram Content Group UK Ltd.
Pitfield, Milton Keynes, MK11 3LW, UK
UKHW021850130926
475466UK00003B/56

9 798765 105481